I0453924

How to Start a Business Complete Guidebook

A Comprehensive Guide for Starting a Small Business, Mastering the Business Plan, Accounting, LLC, Scaling

Marketing Strategies, Exit Strategies and More

David Whitehead

Silk Publishing

Copyright © 2024 by David Whitehead

Silk Publishing

All rights reserved.

No part of this book may be reproduced in any form or by any electronic or mechanical means, including information storage and retrieval systems, without written permission from the author, except for the use of brief quotations in a book review.

Contents

Appendices

Chapter 1
Introduction

The best way to predict the future is to create it.

— Peter Drucker

Welcome to the Entrepreneurial Journey

We will have to first understand what the word "entrepreneurship" means before we look in detail at what an entrepreneurial journey is. Entrepreneurship is all about starting or running your own business. You're responsible for the growth and success of the business from scratch.

It's important to understand that you can't just qualify yourself as an entrepreneur simply because you own a business. That could be part of it. However, as an entrepreneur, you need to have the ability to face difficulties with boldness and have the courage and confidence to achieve your goals.

Also, be ready to take risks because that's what entrepreneurs do. Entrepreneurs are risk-takers and always try to come up with ideas and look out for business opportunities to explore.

Entrepreneurs are known for pioneering changes in society and bringing about economic expansion. They do this through their innovative products, services, and business models. The always set an example for others to follow.

We will look at the entrepreneurial journey now that we have looked at what entrepreneurship entails. Every person starts on this fascinating and unique journey of an entrepreneur. Each business person has their own tortuous and successful stories that they take as they shape their own roads in the business world. A few common threads emerge, though: This includes the high associated with a successful pitch, the low of a rejected plan, the high of a breakthrough, and the low of a setback.

The entrepreneurship journey starts from a mere plan of a business, followed by market analysis and strategy, funding, assembling of a competent team, creating a good product or service, marketing and distribution to the public, and finally growth. The dynamics of challenges and opportunities at each level have deep impacts on the company as well as the entrepreneur.

Understanding Business Opportunities

Business opportunity means a Starter's opportunity to start or develop an existing enterprise to fulfill a need that is yet to be met in the market. For this, you have to take a view of trends, consumers' requirements, and competitors' actions to identify where you can make a difference. One can make money by providing corresponding products or services to fill up these requirements.

Identifying Good vs. Bad Opportunities

Good business opportunities are those that have a high chance of success and expansion. Most of the time, it addresses a particular need or a specific issue that affects many people, and the consumers find the solution useful. For instance, if you observe that citizens in your locality cannot easily access fresh vegetables that are free from pesticides, then it will be a good idea to plant vegetables or start delivering this product to the public. This is a good opportunity because it is evident that there is a market need, and one will be able to meet this need with a product that is marketable.

On the other hand, bad business opportunities are unlikely to succeed most of the time because these are either prospects that do not exist or the prospects are faced with too many issues. For example, in the present times, where the general population gets to observe films on the web, it is a terrible strategy to begin a video rental business. The overall market of video rentals has greatly reduced, and therefore it is rather improbable that your business would be flooded with clients. However, this time, opportunity does not turn into success when the market is saturated, demand is not high, or the cost of risks is more than the returns.

The right business opportunities are important for the success and expansion of the company; thus, it is crucial to identify them. To portray its importance, any budding entrepreneur, irrespective of background, should not overlook these opportunities.

Market Analysis and Validation

Market analysis or validation process is one of the most important activities that an entrepreneur has to conduct. This is a process of investigating a market to see whether there is demand for your service or a given product. This means that one has to focus on the current situation within the market, their competition, and the trends, too. The capability of validating customers' interest and their willingness to make a payment for the products/offering is an affirmation. This can be done by adverts like surveys, comments and others that are forms of direct marketing.

Assessing Risk and Reward

When choosing the appropriate business course, a comparison of the strengths and the weaknesses in undertaking a particular risk is usually carried out as a way of identifying the strengths and weaknesses. Let's assume a person has the idea of opening a coffee house. The capacity of rental costs, competition from other cafes, and the total lack of demand are the issues to consider in such a case. At the same time, there are advantages, such as the ability to earn money, have a loyal following, and advance the business. This will assist you in identifying whether or not managing a coffee shop is feasible and something that you can do.

The Mindset of a Small Business Owner

Frequently, there is strong desire and perseverance in the head of a small business owner. There is determination and passion among business people concerning the merchandise they deal in. They get that they have to work harder if they want their firm to flourish, hence they are not shy to clock many hours. Also, being own-account workers, businessmen can be more flexible and adapt to the setting more quickly. Hypothesis 4: Hardworking students, as they know exactly what is expected of them, will continue to attempt at trying regardless of the failure.

Another important feature of their thinking is their willingness to take risks. Entrepreneurs need to be comfortable with the idea of having to make decisions that may have crucial consequences in the constantly changing environment of starting a new business and managing a small business firm. They can always manage to work with what they have and sometimes come up with out of the box solutions.

Cultivating an Entrepreneurial Mindset

Thus, entrepreneurship requires that one is creative and comes up with great ideas that are new to the market. The greatest challenge any" budding" entrepreneur faces is not coming up with the idea but growing it into a business. To be able to think like an entrepreneur, one has to be very enthusiastic, innovative, and persuasive. But it also means you have to be prepared to fail, and that means to take risks.

Entrepreneurship is more than just possessing a fabulous idea in business. A company's success or failure is usually dictated by the entrepreneurial qualities of its founders. If you want your great idea to become a fully functional business, you have to develop specific traits. Is it true that certain company owners have an innate talent for running a profitable enterprise?

Overall, being successful as a business does not require any magic formula. In order to greatly increase their chances of success, all aspiring business owners should strive to develop specific traits. To put it another way, if you want your firm to succeed or fail within the first year, you might as well adopt an entrepreneurial attitude.

To become a successful business owner, what are the most important qualities one should have? When it comes to managing a company, what qualities usually make all the difference?

- *Have a positive mental attitude*

In order to be a successful entrepreneur, one must be a person with positive thinking and attitudes. The CEO's perception is wrong and it directly affects the culture of the organization because it determines the direction of the corporation on the whole. Negative thinking prevents the development and growth of a company and also affects management's capacity to steer and inspire employees. For entrepreneurs, optimism is part of what enables them to endure economic hard times. Instead of putting your head in the sand, it is important to reframe your

5

response rather than ignoring possible dangers. Focusing on mistakes won't help at all. One way of changing one's mindset could be looking at a negative pain point and asking oneself, "What can I do actively to correct this?" This enables you to develop a positive outlook on change. Therefore, you need to focus this skill on how positive people would use obstacles as an opportunity for growth and learning. Optimism, like all life skills, can be learned. Starting your own business is not for cowards because it entails long hours and uncertain demands that may adversely affect one's family or own psychological health.

Concentrating on the things you can control is one of the simplest strategies to develop a happy outlook. Your ability to exercise, sleep patterns, and food are all under your control. You'll remain optimistic, healthy, and focused with the support of each of these elements.

When you're working nonstop, where can you find the time to take care of yourself? Studies have indicated that a daily stroll of ten minutes or less can improve your mood and lower your frequency of negative thoughts.

- *Cultivate a creative mindset*

In the business world, the phrase "Creativity gives birth to invention" is true in the present time. Consider Apple, Steve Jobs, and the iPhone. The light bulb, and Thomas Edison. The airplane and Wright Brothers. All these revolutionary concepts would not have been introduced to the market without courage.

Creativity is essential for entrepreneurship, even if you don't work in a "creative" field. An entrepreneur's mind is constantly searching for new concepts and inventions. Any entrepreneurial product's fundamental life cycle begins with the idea's inception. It continues with the idea's transformation into a workable product or service.

Being in charge allows you to exhibit your creativity every single day, which is one of its many advantages. You get to test out innovative strategies to improve and modify your business. Finding methods to improve your company's operations is a creative endeavor, even if you don't work in a creative industry.

You may use creative thinking in many areas of running your own business, including IT, hiring, PR, sales, and hiring.

Since most entrepreneurs are naturally creative thinkers, it is unlikely that they would be motivated to take the risky step of starting their own business.

- *Be persuasive*

People who can convince others make the best businesspeople. Your ability to persuade helps you negotiate close deals or get better prices for your stock. Plus, those who know how to sway others often become great bosses because they inspire their teams.

While some folks have a natural knack for persuasion, anyone can learn and improve these communication skills. No matter what business you're in, getting better at talking to people and presenting your ideas will make you a stronger entrepreneur. Being good at convincing others can be the key factor between making money and losing it.

To get the most out of persuasion in the business world, you need to use the reciprocity rule. Research in psychology shows this rule has many uses in business. At its core, the rule means when someone does you a favor, they expect you to return it. As part of your pitch, try to "give" something to the person you want to convince. This might help you close the sale or seal the deal.

Learn to look to others as well. The idea that people look to others for social proof describes how people should act in social situations. In business, social proof can be an effective persuasive technique. Demonstrating the product's success for others can help you close a deal if you're trying to sell one.

Finally, make use of labels. Reputational appeals are effective strategies for persuasion. This kind of persuasion might be employed by suggesting that people behave in a manner that is compatible with a label. Say something like, "We stock our wine in fine French restaurants, and your restaurant is one of them." This is a typical sales-boosting strategy employed in marketing efforts.

- *Learn from failure*

When you start a business, your dream is to make it more successful. While success is certainly wonderful, failure brings change and growth. Being able to admit your mistakes and learn from them can help you grow from them rather than break you. This is the secret to learning from failure.

You will be in good company when you fail, so don't be afraid to fail. The richest businessmen, decorated athletes, and famous artists have had obstacles on their way to success and recognition because everyone is human, and they all make mistakes. Don't put too much pressure on yourself to be flawless when pursuing your company's ambitions. By definition, it is impossible.

Failure is inevitable, but it determines how you respond to it. If you fail, don't blame or judge yourself. Business failure shouldn't make you feel guilty or ashamed. Try to distance yourself from your emotions with the mistakes you make as a professional so that you can think rationally about ways to improve your work and yourself. Instead of saying negative things to yourself, try saying, "Now I see better for next time!"

Furthermore, allow adversity to strengthen you. Your best opportunity to learn how to do something correctly may come from failure. You will experience numerous firsts as an entrepreneur and new business owner, including your first employee hiring, first client, and first business lease. Certainly, some of these firsts won't work out, and that's acceptable. Make use of these setbacks to generate concepts and strategies for your future business operations.

It is also important to understand that failure is a daily process and that other people have gone through the same process before you. To get the other side of the story, you should share the incident with your friends, colleagues, or subordinates, especially your mentor. By discussing that experience, you and your team can work together to come up with an even better way to solve a challenging issue in the future.

In addition, don't be scared to start over and change directions. Sometimes, even the best-laid intentions can go wrong. That's just how life and business work. You might eventually conclude that something is just not working. It could be necessary to change your intended route, reset, and begin again.

Finally, never quit. Never giving up is one of the most crucial rules for entrepreneurial success. You will overcome difficult situations with perseverance. Strive to achieve your goals with perseverance. You can attain them if you have courage and dedication, but it can take some time!

Embracing Innovation and Adaptability

Innovation and adaptability are top priorities for small business owners because they keep the business relevant and competitive. Innovation refers to coming up with new ideas or improving existing ideas, which can help a business stand out from the competition. For example, a small bakery can introduce unique flavors or healthy products to attract more customers. Adaptability means being able to change quickly and respond to new trends, customer needs, or unexpected challenges. Suppose a new technology comes along or a competitor changes its strategy as a small business owner. When that happens, you need to adjust your approach to keep up.

It is important to note that it is important to embrace innovation and change because the business environment is constantly changing.

Markets change, consumer preferences change and unforeseen events can occur, such as economic downturns or supply chain disruptions.

Suppose you are innovating as a small business owner. In that case, you can offer products or services that are in line with the latest requirements. The same goes for adaptability, which keeps your business alive and thriving despite these changes.

Overcoming Fear of Failure

We have already discussed the importance of learning from failure. This needs to be reiterated because it is important to overcome the fear of failure. It gives you the freedom to try new things and take unlimited possibilities. For example, when starting a business, a person worries that things will become obsolete or fail. But if they let fear hold them back, they can miss out on opportunities for growth and knowledge. You can be more confident in your choices and overcome this anxiety to increase your willingness to try new ideas.

Another benefit of being positive in the face of adversity is resilience. While nothing will ever go as planned, it can help to see failure as an opportunity to grow and learn. It encourages entrepreneurs to persevere and never give up, especially in the face of adversity. These considerations are essential to maintaining competitiveness and innovation.

Navigating the Struggles of Entrepreneurship

The unique combination of obstacles that come with being an entrepreneur can be hard to articulate. Starting a company, for example, often takes a lot of time, energy, and possibly money. Dealing with competition, finances, and customer acquisition can all be very stressful. Uncertainty is another challenge; The corporate world can change rapidly, making it difficult to predict what will happen next. There are times when these challenges can make business seem daunting.

As an entrepreneur, you need to meet these challenges because by doing so, you can build a strong and successful company. Understanding the challenges ahead can help you better prepare and find ways around them. Plus, by facing these challenges head-on, you can improve your chances of achieving your goals and building a long-term company.

Let's look at some of the following operational challenges.

Financial Challenges

Financial challenges can be one of the main issues that young and aspiring business people have to face. Businesses and making money can be tough until one can start earning a profit. There are times when you have to use your own money or even borrow from some banks; at times, it may be a challenge to lure investors into supporting your idea. Managing money once the project starts—making sure you have enough cash flow coming in to cover expenses like rent, paychecks, groceries, etc.—can also be stressful. Unmanaged expenses, so in some way or bad sales month can make it even more difficult.

Careful planning and budgeting are essential to meet these financial challenges. Start with a comprehensive business plan that outlines your costs and how much money you'll need to keep the business running for the first few months or years. Find ways to cut costs without sacrificing quality. For example, you can build better deals with suppliers or find cheaper ways to sell your products or services. It's also a good idea to set up a savings account or emergency line of credit to cover unexpected expenses. Finally, keep a close eye on your finances by regularly reviewing your income and expenses to spot any problems early and make adjustments as needed. With proper planning and financial management, you can successfully manage the industry's ups and downs.

Time Management and Work-Life Balance

One more challenge that may be closely related to entrepreneurship is time management, or more precisely, work-life balance issues. Working on a project is usually very time-consuming and there is always more work than there is time to do it. You wear many hats as an entrepreneur; you are in charge of accounting, sales, customer relations, as well as the general running of the business. Due to the numerous activities, one can spend most of their time working and end up working late in the evening or even over the weekends. Non-stop work, however, does not only affect your work life but also your social life and even your family; you have no time for your friends, your loved ones or simply to relax.

Not having enough time to rest and recuperate can lead to burnout. Burnout is the physical, emotional, and mental exhaustion caused by prolonged stress. You start feeling tired every day, you lose motivation, and you have trouble focusing. This type of stress can make it harder to meet the demands of your job, reduce your productivity, and even affect your health.

To meet this challenge, establish clear boundaries and prioritize your work. Start with a schedule that includes work tasks and personal time. Identify the most important things you need to do each day and focus on them first. If possible, learn to delegate tasks so you don't have to do everything yourself. It is also important to take regular breaks and make time for activities that help you relax and recharge.

Dealing With Uncertainty and Setbacks

Business is a quite unpredictable world where one is never quite sure as to what to expect. Markets can shift, customers' needs can shift, and other factors, such as an economic downturn or new laws, can occur that can alter your strategies. This can make it hard to plan for the future and results in the population living in a state of constant flux.

Barriers are common in the workplace as well. Not every idea will work, and you may face failures such as product failures, loss of key customers, financial loss, and more. These setbacks can be frustrating and can shake your confidence. It's hard to deal with these frustrations, especially when you've invested so much time, effort, and money into your business.

While this can be a struggle, it's important to have flexibility and flexibility. Recognize that uncertainty is part of the entrepreneurial journey and strive to be flexible and ready to adapt when necessary. Create a support network of mentors, peers, and mentors who can offer guidance and encouragement during difficult times. Also, a plan should be developed to address potential obstacles such as emergency funding or support mechanisms.

Seeking Support and Mentorship

Not many people will think it would be hard to find help and a guide. The truth is that starting and running a business can feel very lonely at times, and it can be hard to find the right people to connect with and get helpful advice. There are also business owners who wouldn't like to ask for assistance or advice even when they need it. They think it makes them look foolish.

There is also the problem of getting a good role model or people to turn to. This, most of the time, takes time and appears intimidating. Employees don't know where to look for mentors or how to approach potential mentors. Finding someone who really understands the intricacies of an industry or profession can also be a challenge. While help is purchasable, the challenge arises in how to seek help while at the same time attending to the business needs.

You need to realize that it will not be a cakewalk to overcome this challenge; it is crucial to attend such events as conferences, business groups, or online forums. It's a huge advantage when you are willing to listen to what others have to say and not afraid to ask for help. Other people in the business can also help in creating a mutual support system and understanding each other's situation.

Chapter 2
Navigating Your Guidebook: An Overview and User Guide

The Ultimate How to Start a Business Guidebook is an all-in-one guide to understanding, launching, and building a small business, developing a business plan, accounting, LLC, and scaling. This guidebook is designed specifically for would-be small business owners in order to provide them with the necessary knowledge, tools, and confidence required to start, operate, and grow the small business of their choice and dream.

It doesn't matter if you are a rookie entering the business world for the first time or if you have a solid need for improvement of your business to marketing strategies. This guidebook does not only provide you with information on the steps on how to start a business but also presents detailed guidelines and tips on how to be successful.

Overview of Chapters and Sections

To help you navigate the wealth of information contained within this guidebook, here's a brief overview of the main chapters and sections:

- **Chapter 1: Introduction**: This section lays the foundation of an entrepreneurial process, explaining the concepts of business opportunities as well as developing a proper mindset and managing specific difficulties.
- **Chapter 2: Navigating Your Guidebook**: Chapter two of the book offers the reader a guide on how to get the best out of the book as well as on how to set the right entrepreneurial goals.
- **Chapter 3: Legal Framework**: Chapter 3 provides a step-by-step procedure for choosing the right business structure, formation of an LLC, and other legalities.
- **Chapter 4: Financial Foundations**: Chapter 4 is devoted to the primary knowledge of business finance, budgeting, accounting principles, and taxation.
- **Chapter 5: Creating a Solid Business Plan**: This chapter lays down the guidelines for creating a business plan to systematically address the needs of the business venture.
- **Chapter 6: Marketing Psychology**: Specifically, Chapter 6 deals with consumer behavior, cognitive biases, and brand loyalty and trust.
- **Chapter 7: Developing a Marketing Strategy**: Here, you will discover a 7-step guide to not only develop but also deploy a proper marketing strategy.
- **Chapter 8: Operations and Management**: Chapter 8 gives the reader information concerning workspace arrangement, inventory management, hiring employees, and other best practices related to client satisfaction.
- **Chapter 9: Scaling Your Business**: Here, you will be able to learn how to grow your business, how to deal with new tasks, and how to sustain quality.
- **Chapter 10: Legal and Regulatory Compliance**: This chapter covers business laws and regulations for small businesses, compliance issues, and how to protect intellectual property.
- **Chapter 11: Troubleshooting and Problem-Solving**: This chapter provides tips as to how to get over and solve a range

of difficulties and challenges which includes financial and legal issues.

- **Chapter 12: Exiting Your Business**: Chapter 12 is basically about exiting the business, the strategies on how to achieve this, the key issues involved in exiting the business, and also the emotion attached to exiting a business.
- **Chapter 13: Conclusion**: This section summarizes the entrepreneurial journey so far, how to celebrate success, and why there is a need to look forward.
- **Appendices:** Additional resources, templates, and a glossary of business terms

How to Use This Guidebook

1. Set Your Entrepreneurial Goals

Before you proceed to read the chapters, it is important that you lay down your business objectives. Are you in need of starting a new business or expanding on the existing one? Do you want to attain financial freedom, follow your passion, or address a particular need? Know what you want. This enables you to focus on the chapters of this guide that are most significant to you.

2. Identify Your Priorities and Needs

Understand the fields that require your attention the most. Are there questions you have concerning business planning, the legal framework or how to market your product? Each chapter of this guidebook is designed to address specific aspects of starting and running a business. When you pinpoint your priorities, you can tailor your reading experience to focus on the chapters that will provide the most value to you at each stage of your journey.

3. Tailor Your Reading Experience

It is recommended to use this guidebook according to your convenience and preference for learning. You do not have to read it from the first page to the last. To find the part that interests you most, you can use the table of contents, and chapter overviews to directly go to the required section. Thus, every chapter is self-contained and offers its own list of tips and strategies to follow, which makes the resource easy to use.

Maximizing Your Learning Experience

1. Interactive Exercises and Worksheets

This guidebook is filled with practical exercises and worksheets to support the understanding of topics and their implementation in the practice of your company. It is hoped that these tools will help the students to be more engaged and think critically. This will allow you to remember more of what is being discussed and allow you to effectively put the strategies into practice.

2. Actionable Tips and Strategies

Every chapter of this practitioner's guide is full of tips and recommendations that one can apply right away. They are here to assist you in decision-making, staying away from the most frequent mistakes, and obtaining the most efficient ways to succeed. Here are the recommendations you can take from it, as well as how to apply them to your company.

3. Real-World Case Studies and Examples

This guidebook also provides the author's experiences and a number of practical cases and illustrations to explain the principles and strategies described in the guidebook. These case studies demonstrate how different companies have managed to overcome certain problems, seize certain opportunities, and, thus, attain success. Thus, it is crucial to know the stories of other people as they may serve as a source of knowledge and motivation for your business.

Getting Started: A Step-by-Step Approach

1. Breaking Down Complex Concepts Into Manageable Steps

To start a business, one may be overwhelmed with all the details, but this guidebook helps to organize it and make it more digestible. Every chapter is organized in a way that the processes that need to be followed are presented in an orderly manner. This is a great way to approach the problem as you are laying out a strong foundation before progressing to more intricate matters.

2. Utilizing Checklists and Timelines

In order to assist you with the process of keeping everything in order and to a schedule, this guidebook contains checklists and timelines. These tools are intended to help you stick to the fundamental goals and objectives, thus preventing you from overlooking critical aspects. Take these checklists and timelines and use them for measuring your progress and motivation when working on your business objectives.

3. Adopting a Growth Mindset for Continuous Learning

Entrepreneurship is a lifelong process of learning, and an entrepreneurial attitude is crucial for the long-term perspective. Always look for challenges that are potential stepping stones for one to learn and grow, be flexible, especially when changes occur, and always be willing to learn new things. This guidebook gives the reader tools for learning and preventing stagnation, including ways to develop a growth-oriented mindset that will be useful for the lifetime of your business.

Following this user guide and using the knowledge from "The Ultimate How to Start a Business Guidebook," you are already on the right track to creating a successful and profitable business.

REMEMBER: entrepreneurship is a long race and not a short one, which implies that one has to be prepared for the long haul. Don't rush; you have all the tools you need, and do not forget to have fun while building the business of your dreams.

Chapter 3
Legal Framework

Choosing the Right Business Structure

Choosing the right business structure is one of the most important decisions you'll make when starting a business. A business structure refers to the legal organization of your business, which determines how your business is taxed, how much personal liability you have, and what paperwork you need to file.

The reason why you should select the right business plan is that it influences all areas of business, including operations, taxes, and legal requirements. For instance, if you pick the sole proprietor option, you will be held liable for all the expenses and lawsuits of the business; thus, your personal assets, such as your house or car, may be at stake while in a structure like LLC or corporation, your personal assets are protected and you can only lose the investments you made in the business.

In addition, the business plan you choose can have significant tax implications. Taxes vary from plan to plan, and choosing the right plan can help you save money and avoid legal trouble. For example, a corporation may be taxed twice—once on profits and again to share-holders in the shares—an LLC may offer more flexible tax options.

Let's look at the various business structures you can choose from as a business owner.

1. Sole Proprietorship

The sole proprietorship is the simplest form of business. This means one person owns and manages everything. When you start a firm as a single owner, you have full discretion for all events and retain every gain made in the process. Nonetheless, it also implies that you are solely liable to offset any liabilities or lawsuits arising against your company. Thus, if it cannot meet its financial obligations, your personal assets like motor vehicle and house would be employed to discharge them accordingly.

Advantages of Sole Proprietorship

- *It's easy and cheap to start*

Unlike forming a corporation or partnership, establishing a sole proprietorship is usually a simple and affordable process. However, it varies according to the state.

A proprietor just needs to file a small amount of documentation with their local authorities in comparison to other business forms. Consequently, proprietors don't have to wait long to receive authorization to operate a firm.

The cheap start-up costs are also consistent with other government initiatives that reduce the obstacles to launching new firms, stimulate risk-taking by entrepreneurs, and contribute to economic growth.

- *There are fewer laws and guidelines*

There aren't many laws and policies in the country that are exclusive to proprietors. The income from their firm and other sources of personal income require sole proprietors to maintain accurate records, submit taxes, and pay them.

Generally speaking, maintaining records for individual tax filings is not more complicated than record keeping and tax filing requirements. Owners would like to spend money on software and consultants to minimize the amount of time that has to be devoted to administration since this can be rather elaborate.

Some rules and requirements, for instance, the ones related to the financial reporting regulations that apply only to public corporations and other large organizations, require many hours of work and do not pertain to sole traders.

- *You have complete authority over the business*

The production, sales, finances, people, and other areas of a firm are all under the proprietor's control. Since the success of the business also equals personal success, many entrepreneurs find this level of freedom appealing.

To achieve success, proprietors need to be "good enough" in the several areas of the firm that they manage.

Even while some proprietors assign some of their responsibility to their staff, they are still ultimately responsible for all corporate decisions and actions.

- *You keep every penny that is made*

Being that the proprietor and the enterprise are legally the same, all earnings go to the owner. All profits go to proprietors, but tax should be paid once only, whereby every proprietor is answerable for their own taxes.

Owners are required to pay individual taxes on their income as part of their annual individual tax filing (in this case), for example. Also, depending on local tax law, these taxes could be paid more frequently, say quarterly.

In order to avoid heavy penalties and other consequences a proprietor must make timely payments of his taxes. Proprietors can seek help from tax consultants in estimating tax and then putting aside sufficient profit to meet government obligations later on.

Disadvantages of Sole Proprietorship

- *There is limitless legal liability*

The owner and the business are the same legally. Just as all earnings go to the owner, the owner is also the owner of all debts and commitments.

Creditors may seize the owner's assets to recoup their losses if the business is unable to pay them.

Promissory notes, which are legal contracts signed with lenders, explicitly define this accountability. Since a sole proprietorship and a proprietor are the same legal entity for all purposes, an owner is not required to give a personal guarantee to their sole proprietorship.

- *The amount of capital and financial resources accessible is limited*

Owners put their own capital into the business when they start it. They are restricted in their access to credit and have limited financial resources in looking for loan relationships. There is no way a sole proprietor can sell interests or shares of their company to raise money.

Indeed, actualizing ideas is risky and sometimes very costly. Running a business may require a high level of investment. Some costs must be incurred before any sales revenue appears. The working capital must finance both cash expenditures for expenses as well as credit sales. Long-term resources needed for the business, such as equipment, must be funded or hired.

In case proprietors' resources and financing are inadequate to meet the needs of their firm, it might become necessary to limit the purchase of fixed assets and continuously monitor their working capital.

A comprehensive business plan helps owners recognize what funds they need to start, sustain, and develop their businesses.

- *There are backup and succession*

In case the owner cannot or will not operate the business, it becomes closed. Sometimes, a proprietor may fall sick or face unexpected situations when he can choose to delegate his duties to a trusted employee or ask one of the members of his family to stand in for him.

However, insurance for business interruption should compensate for long-term issues, but it is not equal to the work that an owner has initiated already.

Consequently, sole proprietorships are not capable of transferring any intangible assets between different owners without creating a separate legal entity. Beyond fixed assets and tools, the proprietor owns something that ends up being intrinsic.

Therefore, if any buyers fell within this criterion, then a seller would be required to find someone who had acquired such capabilities over time and was ready to buy out its goodwill. Alternatively, if no buyer shows up at all, anyone among these family members passing it on could also take charge of the ownership, provided they were deemed reliable.

2. Partnership

A partnership is a form of business in which two or more individuals own and operate it together. Partnerships come in various kinds, although the general one is the most popular kind where all partners are equally responsible for running the business and sharing any liabilities in terms of debts or legal matters. If, therefore, an entity incurs some debts, all partners have to make good on them personally, even if one of them made a decision that resulted in indebtedness. The pooling together of resources, expertise and knowledge by partnerships can facilitate better management efficiency.

Advantages of Partnership

- *It makes room for shared responsibility*

Tasks and responsibilities in a partnership are shared among the partners. This means that people can specialize in some areas of the business, thereby making it easier to manage everything else. For instance, consider you and your friend who wants to start up a bakery; you may be very good at baking and enjoy spending time in the kitchen, while your friend is an expert in handling finances as well as marketing.

In this situation, you would focus on baking delicious goods, ensuring that the products sold are of high value, and supervising the kitchen staff. On the other hand, your partner could do all the bookkeeping work for you while creating marketing plans to attract customers, such as managing a social media presence for your business. When such duties are divided according to each individual's competencies, it makes workloads lighter, resulting in each partner being able to concentrate on what they do best.

- *Partners can combine skills and knowledge*

In a partnership, every individual has their strengths and experiences that can be useful in the business and can, in turn, assist in the growth of their businesses. For instance, you and your partner are planning on opening a restaurant business. Well, you might be a chef and create incredible recipes, in which case. However, your partner has a business management background and knows exactly how to manage finances and customer service.

Together, you leverage your individual strengths and improve the overall business decisions. When designing the menu, depending on your knowledge of food, you can come up with an impeccable one that keeps the customers coming. Meanwhile, your partner with a talent for business management will keep the restaurant up and running.

- *There is usually more capital available to start*

When many individuals participate in a business, it usually results in a greater amount of capital being accessible to facilitate the firm's initiation and expansion. This supplementary cash may provide several advantages in various ways. For instance, in the scenario where you and a business partner are starting a coffee shop, pooling your resources would enable you to acquire top-notch coffee equipment, cozy furnishings, and trendy decorations, so establishing a more appealing ambiance for your clientele.

Increased capital enables the expansion of the workforce, leading to enhanced customer service and operational efficiency. Instead of personally handling all tasks, you have the option to hire baristas, a manager, and cleaning staff. This enhances operational efficiency and enables you to concentrate on strategic expansion. Furthermore, by acquiring additional finances, you may expedite the expansion of your activities. This might include the establishment of an additional branch, the introduction of novel offerings, or the allocation of resources towards marketing efforts to enhance client acquisition.

- ## *There is more flexibility in management and operations*

Usually, the management and activities in a partnership are more adaptable than in a corporation. This adaptability comes from the ability of partners to make choices jointly without having to go by the rigorous guidelines and official policies often demanded by corporations. Suppose you and your spouse manage a clothes shop and decide to start a new fashion line, for example. In that case, you may rapidly go over and agree on the designs, price range, and marketing plan. You don't have to go through many levels of bureaucracy or wait for the board of directors' clearance.

Making fast judgments may be rather helpful in reacting to developments in the market or grabbing fresh prospects. If a popular trend develops, for instance, you and your partner may quickly decide to stock fresh products that fit the trend so you remain competitive and satisfy client demand.

- ## Partnership offers tax advantages

Under a partnership, the company itself does not pay taxes on earnings. Rather, the gains "pass-through" to the individual partners, who then document their portion on their personal income tax forms. Each spouse so pays taxes depending on their own income tax rate. Because it prevents the "double taxation" businesses experience, this technique may sometimes provide tax savings.

Under a corporation, the company initially pays corporate income tax on earnings. The shareholders so pay taxes on that revenue even as the company distributes those earnings to them as dividends. The same money is taxed essentially twice: once at the business level and then once again at the personal level. In a partnership, you just pay taxes once as the earnings directly benefit the partners, therefore freeing more money in your pocket and simplifying tax management.

Disadvantages of Partnership

- *Partnership has unlimited liability*

In general partnership, there is this concept known as the unlimited liability which means that every partner is to some extent fully responsible for the company's losses and for the company's debts and liabilities. This will also include their investments in the business besides the capital they have invested in the business. If the partnership borrows money, then the company defaults on its repayment; the lender could look for personal savings, real estate and other property of any or all of the partners. This degree of responsibility may be somewhat dangerous as the form of the company does not protect partners and can be individually sued for the debts and liabilities of the partnership.

This limitless liability also covers any legal difficulties the partnership might run upon. All partners are jointly liable if one of them runs a liability while running a partnership firm. For instance, imagine one partner engages in litigation or makes a poor business judgment because of their activities in the company. In such a situation, all partners might have to pay the resultant damages or settlement expenses from their own funds.

- *Partners must reach a consensus on decisions*

Partnership necessitates all partners to agree on important decisions about how the business is run. This means everyone has to discuss and come to a mutual agreement before moving forward with plans or strategies. While this ensures that everyone's opinions are considered, it can slow things down because it takes time to get everyone on the same page.

Disputes and excuses can partially stem from the differences in the perception of the partners as to what needs to be done. For example, it can be that one partner wants to invest in new equipment while the other partner is against it. In such cases they could use most of their time in arguing than in actually doing what they have planned to do. It could be argued that these differences slow down the company's ability to respond to opportunities and threats, thus threatening the success of the organization.

- ***There is potential for conflict***

A number of issues may arise when business partners disagree on crucial issues such as the direction of the company, handling money, or even personal difficulties. These disputes may cause stress and anxiety among the partners, therefore impairing their ability to collaborate.

These conflicts may potentially cause company disruption or slow down. Imagine a situation when partners cannot agree on a new business plan or how to allocate firm funds; this might postpone significant decisions and actions. This can compromise the company's capacity for swift issue-solving, competitiveness, or expansion.

- ***There is limited financial resources***

Since they lack the same choices as corporations, partnerships can find it difficult to raise funds. Unlike companies, partnerships cannot provide shares to draw in businesspeople. Stocks provide companies with a means of selling ownership shares to generate funds. Partnerships have less means to attract significant sums of finance because they cannot do this. This restriction may make it more difficult for alliances to pay for major costs, new initiatives, or growth.

The inherent risks and complexity of a partnership may also make outside investors reluctant to participate. Investors typically prefer the limited liability and structured governance of corporations, where their risk is minimized, and they have a clearer say in the business through shares and voting rights. In a partnership, the personal liability of partners and the potential for internal conflicts can make it less attractive to potential investors. This can further limit the partnership's ability to secure external funding.

3. Limited Liability Company (LLC)

A limited liability company (LLC) is a legal business form that combines aspects of corporations and partnerships. It offers members, or owners, limited liability protection, therefore shielding their assets from the company's debts and obligations generally. Additionally, providing management freedom, LLCs may be run either directly by its members or by selected managers. An LLC's pass-through taxation arrangement, in which the company's revenues and losses are passed through to the member's tax returns, therefore avoiding double taxation at the corporate and personal levels. Small companies and startups especially like this structure for its simplicity in development and running even if it provides significant legal protections and tax benefits.

Let's examine more broadly the features of LLC to better grasp how it runs and what sets it apart as a well-liked company entity option.

Characteristics of Limited Liability Company (LLC)

- *Limited liability*

An LLC's limited liability protection is fundamental for keeping members' assets free from the debts and liabilities of the company. Establishing an LLC results in a separate legal entity capable of owning real estate, signing contracts, and bearing liabilities in its own right.

Generally speaking, this separation assures that creditors and legal claims cannot pursue the personal assets of LLC members to cover debt or liabilities related to their companies. Small business owners and entrepreneurs who want to safeguard their wealth from the financial risks associated with starting a business rely on this defense. It encourages investment and entrepreneurship by providing a degree of security, allowing individuals to take business risks without endangering their homes, money, or other personal assets outside their initial LLC investment.

This, however, does not mean that limited liability protection is absolute. Some of the members may remain legally liable for some matters whereby they will be treated as if they have guaranteed a loan or a debt of the limited liability company. The shield of limited liability may also be pierced by the courts where the circumstances warrant such actions; these include cases of fraud, gross negligence, or where there is no clear distinction between the owner's assets and the company's assets.

Under such circumstances, members can discover they personally bear responsibility for LLC liabilities.

NOTE: Although an LLC offers strong protection for most operational and financial risks, members should nonetheless follow the best standards in corporate governance and maintain a clear distinction between personal and commercial operations to retain the limited liability shield.

- *Pass-through taxation*

Designed to streamline member tax responsibilities, the LLC form offers a major benefit in pass-through taxes. LLCs do not pay taxes at the entity level, unlike corporations, whose revenues are taxed twice at the corporate level—via corporate income tax—and once more at the individual level—when dividends are paid to shareholders.

Rather, the LLC's gains and losses flow through to each of the individual owners. Whether the revenues are paid to members or reinvested in the company, members record their portion of the LLC's income or losses on their tax returns. For members, particularly in situations when the company is not sharing all earnings with its owners, this arrangement might produce tax savings.

Furthermore, enabling additional freedom in tax planning and management is pass-through taxation. On their tax returns, members of an LLC may typically credit company losses against other sources of income, therefore possibly lowering their total tax load. Small enterprises, startups, and partnerships whose income flow might be reinvested into the company instead of being dispersed as dividends especially benefit from this adaptability.

- *Flexibility in management*

This feature of LLC meets the many demands of entrepreneurs. Every member of a member-managed LLC actively contributes to the daily running and business decisions. Small companies, alliances, and startups all have this structure where every member wants a direct involvement in the administration and development of the firm. It encourages people to work together so that choices can be made by using the skills and ideas of everyone.

A manager-managed LLC, on the other hand, gives practical power to one or more managers chosen by the members. When members would like to separate ownership from daily administration tasks, this system helps. Managers could be paid experts with particular knowledge in operating the company or LLC members. Larger LLCs, professional firms, or companies where some members could have passive financial interests and choose not to be engaged in the operational aspects usually preferred this method.

- *LLC can have one or multiple owners*

One major benefit of LLCs is their adaptability in ownership structure, which allows a great spectrum of companies and ownership forms. Since a single person may operate an LLC, they are perfect for small firms seeking pass-through tax advantages and personal liability protection or for single entrepreneurs.

LLCs may also have many owners, often referred to as members, who might be people, other LLCs, businesses, trusts, estates, or even foreign companies.

LLCs usually have fewer constraints than certain other corporate organizations could have regarding ownership forms or demand particular credentials for shareholders. Their transparency helps businesses to be reachable to a wider range of investors and promotes cooperation across many organizational models.

Whether it's a small family-owned company, a joint venture between businesses, or a worldwide company looking for a flexible investment vehicle, the LLC structure offers a flexible platform that may fit several ownership demands and business strategies.

- *Formation and maintenance*

Establishing an LLC is very uncomplicated in comparison to other business entities, such as corporations. Typically, the procedure includes creating and submitting articles of organization to the Secretary of State or a similar body in the state. These articles include fundamental details on the LLC, including its name, address, purpose, management structure (whether it is member-managed or manager-managed), and the names and addresses of its founding members or managers.

In addition to submitting the articles, it is often necessary to pay a filing fee, which varies depending on the state but is normally relatively low compared to the expenses connected with incorporating a corporation.

After being established, limited liability companies (LLCs) have advantages such as reduced procedures and continuing obligations in comparison to corporations. While state-to-state specific rules may vary, limited liability companies (LLCs) usually do not have a requirement to keep thorough meeting minutes or convene regular shareholder meetings as occasionally necessary for corporations.

This reduces the administrative effort and helps LLCs to focus on their daily operations and long-term goals. Furthermore, limited liability organizations (LLCs) provide greater freedom in their internal governance systems, therefore facilitating efficient management techniques and simplified decision-making processes. Small businesses and startups with limited resources may get especially help from this.

- *LCs can have a perpetual existence or a specified duration*

One of the benefits of LLCs is their flexibility in terms of existence. LLCs may be founded with a perpetual life, which means they have no set expiration date and can operate perpetually. This eternal existence ensures stability and continuity, which is advantageous for organizations trying to build long-term relationships with customers, suppliers, and stakeholders. It also opens the door for limited liability companies to take part in investments and strategic planning that focus on the future.

Another option for the formation of an LLC is for the members to agree on a certain length for the LLC's existence. This period may be influenced by the project schedules, certain business objectives, or any other strategic decision.

For instance, a group of investors in a real estate development project, while forming an LLC, may agree to have a specified term of the company, which may coincide with the time the investors may wish to sell or dispose of the property. Owing to the variable duration, LLCs can enhance risk mitigation and opportunity exploitation by adjusting the company's structure as well as its operational strategy according to the objectives of the members.

- *Legal recognition*

The legal recognition of LLCs as separate entities distinct from their owners is fundamental to their operation. It benefits both members and the business itself. This separation means that an LLC can enter into contracts, own property, and incur liabilities in its name.

Consequently, LLC members' personal assets—including houses, money, and other investments—are often kept free from LLC debt and liabilities. Except in cases of personal guarantees or where the "veil" of limited liability is pierced due to misbehavior or improper management, creditors usually cannot pursue the personal assets of members of the LLC to satisfy business debts should legal claims or financial difficulties arise for the LLC.

Furthermore, this different legal position helps the LLC to be more credible in both financial and legal spheres. It guarantees to lenders, suppliers, business partners, and other stakeholders that they are dealing with a legally registered company competent in meeting its responsibilities and commitments.

This credibility may help to lower apparent risks, ease transactions, and build confidence in corporate ties. By guaranteeing a clear separation between the corporate activities and the personal concerns of its owners, it also helps the LLC to be generally stable and long-lived. This advances even further a more predictable and safe commercial environment.

4. Corporation

A Corporation is a legal entity that is separate from its owners, the shareholders, and which is used to carry on business, own property, borrow money and enter into contracts. It fills articles of incorporation with the appropriate forms of the government agency. It is managed by a board of directors elected by the owners of the enterprise. Limited liability companies provide to their owners means that their assets are usually shielded from the debts and legal liabilities of the organization. This arrangement lets companies raise money by selling shares. It helps long-term development and continuation beyond the lives of its founders.

Types of Corporations

- *1. C Corporation*

A C Corporation, also known as C Corp, is a type of business entity that distinguishes the legal entity of the business from the owners of the business. This means that the business can own property, take loans, and be involved in lawsuits without having an impact on the assets of the owners of the business, who are referred to as shareholders. The company's profits are taxed twice: once at the corporate level and again when profits are distributed to shareholders as dividends. C Corporations can easily raise money by selling stock. Still, they have to follow more rules and regulations, like holding annual meetings and keeping detailed records. This structure is often used by larger companies that plan to grow and need a lot of investment.

- *2. S Corporation*

Like a C Corporation, an S Corporation gives its owners limited legal protection. However, the way taxes are handled is different for a S Corporation. It doesn't tax its gains; instead, the money goes straight to the owners. It is only taxed at their personal income tax rates, so they don't have to deal with the double taxation that C Corporations do. Small and medium-sized companies will like this about S Corps. But there are some rules, like the fact that there can only be up to 100 owners, and all of them must be U.S. citizens or residents. There are rules and laws that the S Corps also have to follow, but not as many as the C Corps.

- *3. Non-Profit Corporation*

Non-profit corporations are formed for the purpose of performing some work for the public or for the benefit of the members without the goal of earning profits. These organizations work for the purpose of carrying on activities that are charitable, educational, religious, scientific, or of any other nature for the benefit of the community. All the profits are reinvested in the organization and go towards the achievement of the organization's objectives and not to the owners or shareholders. Non-profits enjoy special tax-exempt status, meaning they don't have to pay federal income taxes on the money they make related to their mission. However, they must follow strict rules and regulations to maintain this status, including ensuring that their activities align with their stated mission and purpose.

How Corporation Works

A company must choose a board of directors before starting a business; the shareholders select those members at the annual public meeting. Each shareholder is entitled to one vote per share; they are not involved in the daily operations of the company. Conversely, shareholders are entitled to run for office and be selected to serve on the board of directors or executive officials of the company.

The board of directors consists of a group of individuals selected to represent shareholders. Apart from creating policies to guide the management and daily activities of the company, they also have to make judgments on important issues affecting the shareholders.

Acting in the best interests of the company and its owners falls on the elected members of the board of directors.

Advantages of Corporation

- *Corporation has a perpetual existence*

Another strength of a company is that it can continue its operations despite having new owners. This means that the firm does not change and continues to operate as before when a shareholder decides to sell their shares, withdraw from the business, or even pass on.

Unlike sole proprietorships or partnerships, where the firm may close or alter significantly should an owner die or depart, this is not the case with other company types. The company is regarded as a distinct legal entity; hence, its existence is independent of personal ownership.

The stability and the long term plans of the companies are dependent mainly on this continuity. For instance, the firm may carry on operating under new management once the founder of the firm retires or dies. This gives everyone the confidence that the business will not just disappear one day due to a change in ownership since this has not been the usual thing to happen.

- *Corporations can raise substantial capital*

Because they can offer shares of stock to investors and, in return, get money from the investors, companies have an added advantage of raising money. For companies, this procedure is much simpler than for other types of businesses, including sole trader or partnership businesses, which will have to rely on loans or personal funds to raise capital.

Selling stock allows companies to rapidly collect significant sums of money that they may then utilize to grow their business, create fresh ideas, or enter new markets.

Stock issuing ability makes companies more appealing to investors. Because they may readily purchase and sell shares on the stock market, investors are more ready to commit money to companies, so their investments are more liquid and maybe more rewarding.

- *Easy transferability of ownership*

Imagine a shareholder wants to sell their shares to another person. In such a situation, they may do this without interfering with the daily company activities. The company keeps running perfectly as the ownership change has no effect on its operations or management. This is so because the company is a distinct legal entity with autonomous existence and operation apart from its owners.

Transferability's simplicity offers major advantages. For instance, it lets owners quickly sell their assets should they want their money accessed. Moreover, it makes it easier for new investors to join the business, thereby giving it additional chances to get money. For corporate succession planning, it also provides flexibility as ownership may be passed without involving convoluted legal procedures or operational interruptions.

- *There is a structured management system*

The management structure of a company, which consists of corporate officers and a board of directors, helps to enable professional and orderly decision-making, therefore benefiting the company. Responsible for reviewing the company's major policy and decision-making projects, the shareholders choose a slate of individuals to serve on the board of directors.

Apart from guiding the strategic direction of the business, they also ensure the fulfillment of the interests of the shareholders. Usually meeting regularly, the board addresses significant issues, approves major initiatives, and evaluates the company's performance.

In contrast, the board of directors appoints corporate officers to oversee the company's day-to-day operations. These executives often consist of positions such as COO, Chief Financial Officer, and Chief Executive Officer.

The smooth operation of the organization is dependent on the individual roles played by each officer. In order to make sure that choices are taken carefully and with enough scrutiny, the board and the officers are separated in this way. This establishes a system of checks and balances.

- *There is tax benefit*

Most of the time, this is true for C Corporations, which can get a lot of tax breaks that can really help their finances. One big gain is that companies can keep their spending out of their taxed income. Some of these costs are rent, utilities, ads, and other fees, as well as salaries and wages. These are the costs that, when removed, allow corporations to reduce their taxable income and, in turn, the taxes they pay to the government.

Another advantage is that tax exemptions are rather simple to acquire. Although tax credits do not affect the taxes that a company needs to pay, they reduce them by the same amount. There are a number of things that these credits can be used for, such as research and development projects, investments in renewable energy, hiring certain types of workers (like veterans or people from disadvantaged backgrounds), or investing in certain areas to help the economy grow.

In addition, companies have the potential to be eligible for certain tax exemptions and incentives provided by the federal, state, and municipal governments. These incentives are often crafted to promote certain behaviors or investments that provide advantages for the economy or society at large. For instance, a firm might be granted tax benefits for making investments in eco-friendly technology, supporting community development initiatives, or generating employment opportunities in financially disadvantaged regions.

- *It offers employee benefits*

One of the employee benefits a corporation offers is the opportunity to provide stock options or grants to employees. Stock options allow employees to purchase company stock at a predetermined price in the future, which can align their interests with the company's success and potentially increase their earnings as the company grows. Stock grants are the actual issuance of the company's stock to employees, which in turn helps the employees to feel that they are part owners of the company and, therefore, they will work towards the success of the company in the long run.

Some of the common retirement benefits include 401(k) plans through which corporations allow employees to contribute part of their salary before tax. Employers may also offer matching contributions, which can significantly boost employees' retirement savings. These plans provide financial security for employees during their retirement years and demonstrate the corporation's commitment to their long-term financial well-being.

There are also health insurance benefits corporations offer. Many companies provide health insurance plans that cover medical, dental, and vision expenses for employees and their families. Access to quality health care coverage not only supports employees' physical well-being but also contributes to their overall job satisfaction and loyalty to the company.

Disadvantages of Corporation

- *There is the issue of double taxation*

We covered this under C corporation as double taxation mostly affects this kind of organization. At the corporate tax rate, the company itself is liable. This implies that the company has to pay taxes on the residual earnings to the federal and maybe state governments after the computation of its income and deduction of its corporate costs. Taxes begin at this level.

Following the payment of its corporate taxes, the company could decide to split part of its residual earnings among its owners as dividends. For the stockholders, these dividends turn into taxable income upon payment. After that, shareholders have to pay taxes on this revenue at their personal income tax rates and document it on their tax forms. This is the second taxing level.

Consequently, the same money—that of the profit of the company—is essentially taxed twice: first at the corporate level and then at the individual shareholder level upon dividend receipt. By having earnings taxed only at the individual level, the C Corporation structure is less appealing compared to alternative company forms like S Corporations or LLCs, which might help to avoid this double taxation and thereby lower the total return on investment for shareholders.

- *More complex and costly*

In contrast to the easier and cheaper forms of business, such as sole proprietorship or partnership, incorporating a corporation is tough and costly. In the past, incorporation involved the submission of articles of incorporation to the state describing the company's details, such as name, objectives, and stock.

Legal advice may frequently help with this procedure; it can be costly and result in varying but rather significant state filing costs. To further add to the initial complexity and expense, companies must create bylaws, call an inaugural meeting to name the board of directors, and distribute stock certificates.

Once set, companies have to follow continuous legal and regulatory rules that add to their administrative load. This includes keeping proper company records, having regular shareholder and board meetings, and submitting yearly or biannual reports to the state.

Companies also have to pay federal, state, and local taxes, which calls for different corporate tax forms and usually calls for professional accounting services. Maintaining thorough financial records and adhering to official governance policies adds even another level of difficulty and expense.

• *Regulatory requirements*

Corporations are required to obey numerous federal, state, and local laws in order to conduct activities legally, which means that they are required to adhere to the laws. This legal environment includes numerous laws and regulations that pertain to various aspects of corporate functions like financial statements, employees' conditions, environmental standards, and consumers' protection.

Companies that want to adhere to these regulations must fulfill several administrative tasks and produce extensive paperwork. For example, they are required to regularly produce tax returns, annual reports, and detailed financial statements, each of which must adhere to certain regulatory guidelines and timelines.

In order to adhere to regulations, corporations must also engage in the challenging task of negotiating complex legal obligations. This includes following labor laws controlling employee rights, benefits, and workplace safety, as well as industry-specific rules perhaps relevant to their activities.

For example, companies in the financial or healthcare industries have strict legal obligations meant to safeguard customers and guarantee moral behavior. Maintaining compliance with these rules usually requires the employment of expert legal and compliance professionals to monitor changes in legislation, guarantee that the corporate policies and procedures match legal requirements, and handle any compliance concerns that develop.

• *There is less flexibility in tax planning*

Corporations, particularly C Corporations, have certain tax benefits like the opportunity to deduct company costs and access special tax deductions. In tax planning, they do, however, sometimes have less freedom than other company forms such as sole proprietorships, partnerships, or S corporations. Their approach to company losses is one of the main constraints. Business losses in a C Corporation cannot be utilized to offset the personal income of the owners; they only help to offset future corporate profits. This implies that should a company suffer a loss, the future success of the company itself alone will be the only advantage in terms of lowering tax obligations.

Other company forms, such as sole proprietorships, partnerships, and S Corporations, let business losses flow through to the owners' tax returns. This implies the owners may use such losses to offset other personal income, including salary, investment income, or other company gains, thereby perhaps lowering their total tax bill more swiftly and efficiently.

Other rules that affect specific credits and deductions are also applicable to C Corporations. For example, they can claim off business costs; however, they have more rigid rules when it comes to what can be claimed as a loss and may not be allowed to claim certain losses that pass-through entities can. As compared to other company structures, this would result in higher total taxes and fewer opportunities for tax planning for C Corporations.

Steps to Forming an LLC

Understanding how to form a limited liability company (LLC) is one of the most significant factors when starting a business.

Step 1: Select a Name

As you choose names for your business, marketing might take the front stage. Apart from branding issues, state legislative obligations also have to be satisfied by your company name.

Many times, state laws prohibit you from choosing a business name already in use by another corporation in your jurisdiction. Most governments also limit using terminology like banking or insurance that would suggest you operate in a certain field. You also most likely have to put the full stop and append "LLC" or "limited liability company" at the end of your business name.

You can know the LLC naming rules in your state, and you can check the availability of the desired name by conducting a name search using the website of the company, which deals with the filings of companies in your state, and this is usually the Secretary of State.

Step 2: Complete the Organization's Articles

To legally create your LLC, you have to submit certain paperwork to the state authority that is responsible for the business entity filings in your state. This document is known as an article of organization in the majority of states; however, some of the states may use different names for it, for instance, certificate of formation. There is a form you can use in each state. Go to the same website you used to look up business names to get the form for your state.

After obtaining a copy of the LLC article of organization form for your state, fill it out. Before submitting your articles of organization to your state, carefully review them. In addition, there will be a filing cost that varies based on the state in which your business is being formed.

The state will grant you a certificate indicating your LLC is officially registered once your formation documents are accepted. The other uses of a business registration agency include processing other important matters, such as applying for a tax identification number and opening a business bank account.

Step 3: Draft an Operating Agreement

The specifics of the LLC member's financial, legal, and managerial capabilities are provided in the operating agreement. In particular, it can establish who contributes capital for the business, the procedure for a member's departure from the LLC, and the distribution of profits. It should, in essence, contain all the information about your LLC's activities.

Although an operating agreement is not compulsory in most states, you should try to have one. LLCs that have more than one partner or member should establish one to guarantee that everyone understands their respective roles and duties. It's beneficial for single entrepreneurs as well to put the specifics in writing.

One way is to create your operating agreement especially if you are forming an LLC with a single member. This is where templates come in handy; there are many free ones available on the internet. Thus, it might be very beneficial to spend more money on a good lawyer, especially in more complicated cases, such as LLCs with multiple members.

Step 4: Acquire the Needed Licenses and Permits

Apart from the documents needed to establish your LLC, you will most likely also have to complete paperwork and pay fees for company licenses and permissions. Usually, you may get this information on the official website or from the same office by looking through the list of company forms and fee schedules.

Check the types of licenses and fees your company has to pay to lawfully do operations in your state. Look for deadlines, as you will most likely need to apply routinely to renew your license or permission. Should renewal requirements not be met, your LLC might lose legal business recognition.

Chapter 4
Financial Foundations

The major issue facing the majority of small businesses is mismanaged finances. The U.S. Bureau of Labor Statistics reports that about 20% of small enterprises fail in their first year of operation. Roughly half of them have shut down by the end of their fifth year.

Many businesses fail as a result of inadequate business financing. However, some fail because there is no market need for their product, fierce competition, or poor marketing. Cash flow was listed as the second-most frequent cause of failure in a CB Insights poll. Cost and pricing concerns also ranked first on the list.

This exemplifies the significance of business finance perfectly. However, what really is business finance?

The money required by a business to operate commercially is known as business finance. It is the capital needed for entrepreneurs to launch, manage, and grow their businesses.

The funds of a business are its most important part. Without strong cash support, it's almost impossible to be successful. Money is used to buy things like raw materials, finished goods, and real estate. Basically, it's anything that will help your business grow.

It's because of this that money and finances are called the heart of any business. You and your business can't run smoothly if you don't have enough money.

Purposes of Business Finance

The most important resource that can be used in order to close the gap between your production and sales is capital. Business finance has the following functions. Among them are:

1. Financial statements

Understanding your business finances involves looking at your cash flow, balance sheet, and profit and loss statement.

These reports, when analyzed together, will provide you with a general view of the financial standing of your business.

Thus, by comparing the balance sheets and income statements, it is possible to estimate the working capital and its sufficiency. Here you will get to know the reasons for the deficiency and thus make ways and means of how to solve the problem.

2. Strategic planning

Every business, therefore, has to have a strategy that it follows. This is the strategizing and seed capital for your goals and estimates.

When thinking about business expansion, business finance will assist in estimating the amount of funding you will require to initiate the process.

You can use the given strategic plans to check how your business is likely to perform concerning the achievement of the set short and long-term objectives.

3. Taking out loans

As we know, cash flow problems are not uncommon. Such a situation requires the application of business finance as a means of managing and understanding the impact of borrowing money.

This information can assist you in arriving at more sound decisions on how much capital to obtain when you include it with your financial information. You can also select the payback plan which you want to opt for and the most effective one.

4. Promotion

Having a fantastic product and business plan is amazing, but to succeed as a firm, you must gain recognition from the public.

Effective marketing and promotion are the greatest ways to accomplish this. Since market research is in high demand, it is typically not inexpensive. To ensure that your product is available and appealing to your target market, you must set aside a portion of your revenues for the hiring of a marketing manager.

5. Managerial finance

Do you own sufficient money to fulfill your financial obligations? Are you in a position to provide the business's expenditures, receipts, payments, and earnings estimates? Are they to generate a profit within the framework of fixed assets?

Through the use of management accounting and financial planning, you can predict better and, therefore, come up with a financial strategy that reduces risks and helps grow your business.

Budgeting and Financing Planning

Financial planning and budgeting are ways through which you may be able to make your money work for you better. However, the two are dissimilar in many ways when it comes to their functions.

What is Budgeting?

Budgeting is a way to handle your money that includes writing down your weekly or monthly income and spending. It is common to divide up money to pay for things like rent, bills, food, gas, clothes, savings, healthcare, insurance, and investments. This lets you have a clearer picture of your spending and the areas that require your attention most, especially at present.

With budgeting, you are likely to be conscious of the areas and ways you have been spending your money; hence, you can eliminate or reduce some things that are not necessary. You can use any extra money you have after using your budget to cut back on costs that aren't necessary to hit your short- or long-term financial goals. A lot of people make their budgets with a computer worksheet, a calendar, or pen and paper.

What is Financial Planning?

Financial planning is a strategic method of organizing one's financial status in order to meet certain financial goals in the future. Thus, proactive financial planning can help to cover the costs of further education, minimize taxes, plan for a wedding, pay off debts, provide for children's needs, manage risks, retire early, and leave a financial legacy. Within your financial plan, you outline the necessary actions to be taken in order to achieve your financial objectives. Consistently or biannually, a sound financial plan should monitor your advancement toward your objectives.

When strategizing your financial management, you may use a portfolio as a means to monitor and manage your assets and cash flow. When you are well aware of your current financial position, then you are in a position to tell what awaits you in the future. You can also get to learn what you want to achieve financially and the most effective way of doing it in a plan that you can afford. Planning your finances can help you set goals that you can reach and give you advice on how to spend your money when making big financial decisions.

Differences Between Budgeting and Financial Planning

- *Scope of goals*

The primary objective of budgeting is to either continue or stop some spending patterns. One can be able to achieve this by reducing their entertainment expenses or depositing more money into their savings account monthly. The purpose of financial planning is basically for the achievement of long term financial objectives such as paying off debts or for the purchase of assets such as a house.

- *Frequency of progress*

Because planning is based on how much you spend, you can check in on your progress every month, every week, or even every day. This happens a lot more often than you might be able to keep track of your progress toward the goals you set in your financial plan. The primary concern of financial planning is the achievement of your long-term goals; therefore, you should review your performance every three, six, or twelve months.

- *Level of detail*

Understanding how much you have to spend in each category could be useful when compiling the budget. Because expenses can mount up, it's crucial to make sure you stay within the spending restrictions you've established. You might even be able to cut your monthly spending by a few dollars. Rarely does financial planning call for the same degree of specificity. There is frequently less benefit to precisely calculating the quantities because the goals are higher and involve more factors.

How to Create an Effective Budget

1. Choose your budgeting method

Choosing the method that best suits you to make your budget and monitor your expenditure will help you create an efficient one. You could want to use a spreadsheet, pen and paper, or a budgeting tool, depending on what you find most comfortable and easiest. Choosing the correct approach can help you to develop and follow your budget more easily.

Imagine you enjoy working with computers and find great satisfaction in using automatically calculating tools. In such a case your best option may be a spreadsheet. It is quite simple to maintain records of income and expenditure using spreadsheet applications such as Microsoft Excel or Google Sheets. The totals will be changing quite frequently as you enter new information.

You can also use pen and paper if you don't wish to type or if you work better that way. This one may look and feel more real and reasonable because you can manipulate and represent your budgeting procedure with it.

The planning app may also be for you if you like to carry your money around and you are grounded on technology. Apps like Mint and YNAB (You Need a Budget) can connect to your bank accounts and keep track of your spending automatically. They can also help you stay on track by sending you alerts and giving you information.

NOTE: It doesn't matter which method you choose; the important thing is that you use it regularly and find it easy to handle.

2. Gather your financial materials

Get materials together, like bills, bank records, and pay stubs. It will be much easier to make a budget if you have everything in one place.

When you get all of your financial documents together, it's easy to see how much money you make and how much you spend. Pay stubs prove that you get paid, while bank records show how much you spend. Bills help you keep track of your usual costs, like rent, utilities, and payments. If you have these papers ready, you can keep a close eye on your money and make sure nothing gets missed.

Putting these papers in order can also help you find trends and places where you could save money. You might find subscriptions you no longer use or notice that you make a lot of small purchases that add up.

3. Calculate your monthly income

Total the income you receive in a month. Do not forget to include any other sources of cash or money from full or part-time jobs.

If you understand how much income you have per month, then you will be in a position to prepare a good budget. This includes your daily pay, such as your income, wages, independent work, and any other money you get. When you and your partner or husband make a budget together, adding up your income gives you a full picture of your family funds. This helps make sure that all the money that comes in is tracked, which makes it easier to plan how to spend and receive money.

Knowing how much money you make in total also helps you set reasonable goals for savings and spending. It tells you how much money you have each month for savings, spending on things you need and don't need.

4. List your monthly expenses

Write down all of your weekly bills. Start with the biggest ones, like your rent or mortgage. Don't forget to add in the cost of things like clothes, fun, public transportation, and car repair.

Making a list of your monthly costs will help you see where your money goes. First, consider the major expenditures such as rent, power, and insurance. These do not change and are essential in day-to-day life. Third, sum up your variable expenses, which are food, transport, and other miscellaneous expenses. These categories include eating out, sports, and services and they ensure that you get to see the total expenditure incurred.

If you have a thorough list of your spending, you can see where you can save money if you need to. It also helps you know what costs you'll have in the future and avoid shocks. You could set aside money to fix your car or save for a trip, for example.

5. Separate fixed expenses from variable expenses

Expenses can be broken down into two groups: We have; Fixed expenses and Variable expenses. These are costs that are incurred in a business and do not change from one accounting period to another, such as rent, electricity, insurance, and loan repayments. Variable expenses are the costs that may vary from one month to the other, such as food, clothing, entertainment, car maintenance, and repair, among others.

When you separate your prices, you can see which ones stay the same and which ones change. Fixed costs are necessary and usually can't be changed. They give your budget a solid base. These are the bills that will always be the same, which makes it easy to plan for them. Differentiable costs, on the other hand, give you more freedom. These are the places where you can change how much you spend the most easily.

You can save money or spend your money differently based on your wants and financial goals if you know what these are.

6. Add your income and expenses

To know your financial situation, you have to add up all your income and expenditure for the month. First, calculate gross revenue for the month, that is, all your income from salaries, wages, freelance, and any other form of income. Then, sum your fixed and variable monthly costs.

Subtract your whole expenses from your entire income to get your net income. This simple analysis shows if your spending is within your means or whether it surpasses your income. Your income exceeds your expenses; you have a surplus—that is, the extra money you may save, invest, or put toward debt cancellation. On the same note, you have a deficit if your expenses are greater than your income and the only course of action that you can take is to either try to increase the income or decrease the expenses.

7. Track your spending to stay accountable

It is recommended that one should track their monthly expenses in order to ensure that they adhere to the set budget. Tracking your expenditure helps you remain responsible and see how closely you are following the spending limits you establish.

There are various methods you could use to keep track of your expenditures, including those we discussed at the start of this chapter. A budgeting tool will automatically classify your transactions, therefore helping you to clearly see where your money goes.

As an alternative, you may hand-write your purchases in a notebook or a spreadsheet. Whichever approach you choose, the secret is to regularly update your data to get a realistic view of your expenditure patterns.

How to Create a Successful Financial Plan

1. You can choose to get a financial adviser

Establishing a robust financial strategy is essential for attaining your financial objectives, whether it is accumulating funds for a house, preparing for retirement, or making prudent investments. It can be done on your own, but a financial advisor brings in skills and experience that are useful. It allows you to understand your financial situation, understand what you want to achieve, and propose the most effective strategy given your circumstances. It may also assist you in increasing your productivity and efficiency when working, as well as ensure that the money allocated for the purpose is properly spent.

Besides, a financial consultant might also help you manage your finances in the future as your financial needs change. A financial advisor can assist you in making sound financial decisions, including taxation, wills and succession, and investments during economic downturns. By offering unbiased guidance, they may give you confidence, as you have a knowledgeable ally helping you accomplish your financial goals.

2. Create a net worth statement

This is where you have to list down all that is yours and has some value, like cash, savings, investment, and real estate, and then subtract from it all that you owe, like credit card debts. This statement enables you to have a clear view of your financial status, be it good or bad. It is perhaps as if one is taking a snapshot of the current financial situation. Utilizing this information, you will be able to set realistic goals that will enable you to make proper decisions in the areas of saving, investing, or even eliminating debts.

3. Clarify your financial goals and objectives

Begin by creating a comprehensive inventory of your desired objectives for your financial strategy. These goals include both immediate and future objectives, such as accumulating funds for a vacation, purchasing a property, or preparing for retirement. Personal objectives are essential since they provide your financial strategy with meaning and guidance. Consider how obtaining financial freedom can help support these goals, be it through the protection of your family, education, or enjoying a comfortable retirement.

Understanding your goals helps one to identify the areas that require the most attention and, thus, the funds. Suppose your goal is to open your own business, then you will need to gather your starting capital and possibly sacrifice some things that you do not need in order to save money. On the other hand, if you want to retire early, then you must try to enhance the amount that is being contributed to the retirement corpus and make sound investment decisions.

4. Create and follow a goal-oriented budget

Budget with your goals in mind. This is a critical piece to the puzzle when it comes to putting any available funds toward your financial objectives. Budgeting with your goals in priority order: pay off debt, save for a house down payment, and build an emergency fund, among others, will help you keep all of your spending aligned to accomplish them. Now that we have a finite plan, we can be aware of our everyday costs and then put the remainder into other things.

5. Monitor your progress and adjust if necessary

In order to ensure that your goals are being met, it is important to do regular reviews of your financial condition, either every six months or every quarter. Check the budget, monitor the expenses, and ensure that assets and savings are in line with the set objectives. Therefore, through this periodical examination, any weaknesses, if any, can be easily pointed out. If such is the situation, it is advisable to revise the financial goals or the amount of money available. There is a possibility that you may be asked to cut your expenditure on the other things that you do not necessarily need, save more of your income, or adjust your goals to correspond with the new conditions.

Understanding Cash Flow

It can be described as a basic measure of the financial status of companies, projects, and financial products, which reveals how money moves in and out during a certain period. It portrays the liquid position, the operating effectiveness, and the general financial standing of a company.

Positive cash flows — when a firm has more than enough cash to pay for its expenses, this may indicate the ability of a firm can generate profits and fulfill financial debts, further supporting growth projects and paying dividends.

Also, negative cash flow might suggest that too much debt is being taken on and spending or income levels are not under control.

Why is Cash Flow Important in Business?

1. It provides financial stability and liquidity

Cash flow ensures that there is financial stability since people and companies are in a position to meet their financial obligations. Making a business have the money it requires to meet its expenses, discharge its obligations, and carry on its operations reduces its likelihood of becoming insolvent.

2. It creates investment opportunities and facilitates corporate growth

Positive cash flow means that a company is in a position to invest in things that will help it to grow, such as expansion, introduction of new products or services, and expansion into new markets. It provides the group with the financial resources necessary for the accomplishment of the planned objectives and for the sustenance of the group's success.

3. Ability to borrow and creditworthiness

Lenders and creditors usually consider the cash flow of a person or a business to determine if the latter is capable of paying back the borrowed amount. Suppose a business has a positive cash flow. In that case, it means that it is in a position to meet all the expenses it has, including the payment of debts; thus, the business is likely to be offered a good deal on loans, and in any other instance, it will be able to obtain more cash.

4. It facilitates financial planning and decision-making

Having timely and correct cash flow information makes it easier to make good financial decisions. It helps people and companies to know how their decisions will impact their cash flow, know which areas to invest in first, and plan for both the near and the distant future.

5. Valuation and investor confidence

Investors and stakeholders regard cash flow as one of the most important measures of a company's worth and viability. This means that if the flow is constant and favorable, the company shall be in a position to earn a profit and thus make a return on its investment. This makes investors have confidence in the company and this increases the value of the company.

Types of Cash Flow

1. Operating Cash Flow

The term "cash flow from operations" (CFO) refers to the money that comes in and goes out of a business due to its regular activities, such as making and selling products. CFO, also known as operating cash flow, indicates if a business has enough income to pay for its daily expenses and other commitments.

To calculate operating cash flow, you subtract the money spent on regular business costs from the money received from sales. A company's cash flow statement keeps track of this operating cash flow. It helps show if the business needs extra money to grow and whether it can generate enough cash to keep its operations running and expanding.

2. Investing Cash Flow

Businesses engage in cash transactions when they invest in long term assets and financial tools known as investing cash flow. This involves receiving money from selling assets such as estate, tools, or investments, like stocks and bonds. It also accounts for the outflow of money when acquiring these assets or securities. This aspect of cash flow is crucial as it reflects the spending decisions made by company leaders to foster growth and enhance earnings.

3. Financing Cash Flow

Cash flows from finance, or CFF, represent the net flows of cash used to fund the firm and its capital. CFI is also known as financing cash flow. Financing operations include the issuing of debt and stock, as well as dividend payments.

The cash flow created by financing operations may provide investors with valuable information about a company's financial health and capital structure management skills.

Small Business Accounting: Managing Finances Effectively

Accounting is often regarded as the backbone of every successful firm, big or small. In truth, since small firms usually have fewer resources and face unique financial challenges, strong accounting standards are even more vital.

The Importance of Small Business Accounting

Finance control and decision-making

Accounting gives a clear picture of the financial state of a small business; thus, it is essential to make sure that accounting is done. This is because owners of small businesses get to know their income, expenditure, and profit through proper recording of the business finances. The use of this data makes it considerably simpler to arrive at well-informed selections about pricing, investments, budgeting, and growth. Without proper accounting, it is comparable to driving in the dark; it is possible that you will not even become aware that your firm is experiencing difficulties until it is too late.

Guarantees adherence to legal requirements

There are numerous tax laws and regulations that apply to small businesses. Accounting assists in making sure you fulfill your legal responsibilities. It is possible to avoid penalties and legal issues by maintaining accurate records, filing taxes on time, and abiding by tax regulations. A skilled accountant can help you optimize your credits and deductions while navigating the intricacies of tax preparation.

Aids in financial planning and budgeting

Small firms can generate financial projections and budgets with the help of accounting. These resources are crucial for managing cash flow, establishing reasonable goals, and making sure the company stays solvent. Precise financial estimates can also be very important when looking for funding or loans to finance expansion.

Helps monitor spending and reduce costs

Since small firms frequently have limited resources, keeping costs under control is essential. Accounting enables you to monitor your spending, spot areas of excess, and put cost-cutting initiatives into action. This can boost profitability and enhance your bottom line considerably.

Promotes the expansion of businesses

Small enterprises get more challenging financially as they expand. Accounting solutions can keep up with this expansion, assisting you in managing more workers, assets, and transaction volumes. As your company grows, a structured accounting system may also make it simpler to get funding or draw in investors.

Performance evaluation

Regular financial statements produced by accounting, such as balance sheets and income statements, offer a historical assessment of the success of your company. You can use this data to determine which areas of your organization are doing well and which require development. It also lets you assess how well your company is doing over time and compare it to industry standards.

Attracts lenders and investors

Small companies must prove their financial stability and growth potential to get loans or draw investors. Lenders and investors will want to examine your financial records and statements to evaluate the prospects and risks related to your company. Your chances of getting the funding you require might be greatly increased by having an accounting system that is kept up to date.

Basic Accounting Principles and Concepts

Naturally, if every business shares its data using its own unique approach, we would have a babel of meaningless financial data.

In the past, most firms were held by partnerships or sole proprietorships. Personal accounting practices are now losing importance in the era of joint stock corporations.

Thousands of investors have invested millions of dollars in these firms, so they need a uniform, standardized accounting system to enable companies to be compared depending on their value and performance.

Consequently, accounting authorities and regulators have established and embraced internationally accepted accounting standards based on certain ideas, practices, and conventions based on which they base.

Referring to themselves as "Generally Accepted Accounting Principles," or GAAP, these rules control financial transaction recording and financial statement creation.

The application of the ideas by accounting experts assures the accuracy and informative worth of financial accounts.

It ensures conformity to common practices, conventions, and regulations, as well as to shared standards and procedures. The adoption of these accounting ideas has helped to create a widely used syntax and language for financial statement recording.

It should be mentioned, although, that depending on the accountant, there might be some variations in how accounting rules and procedures are followed, just as there could be differences in how two people living on different continents use English.

For the same transaction, two accountants could use two equally accurate methods based on their professional judgment and expertise.

Principles of accounting are acknowledged as such if they are:

- Comprehensible to those with a basic knowledge of finance
- Feasible (they can be applied without incurring high costs); and
- Reliable
- Usable in practical situations
- Objective

Below are some basic accounting concepts:

Accounting Concepts

Accrual concept

Monetary inflows and outflows attain acknowledgment upon their attainment or imposition rather than predicated on the transference of liquid assets. This paradigm guarantees that fiscal documentation epitomizes an authentic depiction of a corporate entity's monetary standing and operational efficacy.

Consistency concept

Subsequent to the selection of a specific accounting modality, it necessitates unwavering application throughout ensuing temporal accounting intervals to facilitate comparative analysis across financial statements over progressive durations. Alterations in said modalities ought to be illuminated and substantiated adequately.

Going concern concept

This stipulates an assertion regarding a commercial enterprise's persistence in functional operations ad infinitum without succumbing to insolvency or impending liquidation within any proximal chronological framework. Such presuppositions bear consequential implications for asset appraisals as well as methodologies concerning depreciation calculations.

Matching concept

The expenses should be matched with the revenues they helped to generate within an accounting period. This ensures that earnings are correctly stated in a company's financial statements.

Prudence (conservation) concept

Revenues and profits shall not be anticipated, but expenses and losses are to be deferred unless they become foreseeable. This ensures that financial statements do not show a value higher than the true value of the assets, and it makes sure income is not inflated as well.

Historical cost concept

Current market value is used to record assets and liabilities; they are recorded in the books at face value. It serves as a fair, independent evaluation data point.

Materiality concept

All items significant to affect the judgments and decisions of users shall be disclosed in the financial statements. Some of the entries can be avoided, like nominal entries, as they can clutter a financial statement.

Business entity concept

A business is considered a separate legal entity from its owners. This means that the owners' transactions should not be mixed with business transactions.

Monetary unit concept

Only transactions that can be measured in monetary terms are recorded in the financial statements. It provides clarity and comparability of financial information.

Periodicity (period) concept

The life of a business is divided into distinct and relatively short periods (e.g., months, quarters, years) to provide timely financial information. This allows stakeholders to assess performance and make decisions periodically.

Full disclosure concept

Accompanying financial statements should contain all the information that is required for assessment of the financial condition and results of the company's operations. This entails notes and other additional schedules.

Dual aspect concept

All financial transactions record in the accounting system have at least two accounts that are involved in the recording process, and it will always maintain the accounting equation (Assets = Liabilities + Equity). It makes a point of seeing to it that the balance sheet never aggregates.

Setting Up Your Accounting System

You need to have an accounting system in place if you want your business to run smoothly. No matter the cash flow, setting up a system gives you transparency in your transactions with self-audits and looking for holes.

To most small businesses, bookkeeping and accounting seem to be complex. But you will have to cross this barrier.

Below are action items you can follow to establish your accounting system.

Step 1: Open a bank account for your business

Establishing a separate business bank account is something you should consider doing before selecting and using accounting software. Certain business arrangements, such as limited partnerships, corporations, and LLCs, require the creation of a separate bank account. The IRS advises you to do so even if it's not necessary for your company. It's the easiest method for maintaining organization.

It helps you to predict your cash flow, avoid mixing business with personal accounts, organize your business records, and for easy filing of business taxes.

Step 2: Select a method of accounting

Three accounting approaches are available: accrual accounting, modified cash-basis accounting, and cash-basis accounting.

The most basic accounting method is a cash basis. The single-entry technique of accounting is applied in cash-basis accounting. When using single-entry accounting, every transaction is entered as it occurs. Short-term transactions work well with this accounting system.

A good middle ground between accrual and cash-basis accounting is provided by modified cash-basis accounting. Double-entry accounting is used in modified cash-basis accounting. For short-term transactions, you can use cash-basis accounting; for long-term items, such as long-term obligations and accounts payable, you can utilize accrual accounting. Put differently, you document financial transactions both when money has changed hands and before.

For beginners, accrual accounting may seem difficult. The double-entry accounting method is applied in accrual. Whether or not you have received payment yet, you record transactions as they happen while using accrual accounting. Long-term fund tracking is the most effective method.

Step 3: Select the appropriate accounting software

First, what you need to know is how you can choose the right accounting software for your firm. After all, there are many options. There are so many that it might seem a bit overwhelming. It is not as difficult as you think it would be.

We'll cover the basics so you have some idea of what software to pick. There are two types of accounting software available- desktop and cloud-based accounting. Desktop software generally traps you on the computer or device where you have it downloaded, whereas cloud accounting allows for work at your fingertips from anywhere.

No matter which type of accounting software you choose, there are a few other factors to consider as well. Make sure the accounting software you:

It offers all the features you need, is really simple to use, can change payment education anytime that suits you better, and provides customer support when required.

Step 4: Set up a chart account

Record all your business accounts through the use of a chart of accounts (COA). As in the case of a table of contents, it offers the user an easy way of accessing all of the accounts. Your business transactions will be classified into five major accounts together with any number of sub-accounts, depending on your COA.

This is an illustration of how your five primary accounts and each sub-account may appear:

Asset

- Checking
- Savings
- Petty cash
- Account receivable

Liability

- Accounts payable
- Sales tax collected
- Payroll tax liability

Equity

- Owner's equity

Income (revenue)

- Bank account interest
- Product sales
- Miscellaneous income

Expense

- Advertising
- Equipment
- Insurance
- Supplies
- Payroll expense

Step 5: Find ways to get old records and new transactions organized

The IRS recommends keeping detailed records of any purchases, expenses, investments, or other items you intend to write off. It is important based on common sense. For example, we know you are interested in accounting software so consider digital filing of receipts. Organizing that stuff about is a moot exercise and later unnecessary process soon enough. Well, here in comes the electronic receipts, which can really organize your bookkeeping - if you set it up right.

Whether you store receipts for your business in digital or paper format, the same principles to organize them apply. When organizing your receipts, keep this in mind: sort by type of receipt-i.e., do not mix up invoices with sales slips; then section everything out and place the papers chronologically to be later filed together into a safe spot (a filing cabinet or digital folder). You need to be consistent.

Step 6: Choose the appropriate time to use the new software

An accounting period is a good time to make the change, because you can rely upon closing balances for the previous period end as your beginning balances. Use 13-month accounting cycles so that the end of an account period is close.

And speaking of schedules, keep it high level by setting up a schedule for your bookkeeping tasks and set them to reminders if you wish.

Step 7: Enter the figures in the software

You can now continue business and use your accounting program Cool. Procure being timely, maintain systems, and plug in the numbers.

Bookkeeping Basics: Recording Transactions

Bookkeeping refers to the process of systematically recording, organizing, and maintaining a company's financial transactions. It means recording every money coming in or out, like sales, purchases, receipts, and payments made by an individual; this makes sure that entries occur due to happenings in everyone's life. It is a fundamental process that becomes the cornerstone for generating financial statements and reports. It helps businesses to track their financial performance and manage cash flow, as well it makes easy compliance with legal and tax obligations.

Below is a comprehensive process to record e-transactions:

Step 1: Identify the transaction

The basics of bookkeeping are to identify an individual financial transaction and record it correctly. That is to say that you should pinpoint each place where money changes hands in your business. Such transactions can be sales (when you sell something), purchases or expenditures, receipts of money, and payments. You locate and confirm these transactions by examining source records, which are the sales receipts or evidence of a transaction. These documents are things like invoices (bills you send or receive), receipts (proofs of payment), and bank statements (your records from the bank, not your bills to pay!

Step 2: Note the date the transaction occurred

While writing the Financial transaction date, it is imperative to write its actual and accurate exact data, which helps in keeping a proper track record of all your reports. This 'example date' can be used to order transactions by their chronological alignment. This is required to make financial statements and compliance, and it also provides clear trails for audits/reviews. For example, if a sale was made on June 1st, your journal entry date will be recorded as June 1st.

Step 3: Create a chart account

The next part of the bookkeeping process is to make a chart of accounts. This is a total overview of all the accounts that would enable an organization to trace down its financial activities. The chart of accounts is categorized into asset accounts, liability accounts, equity accounts, revenue accounts, and expense accounts. For instance, "Office Equipment" would fall under asset accounts, "Accounts Payable" would be listed under liabilities, and "Office Supplies Expense" would be categorized as an expense account.

For example, if you want to launch a business called Sunny Days Café. Here's an example of how you can keep track of your finances and improve the finances of your business.

Account Type	Account Name	Description
Assets	Cash	Money in the business bank account
	Accounts Receivable	Money owed to you by customers
	Office Equipment	Computers, printers, and other office tools
	Inventory	Stock of coffee beans, pastries, and other items for sale
Liabilities	Accounts Payable	Bills you need to pay, such as for suppliers
	Loans Payable	The money you owe from business loans
Equity	Owner's Capital	Your investment in the business
	Retained Earnings	Profits that are reinvested in the business
Revenue	Sales Revenue	Money earned from selling coffee and pastries
	Service Revenue	Income from hosting events or catering
Expenses	Rent Expense	The monthly cost of leasing the café space
	Utilities Expense	Bills for electricity, water, and internet
	Office Supplies Expense	Cost of pens, paper, and other supplies
	Salaries Expense	Wages paid to your employees

Step 4: Record in the Journal

The fourth bookkeeping stage is to enter financial transactions with double-entry journals. This dual-entry approach means that every entry should impact at least two accounts-one account is a debit (increase), and another is a credit reduction. Other gets a credit, that is the only case it dropped. By keeping a double entry system, it makes sure that debits must still produce the same total credits which will result in an appropriate view of financials.

Let's say that on June 10, you purchase $500 worth of office supplies from the store using credit this year. The journal entry to record the transaction will be a debit of $500 to Office Supplies Expense and credit for Accounts Payable in the amount of $500.

Date	Account	Debit	Credit
10/06/2024	Office Supplies Expense	$500	
10/06/2024	Accounts Payable		$500

Step 5: Prepare a trial balance

The completeness of the financial records is checked by trial balance. A trial balance is a listing of all accounts and their balances by debit or credit to ensure that the total debits equal the total credits. This process facilitates the determination of mistakes about incorrect postings, omissions or mathematical errors in recordation. This assists in comparing the trial balance against other financial statements, such as income statements and balance sheets, to recognize any discrepancies at an earlier stage, thereby providing more time for the rectification process.

Step 6: Prepare financial statements

Essential financial statements: income statement, balance sheet, and cash flow statement. The whole can provide an overall picture of the past and current financial status and cash flow activities reflecting a business. The income statement combines two extremely broad revenue and expense descriptions that sum up a period, usually a quarter or year, with the aim of showing if you made a profit (positive balance) or lost money. The other statement is the balance sheet, which gives a snapshot of how the company looks at the present moment - what the company has (assets), what the company owes (liabilities), and the difference between the two, which is called equity or net worth. The third one is the cash flow statement, which presents the movement of cash in and out of the business in various activities classified into operating, investing, and financing activities.

Financial Statements: Understanding Balance Sheets, Income Statements, and Cash Flow Statements

Balance Sheets

A balance sheet is a statement prepared at a given time to show the financial health of a company at that time. It consists of three main components:

1. Assets
2. Liabilities
3. Shareholders' Equity

Assets

An asset is a component of the company's balance sheet that has value and can be sold or consumed in the future to generate income. They are typically categorized into current assets and non-current assets:

- *Current Assets:* These are items that are likely to be realized in cash or consumed within one year. Some of them are cash and cash equivalents, accounts receivables, inventory, and short-term investments.

- ***Non-Current Assets:*** Non-current assets can also be referred to as long-term assets. These are resources whose benefits are expected to be received in periods exceeding one year. It includes Property Plant and Equipment (PP&E), Long Term Investments, Intangible Assets (such as Patents and Goodwill), and Long Term Receivables, among others.

Liabilities

Liabilities are the obligations that the company has to the parties other than the company. Like assets, they are also classified into current liabilities and non-current liabilities:

- ***Current Liabilities:*** These are payables that are due within one year. Some of them are accounts payable, which is the amount owing to the suppliers, short-term borrowings, accrued expenses, and the current portion of long-term borrowings.
- ***Non-Current Liabilities:*** These are also long-term liabilities on the company's books. These are the obligations that are maturing after one year. They consist of the non-current portion of borrowings, deferred tax liabilities, and a non-current portion of lease liabilities.

Shareholders' Equity

Shareholders' equity or what is commonly known as net worth or book value, is the portion of the total assets of a company that the share-holders own after accounting for all the liabilities. It is the measure-ment of the company's worth, the company's total assets minus the total liabilities; it shows how much capital has been put into the company by the shareholders.

It is calculated as:

- Shareholders' Equity = Total Assets − Total Liabilities

Shareholders' equity consists of two main components: The fundament of the company's equity, which includes the primary investment made by shareholders (common stock) and the profits or losses that remain in the business and have not been distributed in dividends (retained earnings).

NOTE: The balance sheet follows the accounting equation, which states that:

- Assets = Liabilities + Shareholders' Equity

This equation must always balance, hence the name "balance sheet."

Income Statements

An income statement is a financial statement that discloses the revenue and expenses of a company during a given period or a year, hence the name of the profit and loss account. It reveals the financial health of a business organization to a certain extent. It is usually made on monthly, quarterly, or annual basis.

Income statements involve the following key components:

1. Revenue
2. Expenses
3. Gross Profit
4. Operating Income (Operating Profit)
5. Non-Operating Items
6. Net Income (Net Profit)

Revenue

This is the total revenue that has been realized on the sale of goods and or services within the specific time frame of the income statement. It forms the first line of the income statement.

Expenses

These are the costs borne in the course of deriving revenues. Expenses can be categorized into several types:

- *Cost of Goods Sold (COGS):* This encompasses the costs of manufacturing the goods or offering the services that are sold to clients by the company. For a retailer, this may imply the cost of acquiring the merchandise to sell. It could contain direct labor costs for the business that is based on services.
- *Operating Expenses:* These are costs that are not related to the production of goods and services for sale but are required in the normal running of the business. They include wages/salaries, rent, electricity, advertising, wear and tear/depreciation, and other general expenses.

Gross Profit

This is done by subtracting the COGS from the total sales made. It depicts a company's direct cost of production management's effectiveness.

Operating Income (Operating Profit)

This is done by subtracting what is known as the running costs from the gross income. It displays the profit that is made before considering the interests and taxes of the basic operations of a company.

Non-Operating Items

These are the expenses and revenues not associated directly with the primary business operations of the company. Other non-operational income or costs include interest income, interest expense, and profits or losses on investments, among others.

Net Income (Net Profit)

This is the last line in the income statement and illustrates the profit or loss the firm makes after all costs have been charged off and tax and interest have been deducted. It is described a lot as the bottom line.

Cash Flow Statements

A cash flow statement is a financial statement that describes cash inflows as well as cash outflows of a business in a specific period. Appreciation of the solvency and liquidity status of a corporation cannot be complete without this important tool. Being a record of the company's cash, this paper ranks second after the balance sheet and before the income statement in the triumvirate of the most credible financial statements.

The Cash Flow Statement is divided into three main sections:

1. Operating activities
2. Investing activities
3. Financing activities

Operating Activities

Operating activities are the actual business activities that are carried out by the company to generate the main source of its revenues and are directed toward creating value for the clients. Such activities involve the use and generation of cash as the main asset. It presents the amount of cash that a company collects as well as the amount of cash that it pays out. Cash inflow from operating activities: This association's cash inflow usually comprises dues from customers in regard to the sales of goods and services that the company has produced. Others could also include other operating cash receipts such as interest received, dividends received, etc.

Operating activities have some key components, which are:

1. Revenue generation
2. Cost of Goods Sold (COGS)
3. Operating Expenses
4. Depreciation and Amortization
5. Changes in Working Capital
6. Other Operating Income and Expenses

- **Revenue Generation:** This includes the revenues or the fees that the company gets in return for the products or services it offers. Operating revenue is the most important factor of most organizations since it provides the main source of income.
- **Cost of Goods Sold (COGS):** For business entities dealing with products, COGS is the actual costs that are incurred in the production or acquisition of the goods sold within a given time frame. It comprises costs such as the cost of materials, the cost of labor, and the manufacturing cost.
- **Operating Expenses:** These are the expenses incurred in the normal course of the business's operations, excluding COGS. Some of the operating expenses include salaries, rent, electricity, advertisement costs, administrative expenses and the cost of the assets deterioration.
- **Depreciation and Amortization:** These are expenses that do not involve the immediate exchange of cash and relate to the systematic consumption of the asset's cost over time. It is subtracted from revenues to arrive at the operating income.
- **Changes in Working Capital:** These are the changes in the current assets, such as accounts receivables inventory, and current liabilities, such as accounts payable and accrued

expenses. Cash expenditures usually characterize positive changes in working capital, while negative changes lead to cash receptions.

- ***Other Operating Income and Expenses:*** Alongside typical income and spending, this category encompasses any income or expenditure from operations outside of the company's core, for instance, income from the sale of assets or expenditure from the closure of certain operations.
- ***Income Taxes:*** The income tax expense relating to operating activities is recognized as the amount of tax payable on the basis of the taxable income from ordinary activities reduced by all the allowable expenses. This shows the income taxes, which are linked to the profits from normal business activities.

NOTE: The sum of operating activities is called operating income or operating profit, which is one of the most important financial performance metrics reflecting the efficiency of a company's main business. It does not comprise revenues or expenditures from investments or financing, which are disclosed under the income statement.

Investing Activities

Operating activities measure the cash flow generated or used by a company's core business operations. This section is crucial because it shows whether the company's regular business operations are generating sufficient cash to sustain the business, pay its debts, and invest in future growth without relying heavily on external financing. A positive cash flow from operating activities is always an indication that the business is in good shape. However, suppose the negative cash flow is constant over time. In that case, it may suggest that there is something wrong with the business model or the firm's operational strategy.

The investing activities include the following components:

- ***Cash Receipts From Sales of Goods and Services:*** This depicts the revenues a company gets from its clients in relation to the sales of goods or services that the company offers. It is a vital measure of the company's revenue generation capacity from its core business activities. This component contains all the cash sales and collections from the accounts receivable.

- ***Cash Payments to Suppliers and Employees:*** This includes the payment for the operational expenses for the day-to-day running of the business. Payment to the suppliers is made with respect to the costs of the raw materials, stocks, and other materials that may be needed in the production process. Salaries and wages are the most common payments that are made to employees of an organization. These payments are vital to support the company's activities and production functions.

- ***Cash Generated From Other Operating Activities like Interest and Dividends Received:*** Firms also get interest on cash balances or investments and dividends from other companies in which the firms hold stock. These are operating cash inflows because they result from the company's normal, recurring activities, although they are not directly related to the company's primary business.

- ***Cash Paid for Interest and Income Taxes:*** **1. *Interest Paid:*** This includes payments for interest on any borrowings, including loans, bonds, or any other liabilities. Interest expenses are classified as operating because they are part and package of the business's cost of doing business. **2. *Income Taxes Paid:*** This includes the cash expenditures on the payment of corporation income taxes. Taxes are critical in the running of any business and as such, they have been captured in this section.

Financing Activities

Financial activities can be defined as the transactions that a company goes through with the aim of raising capital from its owners and creditors for its operating and expansion needs. These activities affect the company's cash flow and are captured in the cash flow statement.

Financing activities involve the following components:

- *Cash Proceeds From Issuing Shares or Other Equity Instruments:* If a company has a requirement of raising capital it may float new shares of stock. The money that is obtained from investors when they buy these shares is reported as a cash inflow in the financing activities section. This improves the firm's capital and gives it the financial muscle to expand, invest, or meet any other operational demand.
- *Cash Payments to Repurchase Shares (Treasury Stock):* At times, a firm may reach a conclusion that it is more profitable to purchase its own shares from the market, also known as share buy-back or acquiring treasury shares. This is reflected as a cash flow of the financing activities section as it is a payment made for the purchase of the company's own shares. Some of the reasons that companies may engage in this process include decreasing the number of shares outstanding in the market, thus making the available shares be priced highly to avoid dilution of existing shareholders' stakes.
- *Cash Proceeds From Issuing Debt (Bonds, Loans, etc.):* It is quite common for organizations to require funds to implement new projects, expand their business, or pay off previous debts. This can be done through floating bonds or getting a loan. The actual cash generated from such instruments is reported as financing activity cash inflow. This results in enhancing the company's liabilities but provides funds to the company at the required time.

- **Repayments of Amounts Borrowed:** The repayment of the amount borrowed by a firm in the form of a loan or a bond is recorded under the financing activities as a cash flow outgo. Debt repayment decreases the company's liabilities and may enhance its credit standing.
- **Dividends Paid to Shareholders:** Business organizations that make a profit may decide to share some of the profits to the shareholders in the form of dividends. This distribution is reported as a cash outflow in the financing activities section. Dividends are payouts made to shareholders, which helps in giving them a return on the investment made. Nevertheless, it decreases the amount of cash that a company has for reinvestment into the business.

Tax Compliance and Planning for Small Businesses

As anyone who's ever opened a small business can tell you, it's definitely one of the most rewarding things you can do with your life. It also happens to be one of the hardest things to do, however. In addition to the myriad of hats that you'll be wearing, you'll have to do those jobs efficiently, too. One of those most noble hats is tax compliance and planning. Appropriate tax compliance and planning can help your business grow financially and be sustainable. Unfortunately, tax laws and regulations are too broad and confusing to read, especially when you're keeping your business day-to-day. We have several strategies for you to consider on how to comply with taxes and prepare for them as a small business owner.

Strategies for Tax Compliance

Understand Tax Obligations

Small businesses must follow many federal, state, and local tax rules to guarantee compliance and minimize fines. Businesses report their earnings and pay taxes on profits for income tax; payroll tax, whereby taxes are withheld and remitted from employee wages for Social Security, Medicare, and income tax; sales tax, applicable if goods or services are sold subject to taxation; and perhaps property tax, paid on business-owned real estate or personal property. Compliance is promptly submitting tax returns, properly reporting revenue, spending, and deductions, and following certain tax rules pertinent to their company type and location.

Choose the Right Business Structure

In Chapter 3, we discussed choosing the appropriate business structure. The form of a business—whether it is a sole proprietorship, partnership, LLC (Limited Liability Company), S corporation, or C corporation—determines how it is taxed and what compliance duties it must meet.

Most of the time, sole proprietorships and partnerships are easier to set up. Profits and losses go straight to the owners' tax returns.

LLC owners can choose whether to be treated as a partnership, company, or single proprietorship, which gives them tax freedom. S corporations and C corporations are two different structures of business entities. C corporations are taxed twice, at the corporate level, and once more on the money to be distributed as dividends. However, they may be granted some forms of tax exemptions, including the right to claim employee benefits.

S Corporations avoid double taxation by paying money directly to shareholders, who then report it on their tax returns. Each structure has its own set of compliance standards, which influence how company owners handle taxes, deductions, and other financial elements.

Register for Taxes

Small businesses have to follow federal, state, and local tax rules; hence, registering for taxes entails multiple processes. First companies must get an Employer Identification Number (EIN) from the IRS. If your company employs people, runs as a corporation or a partnership, or satisfies other IRS requirements, this nine-digit number— which functions as your social security number—is mandatory. Some of the federal tax filings include income tax returns, payroll tax returns, and other employment tax-related forms where the EIN is used.

Also, it is mandatory for businesses to obtain local and state tax registration depending on the area of business operation. Of course, depending on the type of the company and the region it operates in, this entails sales taxes, payroll taxes, and possibly other taxes. Should the company provide products or services liable to sales tax, sales tax registration is required. Payroll tax registration is the withholding and remittance of federal and state income taxes, Social Security, and Medicare taxes from employee earnings and the employer part of these taxes.

Know Your Filing Requirements/Deadlines

Small businesses need to know their filing deadlines to avoid penalties and ensure compliance with tax obligations. Some of the key deadlines you should be aware of are:

- *Quarterly Estimated Taxes:* If your business expects to owe $1,000 or more in taxes when you file your annual tax return, you generally need to make estimated tax payments throughout the year. These payments are typically due four times a year: April 15, June 15, September 15, and January 15 of the following year (adjusted if these dates fall on weekends or holidays).

- *Annual Tax Returns:* Businesses must file various tax returns annually. For example: **1.** Income Tax Return: Sole proprietors file Schedule C with their tax return (Form 1040). Partnerships file Form 1065. Corporations file either Form 1120 (C corporations) or Form 1120S (S corporations). **2.** Employment Tax Returns: Employers must file Form 941 quarterly to report income taxes, Social Security, and Medicare taxes withheld from employees' wages, as well as the employer's portion of these taxes. **3.** Sales Tax Returns: Depending on the state and local regulations, businesses that collect sales tax must file periodic sales tax returns, typically monthly, quarterly, or annually.

Maintain Accurate Record-Keeping

This guarantees conformity and helps to simplify tax preparation. Comprehensive records provide a clear financial trail, which lets companies fairly record revenue and make qualified deductions. This procedure not only streamlines the tax filing process but also helps the company audit tax authorities. Good record-keeping methods involve methodically arranging receipts, invoices, bank statements, and financial records all year long.

Payroll Taxes

Should you have staff, you have to withhold Medicare taxes and federal and state income taxes from their pay and provide a matching contribution. Tax compliance depends on this as it satisfies the legal need to collect and pay taxes due by workers to federal and state governments.

Employers guarantee that the right amount of tax is paid throughout the year by excluding these taxes from employee pay, therefore avoiding the need for workers to pay a large sum during tax season. Moreover, remitting the employer's share of social security and Medicare taxes is in conformity with employment taxes, thus assisting in the avoidance of penalties and audits from the tax authorities.

Also, appropriate observation of the payroll taxes contributes to the compliance of the tax laws by the company and its employees. This enhances the company's accountability and transparency in the financial aspect.

Sales Taxes

If your company sells taxable products or services, then you need to collect sales tax from customers at the time of sale. The tax amount depends on the authority and the type of goods or services that could be offered for sale. Once gathered, companies have to routinely, usually monthly, quarterly, or yearly, send these taxes to the relevant state or municipal tax authorities as local laws specify. Inaccurate collecting and remittance of sales tax may result in fines and interest charges as well as possible tax authorities' audits.

Tax Planning Strategies

1. Consider a change in tax status

When it comes to organizing a small company, you have several options. You could run the business as a sole owner, LLC, S corporation, C corporation, or limited liability company (LLC). Your company structure will determine how you submit your small business taxes.

If your current company structure has grown too large for you during the last 12 months, you may be able to change to one more fit for you. For example, LLCs may decide to be treated like C companies by turning in Form 8832 to the IRS.

Such an election was unusual before the Tax Cuts and Jobs Act of 2017 (TCJA), when the highest corporate income tax rate was lowered from 35% to 21%.

Corporations versus pass-through entities

Various entities such as partnerships, LLCs, sole proprietorships, and S corporations do not have to pay corporate income tax because they are pass-through entities. Instead, the owner's tax return, which is subjected to the highest tax rate of 37%, receives a pass-through of the net income of the business. In the case of the latter, the LLC members at the highest tax rate might be able to save a significant amount of taxes.

Reversing the corporate alternative minimum tax, or AMT, the Inflation Reduction Act of 2022 was restored. Small businesses won't suffer, however. The new 15% corporate AMT applies only to C companies with an average annual revenue of more than $1 billion.

Choosing a structure for a small firm naturally entails more factors than just tax savings. Before changing your tax status, consult a tax professional who can help you crunch the data and do a cost-benefit analysis.

2. Utilize tax deductions

Pass-through business owners can deduct up to 20% of their portion of the business's income under the qualifying business income (QBI) deduction. However, there are a lot of restrictions and guidelines.

Suppose the income of the owners of specified service trades or businesses (SSTBs) is too high. In that case, they are not eligible for the deduction. Any service-based company, except engineering and architectural firms that depends on the skill or reputation of its owners or workers is considered an SSTB.

These kinds of SSTBs include, for example:

- Law firms
- Medical practices
- Consulting firms

- Professional athletes
- Performing artists
- Accountants
- Financial advisers
- Investment managers

If your business is an SSTB, your QBI deduction starts to be reduced once your total taxable income is more than a certain amount. The standard deduction for an individual taxpayer is $182,100, while for a married individual filing a joint return, the amount is $364,200 for the year 2023. To calculate the deduction, use Part II of the Form 8995-A. Still, you are unable to take the deduction if your income is over $232,100 for single persons and $464,200 for married couples filing jointly.

You may claim the deduction if your company isn't an SSTB and your total taxable income exceeds those upper limitations, but the following restrictions apply:

52 percent of your portion of the W-2 wages that the company pays you, or twenty-five percent of those wages plus an additional 2.5% of your portion of qualifying property

Confused? It's not just you. For small business owners, the QBI deduction can offer a sizable tax advantage; however, determining who is eligible to claim it and figuring out the deduction itself are difficult tasks. See your accountant if you believe you may be eligible.

3. Make use of tax credits

A tax credit is another tool that companies have at hand to help with their tax load. Tax credits reduce the total amount of tax payable, unlike tax deductions, which reduce a person's or company's taxable income. These ideas should help you.

Work opportunity tax credit

The Work Opportunity Tax Credit (WOTC) aims to help companies recruit and keep members of certain target groups who have constantly faced significant employment challenges. This covers veterans, families getting help under the Temporary Assistance for Needy Families (TANF), criminals, and members of other target groups.

Up to $2,400 can be credited to each qualified recruit. Small firms that recruit people who belong to one of these target groups must fill out Form 8850 and submit it to a specific local state agency within 28 days of the new hire's start date to be eligible for the WOTC.

The business can take the credit on the next regularly filed return if the state agency confirms that the employee is qualified for it.

Disabled access credit

The objective of the Disabled Access Credit (DAC) is to help small business owners cover some of the costs they incur when providing accommodations for the disabled. You cannot claim the credit on the first $250 of qualifying expenses. Still, it is worth 50% of eligible expenses up to $10,000.

To be qualified for the credit, your company has to have less than $1 million in income and no more than 30 full-time staff.

Among the expenses supported by the DAC include modifying present facilities to make them accessible to persons with disabilities, providing information in Braille, big print, and audio, assigning a sign language interpreter or reader to consumers or staff, or purchasing adapted equipment.

Credit for low-cost employer-sponsored health insurance

Small businesses that provide their employees health insurance might be eligible for a tax credit to help somewhat offset some of those costs.

To be eligible, you had to:

- Pay an average salary of less than $62,000 yearly per full-time equivalent in 2023 (this figure is adjusted annually for inflation)
- Employ less than 25 full-time equivalents
- Use the Small Business Health Options Program Marketplace to buy group health insurance.
- Cover each employee for a minimum of 50% of the total cost of employee-only insurance.

The credit is worth up to 50% of the annual premiums you paid if you are eligible for it. The credit is available for two consecutive tax years.

4. Set up a retirement account

One can reduce taxable income by opening a retirement account or making contributions to it. Below are some of the available retirement savings options that are suitable for business people as well as their employees.

- It is allowed to deduct all the contributions made to a 401(k) plan during the filing of taxes if the account was established prior to the end of the tax year. Some of the clauses of the plan state the limit of the contribution that the employer can make. The total contributions from the employer and employee for the year 2024 are limited to $66,000 or the employee's wages.
- Suppose the deadline for the year 2024 for implementing the 401(k) plan is missed. In that case, there is still a possibility to opt for SEP or a simplified employee pension plan. One can set up a SEP up to the time of filing their return or even beyond that in case they have requested an extension of time to file the return. The contribution limit for the employer in a SEP is $25,000 or 25% of the employee's salary as of 2024.

In addition to being able to deduct contributions to a 401(k) or SEP, you may be eligible for the retirement plans startup expenses tax credit, which is offered to companies who:

- Had at least one non-highly compensated employee covered under the plan;
- Employed not more than 100 persons who were paid remuneration of not less than $5,000 in the financial year;
- Did not have any other employer sponsored retirement plan during the three years before the date of joining this plan.

The credit can be as much as half the startup costs of the plan, or $5,000.

Chapter 5
Creating a Solid Business Plan: A 10-Step Process

Step 1: Executive Summary

This is a vital statement that should contain brief information about your business venture and the goal you are going to accomplish. It should describe the nature of the business, the product or service it will provide, the client base, and the main objectives. You know, if it is like a way to hook someone so that they will be interested in pursuing your business, it must be simple and must be in a way that anyone who will read it will easily understand the business and the interest it holds.

Highlight Key Points of Your Business Plan

This relates to outlining the key issues that characterize and shape your business. It contains your value proposition that defines what makes your goods or services special and why clients should go for your company. It also encompasses your competitive edge or your distinctive selling proposition as the strategic marketing management tool refers to special features or services that your business offers and which the competitors do not, or are incapable of, providing – this can include new product or service features, product or service quality or new technology, or outstanding customers care.

Also, you should briefly provide your forecast of revenues, profits, and growth rates to illustrate the likely financial returns of the business. Finally, copy down your financial needs and specify the amount of money that you will need, the rationale of the amount, and the ways in which you will utilize the funding to expand your business.

Step 2: Company Description

Provide an Overview of Your Business

This part of the business plan provides the specifics about the business that you are undertaking. You should start by presenting the general data of the business that you are running, such as the business name, the physical address of the business, and the legal status. For instance, you might write: "GreenThumb Landscaping' is a business based in Austin, Texas, operating as an LLC. " This will make the reader aware of where and how your business began and is established.

If you are already running a business, it should be accompanied by a brief company history. For instance, you could describe the history of the business, perhaps including when and how it was established key accomplishments, and the evolution of the business. For instance, "It started with GreenThumb Landscaping, established in 2015 by Jane Doe, and has grown from just offering traditional lawns to the surrounding residential homes to offering our services to commercial buildings as well; the company has grown from two employees to twenty."

Describe Your Mission, Vision, and Values

The next one that you should focus on is the mission, vision, and values. Every organization needs to understand that goals and objectives are some of the key components as they set the areas of focus for a business. To be specific, the aim and objectives of the mission statement should point to what a business seeks to accomplish every day. An example of such a statement is, ''At GreenThumb Landscaping, our vision is to be the leading landscaping company offering quality and environmentally friendly services to our clients."

The vision statement, on the other hand, should define or give an idea of the current place of your business, while the vision statement should show where the business plans to be in the future. It conveys your life's ideal. For instance, "Our vision is to become the premier company offering sustainable landscaping services in Texas characterized by 'x' level of innovation and environmental conservation." The above statement indicates the next course of action of the business. Understanding core values is normally correlated to the set of principles and standards that form the basis of your business. For instance, "Some of our goals are integrity, customers, environment, and improvement goals." These values outline the principles the business implements in its daily operations.

Step 3: Market Analysis

Conducting Market Research and Industry Analysis

Here, what you've to do is collect and analyze data to gain knowledge of the trade your business venture operates. It begins with identifying if the market is large or small, in order to find out the size of the industry and whether it is growing or declining. Another source of information that you should consider is the current trends in an effort to find out what looks trendy and what may be transforming the market. We can continue the example that we previously used, landscaping. Hence, when starting a landscaping business, the topics to investigate could be the number of landscaping firms in the region, consumer interest in environmentally sustainable services, and the trend in backyard living investments.

For this purpose, incorporate data and statistics from authentic sources such as industry research papers, government reports, and market research studies. For instance, in predicting cases, you could gather facts that indicate that the landscaping industry is likely to expand at a rate of 5 percent per year in the next five years.

Secondly, determine your competition's characteristics by establishing who they are, what they engage in, and what their charges look like. It assists you in identifying your business's position in the market and how best you can set it apart from others.

Identify Target Market Segments and Customer Needs

Here, one has to identify and define the target customer base, as well as group the customers according to certain features. For our comparison, let's take a coffee shop as our case study. The different classifications of the target market segments are Age, Gender, income, Education, and geographical area. For instance, your target group may be professionals, males or females, between 25 to 40 years of age, living in urban settings, and with fair to good levels of income. Demographic information assists a business by giving details about the status of its customers and their geographical location.

Second, the demographic feature is the psychographic and behavioral characteristics of the target audience, which are the preferred lifestyle, hobbies, beliefs, and buying patterns of the consumers. For instance, your target customers might appreciate Convenience & Quality, coffee, and, best of all, a comfortable environment to work or unwind in. Know their particular requirement; for instance, they want a quick and quality coffee while on their way to work, a comfortable environment to meet friends, or a quiet environment to work from. Describe how the business will fill these needs with gourmet coffee choices, free internet, and comfortable chairs, a friendly atmosphere.

Step 4: Competitive Analysis

Competitive analysis is the process of identifying your competitors' strengths, weaknesses, major selling points, and drawbacks when compared with your brand. It can give details about each competitor's market status, its sales and marketing planner, its growth concept, and any other business component that can help determine opportunities for improvement and potential opportunities.

REMEMBER: This way, competitive analysis brings you a clearer view of the environment in which you are to expand, helping you with the right decisions.

You must keep in mind that even though competitive analysis gives you an opportunity to gain some knowledge of others, it isn't:

- Strictly copying the strategies of successful competitors.
- Attempting to outbid competitors on price.
- A one-time-only task.

Why Should You Carry Out Competitive Analysis?

- *Identify your differentiators*

Consider competitor analysis as an opportunity to take stock of your business and identify your unique selling proposition. Additionally, it assists you in coming up with ideas for how to best set your firm apart if you're just getting started.

- *Find competitors' strengths*

What are your rivals' successful strategies for expanding? You can find out what an industry leader did successfully to become a market leader by thoroughly examining them.

- *Set benchmarks for success*

Competitor analysis helps you map your development against success metrics. Even if every business has a unique road to success, you can always determine whether you're headed in the correct direction by examining the trajectory of your competitors.

- *Get closer to your target audience*

The primary aspect that should form the basis of a competitive analysis is the target audience. Gauging what consumers like and appreciate, what they do not like as much, what they prefer, and what they have issues with concerning your competitors' products gives you a true picture of your target market.

REMEMBER: competitive analysis eliminates ambiguity and supplies you with definite details to form your business technique no subject how new you are as an entrepreneur or if you are revamping a previous business.

Let's take a look at the key elements that each competitor should have before we go into the systematic methodology for performing competition analysis:

1. Overview. An overview of the business, including its location, target market, and target audience.
2. Primary offering. A summary of their offerings and how they stack up against your brand.
3. Pricing strategy. A comparison of your price and theirs for several products.
4. Positioning. an examination of their main messaging to determine their positioning.
5. Customer feedback: an assortment of consumer reviews for the brand.

How Do You Carry Out Competitive Analysis?

1. Identify and categorize all competitors

The first step is straightforward yet well-thought-out. You must ascertain every potential rival in your sector, including the less well-known ones. Being aware of every player in the market is the aim here, as opposed to picking and choosing to ignore some.

As you discover more and more competitors, classify them into these categories:

- *Direct competitors.* These are the competitors that sell the same goods or services as you do and target the same audience as you do. These brands are often benchmarked by consumers when making a decision about what to purchase for themselves. For example, in the demo automation industry, Arcade and Storylane are head-to-head rivals.
- *Indirect competitors.* These companies provide distinct solutions to the same problem. They give you chances to increase the scope of what you provide. For instance, Scribe and Whatfix address the issue of internal training plus documentation, but in different ways.
- *Legacy competitors.* These are recognized firms that have been operating in your industry for some time now. People view their name as credible, and it has a good standing in the market. For example, Ahrefs is a direct competitor in the sphere of SEO services.
- *Emerging competitors.* These are new entrants in the market to established firms with unique value propositions and a creative business model. For example, ChatGPT overtook many brands and appeared in the conversational AI market as a challenger.

2. Find out where each competitor stands in the market

Once you have identified all your competitors, begin sorting them out according to the industry categorization. This stage will help you define your current market share and view the level of satisfaction of your clients. It will also indicate your main competitors in your field, to whom you should pay preference in the analysis report.

Also, you can determine what is missing in the existing situation by studying the market environment. Of course, in any market, there are niches and opportunities for your business, even for a single individual.

One should use the market presence as the Y-axis variable and customer happiness as the x-axis variable in order to plot the competitors' positions in the market. Now, place competitors in one of these categories:

- *Niche*. These are the brands that are relatively less popular, but the customers are highly satisfied with the products. It is most likely that they are targeting specific demographics successfully.
- *Contenders*. These brands are well placed in the market but customers' satisfaction surveys put them low. They could be recent competitors with a potent sales and marketing plan.
- *Leaders*. These companies have a significant market share and very happy clients. They are the main participants and well-liked by your viewers.
- *High performers*. These are yet another group of recent arrivals that have a low market share yet strong customer satisfaction ratings. They help in providing a good option for those who do not wish to purchase from high branded companies.

This will assist you in determining the market penetration in detail. However, it will also describe how the business can build momentum and challenge incumbents in the market.

3. Extensively benchmark key competitors.

This would assist you to narrow down your competitive focus in Step 2 to the key competitors you need to target among the other dozens of competitors. Now it is necessary to develop a benchmarking study, and perform the analysis of each competitor in detail.

Remember that the purpose of this exercise is not to bring out every one of the competitor's flaws. Each brand must be described with its strengths and weaknesses without showing any bias.

The following are the main things to think about when comparing competitors:

- *Quality.* Determine the quality of the products and services of each rival. Identify the features of their products and see what makes them stronger than you. Besides, one can also find out the quality of an organization's offering by assessing customer reviews.
- *Price.* To understand how your competitors are pricing their products, ensure to lay down their price points. Here are some recommendations on how one can obtain information on value for money from the users' perspective, specifically through interviews with customers.
- *Customer service.* Check out what support channels they have, for instance, chat, phone, email, knowledge base, and more. Customer feedback is also posted on several other websites as well.
- *Brand reputation.* To understand consumers' perceptions of the brand, it is also necessary to determine the position of each competitor within the market. Watch for any comments about some specific competitors that are not very positive.
- *Financial health.* If at all possible, look for financial performance measures that can be used to assess a brand's development over time. Information on such parameters as the profitability and the rate of sales can be obtained.

NOTE: Primary and secondary data will be utilized in this bench-marking exercise. Ensure that you give this stage enough time so that your competitive analysis is correct.

4. Examine their marketing strategy in detail.

Although the first few steps will help you identify areas for improvement in your main offering, you also need to research the product marketing strategies of your rivals.

To understand how they approach customers, you must go deeply into their marketing tactics. Consequently, you can assess each marketing channel and note down the observations regarding how they engage with the target audience and highlight their brand's values.

A few important marketing avenues to consider are as follows:

- *Website.* To know the positioning and brand voice, one has to look at the copy and structure of the website.
- *Email.* You can subscribe to their newsletters to learn more about the tone of writing, the type of copy that is used, and the kind of topics that are covered.
- *Paid ads.* To check if any competitors are using paid search engine ads, you can use Ahrefs and Semrush.
- *Thought leadership.* Some of the digital assets that can be used to measure a brand's thought leadership are podcasts, webinars, courses, and so on.
- *Digital PR.* Determine if a brand has spent money on digital PR as a means of creating awareness for the brand and analyze the strategy that has been adopted.
- *Social media.* Find out how often companies engage in the different social media platforms and which type of content is most engaging for the brands.
- *Partnerships.* In the cases of partnerships with high value it is necessary to check for the presence of close relationships and mutual benefits of cooperation with any businesses.

It is quite feasible to develop a detailed analysis of the competitor's advertising strategy that covers all the necessary aspects. This will put your marketing strategy on the right track.

5. Conduct a SWOT analysis

The creation of a SWOT analysis matrix for every organization is the last stage in a competitive analysis process. This means that you will track the strengths, weaknesses, opportunities, and threats of the competitor as presented above. Consider it the last stage in compiling all of your research to provide answers to the following questions:

- What are you not doing that your competitor is doing, and to what effect?
- In what way are they better than your brand?
- What can you claim as the weakness of your competitor?
- How is your brand better than the competitor?
- In which industries do you consider this rival as a threat?
- Has your competitor been able to discover any gaps in the market?

This data can be depicted with the help of tools like Miro. You will be able to identify the areas of competitive advantage over each of the competitors in the future after representing the given data in a presentable format.

Step 5: Organization and Management Structure

The business plan's organizational and management section should describe your team and its structure. It is usually positioned after the market analysis section of a business strategy. For instance, you run a limited liability company (LLC) with several members or a partnership type of business. In that case, you have to include it.

The following information should be included in this section of your business plan: These are the organizational structure of your company, the ownership details, the management team, and the board of directors' details.

When people read your business plan, they will be seeking information concerning key issues within your business, for instance, who will be in charge of what and why they are joining the board of directors or the staff and what they are expected to do. The functions of each department or division should be well articulated and explained about the work that is expected of them.

In case your organization has an advisory board, this part should describe the members that you intend on having on the board and how you will ensure this. What form of compensation and other reward packages are given to the employees of your company? What incentives do you have? What about promotion? Reassure your reader that your employees are not faceless names on a piece of paper.

What to Include in the Organization and Management Structure

Outlining your business structure through an organizational chart with a narrative is a simple but effective way of presenting your company's structure. This will show that there are no gaps, that you have thought through who will do what, and that each department in your business has a manager. That is vital information to any employer or investor who may be interested in the individual or organization.

- *Ownership details*

Your company's legal structure and any related ownership information should also be included in this section. Has your company been incorporated? Is it a C or S corporation if that's the case? Or maybe you and someone else have partnered. If so, what kind of partnership—general or limited—is it? Perhaps you operate as a lone owner.

You should include the following crucial ownership details in your business plan:

- Ownership forms (i.e., common stock, preferred stock, general partner, limited partner)
- Outstanding equity equivalents (i.e., options, warrants, convertible debt)
- Owner names
- Percentage ownership
- Level of participation in the company
- Common stock (i.e., authorized or issued)
- Management profiles
- Share with your reader the qualifications and experience of your company's owner/management team, as this is considered one of the most important success factors for any growing business.

Provide resumes with the following details included:

- Name
- Position (provide a brief description of the role and its main functions)
- Primary responsibilities and authority
- Education
- Specialized experience and skills
- Previous employment
- Particular skills
- Previous performance history
- Ensure that you put figures on your accomplishments such as; 'Supervised a sales force of ten people,' 'Supervised fifteen employees,' 'Increased revenue by 15 percent within the first six months,' 'Increased the number of retail outlets per year to two,' 'Raised the customer satisfaction from sixty percent to ninety percent.'
- Industry recognition

- Community involvement
- Years with the company
- Compensation basis and levels (make sure these are reasonable – not too high or too low)

Emphasize how the individuals around you enhance your abilities as well. If you're just getting started, demonstrate how each person's distinct experiences will add to the venture's success.

- ***Your board of directors' qualifications***

An unpaid advisory board's main advantage is that it can offer knowledge that your business otherwise cannot afford. A list of well-known, prosperous firm owners and managers can significantly improve the credibility of your business and the opinion of your management team's skill.

When creating the blueprint for your business plan, make sure to collect the following data if your business has a board of directors:

- Titles
- Board positions
- Level of involvement with the company
- Background
- Past and future contributions to the company's success

- ***Support professionals***

Let prospective investors know that you keep a close check on the lawyers, accountants, and other experts who are involved in your business, particularly if you're looking for finance. This is where you should include any contractors or freelancers that you employ in your business. As with the previous parts, you should include:

- Name

- Title
- Educational background
- or certifications
- Services rendered to your business
- Details about the relationships (retainer, as-needed, regular, etc.)
- Any other thing that would make them stand out as great professionals, for instance, any award or experience that makes it right to hire them for the work you need to be done.

Step 6: Products or Services Offered

The goods and services section of your business plan is more than the summary of the products your company will produce. Who gets what at what cost: the information investors need to have so that you can get their money should be included in this segment of your business plan, including the pricing of goods and services and the order fulfillment procedures, among others.

It should also provide details of the company's products and the company's unique selling proposition (USP) in relation to competitor firms. Potential factors that enhance this segment include elaborating on the awards activists have gained, prospective vendors, and production processes which may help in building investors' confidence.

What You Need to Include in Your Products and Services Section

1. The Description

Provide all the pertinent information about your offerings in this section. Use the 5W2H (who, what, when, where, why, how, and how much) method to answer the following questions in order to produce an appropriate description:

- *Who*. Who is eligible to utilize this product? Talk about the specifics of your ideal client.
- *What*. What core features make up your product? Features, materials, substances, prices, dimensions, and so forth are examples of these.
- *When*. What is the ideal time to utilize this product? If the product is seasonal, mention the season or the occasion. You can also state whether or not it is intended for a certain use.
- *Where*. Where are your clients supposed to use the product? Is it utilized outdoors or indoors? Give these specifics.
- *Why*. Why should your clients utilize your products? Talk about how the product meets their needs.
- *How*. How should they utilize your product? If there are any crucial user instructions, mention them.
- *How much*. How much of it should they use? Mention the recommended usage frequency that users of your product must adhere to.

2. Pricing Strategy

The methods you employ to determine a price for your goods and services are referred to as your pricing strategy. You can choose from a variety of tactics, but knowing which one best fits your business model will require you to do a price analysis.

Follow this step-by-step procedure to conduct a pricing analysis:

- *Determine cost of goods sold (COGS)*

You add all of the expenses you incurred before the sales to arrive at the total cost of your products and services. This will include wages for labor, cost of production, distribution costs, cost of packaging, cost of labeling, advertisement, and cost of warehousing. While setting the final price of your products, take the amount of profit that you intend to make and add it on top of your COGS.

- *Collect data about the price preferences of your customers.*

It is important to get an impression about the price through the target customers, and for this, questionnaires and surveys must be taken. This assists in deciphering how much the consumers are sensitive to the prices of the various products and services you intend to offer. Using this information one can be able to identify an appropriate price to charge that will help them make a profit but at the same time keep the demand up.

- *Study your competitors' prices*

Examining the prices of your direct competitors is possibly the greatest approach to determine whether a price is effective.

Those that sell similar goods to yours are your direct competitors. You can learn more about the price range for comparable products in the market by examining their pricing approach.

You can adjust your prices to establish a competitive price using this information.

- *Consider all the legal and ethical aspects*

It is necessary to set a pricing strategy that encourages sales. But do not price your product too low; this may lead to you slicing through the prices of your competitors. This technique is, however, not allowed in certain industries and is, at times, termed as predatory pricing. Thus, it is important to familiarize yourself with the laws that govern your business to avoid such concerns.

The following are the pricing strategies, and you can choose one for the firm after conducting the pricing analysis.

3. Product Comparison

Whatever you're selling, it's possible that someone else in the market already has it for sale. Indirect competitors, as opposed to direct competitors, market comparable products with slight variations.

You can make a comparison by looking at your competitors. Examine their offerings and make a list of the parallels and divergences to accomplish that.

Organize this data in tables by categorizing it into two groups: the qualitative and the quantitative. In the final paragraph, it is recommended to list the competitive advantages you have. Explain how you will apply those to counter your disadvantages.

4. Sales Literature

The written or graphic information that you use for the purpose of persuading, informing, or educating consumers so that they can buy your products is called sales literature. These consist of price lists, brochures, catalogs, newsletters, client endorsements, and case studies.

Make a list of all the sales literature you utilize to promote your products and services, along with a brief outline of the messages they contain. Your website is a crucial component of your sales literature; describe its impact on sales.

Maybe you have a blog where you tell your customers about new releases and market your products. Your sales literature will go there if you offer your goods and services exclusively through your website.

5. Order Management

Order processing includes all aspects of a customer's experience, from the time they make an order to delivery and post-purchase assistance.

This is where you explain the method of delivery to the clients and how they will place their order or make the purchase.

For example, order processing for an online retailer might have stages like these:

- Order placement
- Order processing
- Picking inventory
- Sorting
- Packing
- Shipping
- Product delivery
- Customer support
- Returns

The actions that must be taken in your order processing procedure will differ based on your services. Give a thorough explanation of each phase and specifics regarding its implementation.

6. Delivery Requirements

List any input factors that are necessary for the production and or marketing of your products and services here. Some of them can be equipment, vehicles, software, and technology, among others.

For instance, to run the café business and provide services to clients, it will need culinary equipment, and information technology solutions. In this area of the products and services section, one should point out all these aspects.

Another example is that in order to produce its goods, a consumer electronics company needs both a production site and an IT infrastructure. Such necessities as cars for the delivery of the products and computers for the clients to place their orders online are essentials of this type of business. All of these are elaborated in this passage.

7. Intellectual Properties

This should include referring to every Intellectual Property (IP) document that you have for your specific goods and services. These consist of patents, seller permissions, trademarks, licenses, and so forth.

In this section, you can also list any legal problems you're currently having and describe how you're handling them.

Enumerate possible negative consequences in the future and the preventive actions to be taken to prevent their occurrence. These are opting to buy an insurance cover and opting for safety labels and disclaimers.

8. Future Offerings

This is your chance to introduce the upcoming goods and services to potential partners or investors to influence them positively.

NOTE: If your future products are an upgrade of the existing products you have created, state the changes you wish to incorporate and whether the items are in the development process or complete.

Step 7: Marketing and Sales Strategy

The marketing and sales strategies of your business plan ensure that your business not only reaches the right audience but also successfully persuades them to purchase your products or services. Let's take a look at what each one stands for before we go further.

Marketing and sales strategy entails the set of plans and the course of action that a business devises to reach out to its target clientele and consumer base. This includes defining how one can advertise products or services, establishing how to get to the target market, and what type of wording would likely appeal to or attract the targeted clients.

The marketing with regard to the exterior domain involves advertising, social media marketing, content marketing, and public relations. It is concerned with the creation of awareness of the company and interest in it, as well as ensuring that consumers have a favorable perception of the business.

Whereas the sales strategy describes the directions and plans of how to turn potential customers into paying clients, including the patterns deployed to achieve the same. This comprises sales targets, scope of sales, sales force, the company's methods of pricing, and establishing outlets for the products. Some of the main steps in selling usually include selling presentations and contacts, selling negotiations, and selling follow-ups.

How to Develop a Marketing Plan

1. Identify your target audience

Your target market specifies your ideal customers by analyzing factors like demographics, psychographics, and behaviors of the relevant population. Examples of demographics are the age, gender, income, level of education, and geographical location of the receivers. For instance, nurture an MBA-endorsed pet-washing business. Your target audience might be families who have pets and are in the age category of 25-50, with a higher income level and residing in urban or suburban regions. It is basic demographic information or, in other words, a rough idea about the identity and location of your potential consumers.

After examining demographics, it is critical to analyze psychographic and behavioral factors to get a better understanding of the target population. Psychographics are about behavior and concern, lifestyle, interests, values, and attitudes. Concomitantly, behavior relates to buying patterns and the overall mode of handling similar goods or services. For instance, the Pet grooming service's target market could be clients who are willing to pay a lot of money for their pets and are willing to go the extra mile to get the best services for their pets. When it is possible to establish such needs and preferences, for instance, individualized pet care and convenience, the marketing and business can address them. This makes your business more attractive to the target audience and, hence more competent as per the needs of the market.

2. Clarify what you want to achieve with your marketing efforts

The major reason why it is important to define the goals of your marketing activities is the fact it provides your strategy with direction and also provides you with a benchmark to work towards. Your objectives should be specific, measurable, achievable, relevant, and time-bound, better known as SMART. For instance, if your business is selling clothes online, one of the goals could be to promote your brand. This might mean having the objective of raising the number of the organization's followers on social media platforms by 20% within six months by using effective ads and good content.

Another objective could be to create leads. As an example, you may be planning to attract 500 new email subscribers in the next three months via website pop-ups, social media posts and giveaways, and a free trial of the company's products for those who will subscribe to the company's newsletter. Finally, an objective to promote selling could entail the prospect of selling 15% more products per month in the coming quarter as the organization is planning to run a sequence of promotional emails about the availability of numerous products in the store and give discounts for the next 30 days for the repeated customers. These all assist you in directing your marketing operations in the right direction and help you measure the efficiency of the marketing strategies in achieving your business objectives.

3. Conduct market research

In this stage, it is necessary to gather and process all the data about the industry, tendencies in the current market, and competitors to make the right business decisions and possible opportunities. For instance, if you want to open a new coffee-selling shop, you are likely to undertake the following steps: examining the existing data regarding the coffee-selling business in terms of its size and growth rate and the likely consumer tastes. This might entail finding out what is written on the industry in analytical reports, following the trade fairs, or statistics on coffee consumption.

Secondly, it would be to synthesize the patterns in the market in relation to purchase behaviors and trends of the clients in order to spot gaps or new opportunities. For instance, it is possible to observe that the market is becoming more attractive to specialty coffee and goods that are friendly to the environment. Last of all, you would investigate your competitors to establish what they have to offer, what their price range is, and what their strong and weak points are. This might involve going to the nearest coffee shops to overview their menus and the kind of meaty service they offer to their customers. It assists a coffee shop in finding loopholes that exist in the market and takes an opportunity to start the coffee shop to fulfill the needs of the people. In due course, this will provide you with that much-desired competitive advantage.

4. Select the most effective channels to reach your target audience

Choose the appropriate methods of communication with the intended target market. The aim is to understand where your audience is or where your potential clients are and how they consume content. For instance, if you are trading in fashionable wear via an online store and your target audience is young adults, then you may use Instagram or TikTok. They make it possible to post presenting information, such as new collections' photos or videos, to an audience that is always active with such media.

Also, it is crucial to apply email marketing to keep communicating with the target audience and present special offers to them. For example, you can send bulletins with new products, special offers, and recommendations on how to dress stylishly. Another relevant channel is the so-called SEO in order to guarantee that your store shows up at the SERP when people search for specific pieces of clothing or tendencies in the fashion industry. This is because through SEO, it will be easier to include your site's relevant keywords hence being easier to find by users. Print media advertising like magazines, newspapers, or even business events directly associated with the fashion line also works if a particular audience mostly refers to specific magazines or if the business is involved in a particular event.

5. Create a content strategy

Your content needs to be in line with your UVP and aimed at saying something to your target market. Begin with the differentiation of the relevant themes and topics to your basic business values and the interests of the target audience. Your content may, therefore, be geared towards natural beauty, the advantages of using organic products, and skin care among organic skin care firms. It is important that this content be dedicated to informing, educating and even entertaining your audience while at the same time reminding them of the value and reasons for patronizing your products.

Then, choose what types of content will be more effective in disseminating your messages and appealing to the audience. Such may contain; 'Blog articles' which offer detailed information and are optimizable for SEO; 'Videos' as people like to see how to use the product and how satisfied customers are; 'Infographics,' which entail facts and tips in simple formats; 'Social media posts,' which converse with your audience on their preferred platforms.

REMEMBER: Consistency is key, so create a content calendar to schedule and plan your posts regularly.

NOTE: We will talk more about what your Unique Value Proposition (UVP) is and how to create it in Chapter 7.

6. Allocate resources for your marketing activities

Therefore, it is imperative to define your spending limit for your marketing activities in order to make good spending. This is the first and the primary step to take when engaging in marketing since it will enable one to evaluate the overall financial situation and, therefore, come up with a figure that one can set aside for the marketing process. Such aspects can include, but are not limited to, the annual revenue of your business, its profitability, and aimed growth rates. For instance, if you are a start-up or [small business], then. If that is the case, then you might start with a slightly low budget at the beginning and increase as you gain more sales and profits.

After identifying your budget, spread the money toward the various marketing activities to its proportion of relevance and any probable ROI. Budgeting entails assigning funds for advertisement purposes, content in the form of tweets, blogs, videos, and images, and all the tools that will enable the efficient running of the marketing plan, such as e-mail marketing platforms and tools to help manage social media accounts. One has to pay a lot of attention to how he spends his money and also to how each marketing communication tool is performing so as to effectively achieve the set marketing goals.

How to Develop a Sales Approach

1. Understand the sales process

Conventionally, business lead generation precedes the sales process, where potentials are sourced from marketing initiatives, words, and referrals. The first step after lead capture entails lead qualification; this is where the sales professionals assess whether or not the lead could adopt the company's product or service and whether this is viable through budget, need, and time. For instance, the Internal Quality Control of a software manufacturing firm may filter out its leads' sales to ascertain whether or not they have a challenge that the software can address besides whether they can finance it.

This is followed by the qualification process and the discovery stage, where the actual probing and understanding of the prospect's pains and goals takes place among the sales representatives. This stage is often characterized by asking more questions to clients, especially to identify their needs and concerns, while at the same time trying to establish a good relationship with the clients. For instance, a salesperson might conduct a detailed needs analysis to determine exactly how their product or service can address the prospect's pain points. Following discovery, proposal and presentation stages may occur, where a tailored solution is presented to the prospect, highlighting how it addresses their specific needs and offers value. Last but not least, the cycle is concluded by the closing phase, in which the bargaining is done and the contract is sealed. Every step in the sales funnel must contain specific activities and a properly planned strategy to help the prospect move through the funnel and make the desired decision.

2. Identify sales techniques

In order to determine which of the selling strategies your company has to use, one has to take into consideration several factors: the audience that has to be targeted, the goods or services that are being sold, and the general environment. The first one is consultative selling where the focus is put on gaining profound knowledge of the client's demands and providing individual approaches. This technique is best used when the client's issues are intricate and connected to the selection of a product or service to purchase. For instance, consultative selling in B2B software sales entails an exhaustive analysis of the customer's needs and the precise ways that the merchandise in consideration can meet those needs.

Another useful method is relationship selling, that is selling based on long-term cooperation with buyers. This approach works well in industries where the customer needs to trust the service provider and require constant assistance from the same provider for a long time, for instance, in the backbone industries like insurance, banking, luxury, or any other service industry. Relationship selling focuses on the development of long-term personal interaction routines, a general understanding of the buyer's needs, and the primary aim of offering more than mere products to the customer. For example, in relationship selling, a person, for instance, a financial advisor, might assist clients using financial planning services and follow up help.

REMEMBER: the best sales techniques for your business should align with your company's strengths, the nature of your products or services, and the preferences of your target audience.

3. Train your sales team

The sales people in your team must be armed with information and proper tools to enable perform their duties effectively. Some of the ways that you can accomplish this are to make sure that they are well informed regarding the sales process in its full cycles, starting from the acquisition of leads to the conversion process. That fundamental learning assists them in leading prospects through the sales funnel, strategically. For instance, facilitate awareness sessions or develop online learning tools to train them on how to prospect, qualify, conduct detailed sales calls, and present.

After that, move with teaching techniques apt for the business, like consultative selling or relationship selling in case of a given product or service type going for the target group. Such techniques can be rather helpful in terms of making role-playing exercises more special and intense while using them when role-playing: Offer them means that make their work easier, for example, Customer Relationship Management systems to deal with clients or sales tools that would grant the access to online resources containing marketing content and scripts.

Then, the extent to which one should explain and communicate their Unique Selling Proposition (USP) should be highlighted. Make sure your team can effectively communicate to your customers why your product/service is different from the rest in the market and why it speaks to customers' pain. Furthermore, train them how to deal with objections because you can act out the common objections and use the appropriate response, which has to be focused on the benefits of your product.

REMEMBER: When you invest in comprehensive training that covers these aspects—sales process, techniques, tools, UVP communication, and objection handling—you empower your sales team to perform at their best. This will eventually drive increased sales and customer satisfaction.

4. Develop sales scripts and materials

Equip your salespeople with the tools that will allow them to connect with a buyer and calm him down if needed. One of the approaches to this is preparing the sales scripts that detail the general points to be made and the responses to most likely questions or concerns. These scripts should, in one way, be more elastic in order to enable them to cater to various situations, but at the same time should present some measure of standardization in their message. For instance, create a script to incorporate into the sales reps' first call, the product pitches and closing conversations to ensure that they can speak the UVP of your product with full understanding and also be in a position to deal with the likely objections.

Finally, create sales pitches that are convincing in order to convey the advantages and the seller's offerings. Such presentations should be visually appealing and logically built in a way that would emulate the prospect's attention while presenting you and your offering as the ulti-mate solution to their issues. Add more examples with our service, testimonials, and statistics that would help to make your statement more credible.

It is also possible to hand over additional marketing material, which can comprise brochures, case descriptions, or white literature papers, which the sales representatives can use to convey personally or e-mail to potential clients. These materials should build on the points told in your scripts and presentations and complement the information that a prospect needs to make a decision.

NOTE: Revise and edit these sales scripts and other sales-related materials to reflect feedback from your sales team as well as from customers from time to time.

5. Implement a customer relationship management (CRM) system

A CRM system consolidates each prospect and customer's data, behaviors, history, and preferences into one system. This centralized database significantly improves the communication of sales with clients, tracks leads through the pipeline and controls real-time selling activities.

The advantages of CRM in selling are as follows: The leads obtained from marketing campaigns, advertisements, and other sources can be sorted according to parameters such as lead quality, quantity, and location and be assigned to the right sales officer based on rules that have been set earlier. This way, leads are followed up on time and given personalized attention, which helps in increasing the conversion rate. For instance, when using the CRM system in the business, it is possible to program the sending of emails based on the prospects' behaviors and actions, resulting in an improved probability of making prospects buy the company's products.

Another benefit of a CRM system is that it keeps track of the flow of the leads and gives a view of where every single lead is in the sales funnel. Sales reps are able to record calls and partake in notes while on a call or meeting, as well as set follow-ups to any leads, which means that leads do not go unnoticed and opportunities are everything is made easy in a bid to ensure they do not slip through the cracks. It also assists in projecting the sales revenues ahead of time and in determining the areas of constraints or opportunities for enhancing the sale process.

In addition, it is important to note that CRM includes reporting and analytical tools where the sales managers can create detailed reports about such parameters as conversion ratio, the rates of sales for the teams and particular members, and others on the revenues by periods. With these, business decisions are informed and accurate, and your sales team would know which areas to target, which strategies to adopt, and most optimally, how best to use available resources in order to have the greatest effect.

6. Establish follow-up procedures

Enumerating proper follow-up processes also enables organizations to continue contact with prospects and captures the lead agenda of changing them into consumers. Initially, you have to establish how you are going to follow up depending on the steps of the selling process and the level of interest of the prospect. For example, if you met or demoed a product and then said that you would get in touch in a week or so, follow through and call or email the client within the timeframe.

Next, always give individualized follow-up messages that show good listening and acknowledgment of the prospect's requirements to show consistency in meeting their needs. Retained communication history of the customer should be used to decide on the right messages to send to the target customers. For instance, return to those points that the prospect may have raised in previous discussions and address them to indicate that you have been following the conversations and are in touch with their concerns.

Leverage the automation components of the CRM system to set up reminders on follow-ups and regular messages. This ensures that follow-ups are proper and timely even if there are many leads that need to be followed up. Automation can also lay down the processes of sending follow-up e-mails to prospects depending on their actions or even certain events, such as downloading a white paper or visiting the pricing section of your website.

Then, update all progress and results of follow-up processes in the chosen CRM or other sales monitoring systems. This makes it possible to continue with a series of communications with fellow team members and enables everyone to have a record of the flow of the interaction with each of the prospects. It also determines if there are any certain patterns or trends that are likely to help in formulating strategies on when to follow up in order to enhance the impact of the sales.

7. Evaluate and optimize

You still have to remain competitive and attain this growth in the long run. This is only possible when or if they estimate and measure or if they have incorporated the evaluation and optimization processes. Get opinions from your salespeople frequently on the obstacles they encounter, the success of certain sales approaches, and from the customers. The other approach is a direct approach where one gets to ask the customers directly about their buying experience and level of satisfaction and point out the areas of discomfort. Formulate some of the insights to improve the strengths and weaknesses identified in your sales and develop or alter strategies as needed to respond to customers' requirements or to improve on the general sales procedures.

REMEMBER: Thus, adopting the culture of constant improvement could help you react quickly to the changes in the market, increasing sales effectiveness and nurturing effective customer relationships in the long run.

Step 8: Financial Projections

A financial projection takes figures from existing knowledge of revenues and expenditures of the business to forecast fixed cash inflow and outflow for the next months. These financial projections can be used internally by designing goals and processes of businesses depending on season, trend, and financial background. These are known as cash flow projections, which cover a period of three to five years and are useful in explaining and justifying financial decisions.

Consequently, expecting financial situations can also be used with the aim to prove investors' actual anticipated development as well as the profits of your business. Many facts, which need to support your projection, are utilised in both documents though a financial statement is more appropriate for most of the lenders.

While such calculations are not always accurate, projections are great for getting an idea of how financially solvent your business will be in the future. A number of factors can impact your revenue performance, and financial predictions highlight these particular factors:

- Internal sales trends
- Identifiable risks
- Opportunities for growth
- Core operation questions

NOTE: You should review and update your report on a frequent basis, not just once a year, to assist in managing unforeseen risks and variables that could affect your financial projections.

How to Create Your Financial Projection as a Startup

Business forecasting is carried out in the same manner, no matter the fact that you are projecting for an already existing enterprise or writing a business plan.

The fundamental difference is whether you gathered historical information (existing enterprises) or made the information (new or startup organizations) from your study and previous work.

Bear in mind that although you will be having the preparation of these papers all by yourself, the probability is you will be finalizing each of them by using the reference of each name. For example, if you are preparing your cash-flow statement, sources of revenue estimate may differ.

To guarantee that you can put together clear and comprehensive financial projections, it is best to consider each document as a reference for the others as well as as a piece of the financial projection puzzle all on its own.

1. Start With Sales Projection

Developing your income statement begins with a sales forecast. Using a time horizon of 12 months and 36 months or 60 months can be a starting point, though you must expect that the precision shall gradually deteriorate if there is no preceding financial data.

It is recommended to act in accordance with the utilization of monthly income statements until the estimated break-even point, where sales exceed all the costs and there is a demonstration of profit. Using the Annual income statements is possible after attaining the break-even point with your business.

Also, exclude all the aspects that do not involve sales increases. Your perfectly brewed forecasts are vulnerable to market forces like market concern, international environment, political and health factors, and other business occurrences like the problem of sourcing where price fluctuates and the variable costs increase can annihilate your projections if considered.

Divide the sum of the net sales to be realized over the projection period by the most probable number of units for the purpose of arriving at the per-unit price. Capitalization is done against your entire period's sales.

Subsequently, to find the total costs of making these units, called the cost of goods sold, or COGS, sometimes known as the cost of sales, the per-unit cost needs to be multiplied by the total amount of units that have been produced.

Your gross profit margin is, therefore, obtained when you subtract your COGS from your expected sales. Deduct all running expenses such as wages, advertising expenses, rent, and all other expenses from the gross margin. The estimated operational income, also known as the net operation income, is the resulting figure you arrive at.

2. Cash Flow Statement

A cash flow prediction has the ability to monitor your expected cash receipts and payments from finance and investments, and monetary generated from operations.

Purchasing property or supporting research and development, besides the primary business processes, are examples of investment activities.

The flow of cash received from a business firm for giving corporate loans or received by a company from investors is a financing operation, whereas the payment of cash to redeem the bonds or to distribute the dividends to the shareholders is an example of a financing operation.

This enables you to forecast the specific amount of money that you will require to meet your daily expenses or the cost of supplying working capital, funding growth and innovation, and or handling an emergency, hence the need for a good and accurate cash flow forecast.

3. The Balance Sheet

The balance sheet provides a general picture of how a company has fared in a certain period by itemizing its assets, liabilities, and owner's equity.

Liabilities on the balance sheet refer to the organization's obligations, which include bank loans, other loans, and account payables. Assets are things such as capital, houses, and stocks, among others. Adding to it, owner's equity is the total amount remaining out of the total liabilities.

Of course, when you grow you expect to see your company's Balance Sheet pulling it off through reduction of liabilities and enhancement of owner equity.

Step 9: Funding Requirements

Funding needs in a business plan relate to the money an entrepreneur or a business needs to commence or expand an enterprise and how such money will be used. This section explains the requirements of funds needed for the operation and accomplishment of the company's goals involving equipment, stock, advertisements, employees' salaries, and overhead. It also defines where the funding is to be sourced; this could be from equity investment, loans, grants, or any other financing. It elaborates cash flow expectations from operations in terms of repayment or return to the expected investors or lenders.

Determining Capital Needs and Funding Sources

First, you need to determine the amount of capital you need for your business by identifying start-up costs as well as business operational expenses.

Startup costs include all the costs that are incurred when starting up a new business or when undertaking a new business venture. These costs are occurred before the establishment of the business and most of them arise from acquiring items and expenses which are necessary for the smooth starting up of the business. Other examples of start-up costs would be costs associated with equipment rental or purchase more than the first period of use, initial stock, professional fees including legal, fees for conducting research and studies on the market and clients, costs that may have accrued on designing brand and logo, developing a website, creating advertising campaigns, nominal costs that are incidental to getting the permits and licenses, and working capital that will cater for the first several months of operation.

Fixed costs are costs that are predictable and are repeated to be paid out in the process of operating an already-existing business. These are known as operating expenses and are costs that are widely expected to be used frequently so as to keep the business running. For example, when starting the bakery business, the amounts spent on the equipment, such as ovens and utensils, among others needed for the production, will be considered startup costs. Comparatively, operating expenses in the subsequent periods would provide for daily and frequently occurring costs like buying more ingredients for baking, paying employees' wages, catering for rent or lease on the bakery space, and promoting the bakery through media frequently.

After that, the sources of funds which are able to satisfy such capital requirements should be identified. Below are various funding sources you can consider:

Personal savings

Personal savings are the savings in one's capacity as an individual, which may include saving up money. Beginning a business using your savings means that you shall not be indebted to anyone for the business capital. This means that there is full control of the business activities without being a debtor to banks or investors. You remain in full control and are the one who makes all the choices. The obvious advantage of this approach is that you can finance your business and remain flexible and independent.

Loans from banks or financial institutions

Funds borrowed from a bank or any financial company are one of the means of obtaining larger sums of funds for your business. They entail certain legal requirements that you have to fulfill as to the mode and schedule of the repayment of borrowed funds, together with the agreed rates of interest. They are particularly useful in business that requires a lot of capital at the beginning, for instance, the purchase of equipment, replenishment of stocks, or control of market expansion. Banks and other related financial institutions evaluate your creditworthiness and your business plan to arrive at the amount and the rate of interest to charge. Able to create the credibility of your business when repaying the debts may lead to the unlocking of further credit for your business.

NOTE: it is crucial to look at repayment and review your business's ability to meet the required monthly payments you commit to without and struggle or default.

Investors (Angel Investors or Venture Capitalists)

Investors are also an important source of funding your business since they will provide the funding you need in exchange for a percentage of equity in the business. Angels and venture capitalists are participants who carry out funding of start-ups or companies that are growing. Angel investors put their own money into new businesses to help finance their operations in return for shares in the company or expected earnings.

They can join in during the business-sourcing stages and provide advice and leads on prospective projects due to their experience; hence, they can be of great influence. Venture capitalists, on the other hand, work for firms that assemble capital from various investors for the financing of business enterprises with high growth prospects. They bring in bigger cash to the company they expect a share of the firm in return as well as high returns on their capital. Each is vital in supporting the expansion of enterprises and not only incorporating a financial contribution but also generating ideas to counteract the difficulties and capitalize on opportunities in the stipulated domain of operation.

Grants from government agencies or nonprofit organizations

Government or non-profit organization's funds are referred to as non-repayable funds as they are provided to the businesses for a particular purpose. These grants are typically given based on criteria such as the business's potential for innovation, its impact on the community or industry, or its alignment with social or environmental goals. They can be used to fund such business undertakings as research and development, entering new markets, products or services, geographical expansion, or charitable giving projects.

Grants are essentially a type of funding that do not minimize any stakes in organizations or businesses or result in a business accruing more debts, as is the case with loans: that makes grants specifically helpful for startup companies or firms interested in funding projects that will benefit society or address environmental issues.

How Will Funds Be Utilized?

Next, it will be crucial for you to know/convey how funds will be used once you have identified sources of funds. This includes a projection of how the capital that you need will be utilized in order to fund different sectors of your business. First of all, it is useful to define concrete costs, for instance, identified as the necessary equipment to perform the production or deliver services that would be considered major investments in the context of the business. This helps your business acquire the infrastructure it needs to run without hitches from the onset. Secondly, future investment in advertisement and other promotional schemes should be made to let more and more people get to know about the company and its products and thereby increase its sales. This might involve web-based advertising procedures like search engine marketing, social media marketing and usual marketing in targeting your clientele.

Also, the direct expenses for personnel costs should be included to fund the employee's wages and salaries, including those employees crucial to the running of the business. This helps in having a competent team to address the tasks at hand and contribute to the organization's development. Finally, if included within your business plan, set money aside for research and development — this means money to be spent on growth, new ideas, or enhancement of an existing product or search for new markets. This is a preventive measure that micro business owners can take in order to ensure that they are operationally competitive in the existing market structures.

Step 10: Appendix

Lastly, there is the appendix section within a business plan where all such data and any form of backup information for the statements made in the plan will be placed.

Some of these technical reports and papers, solid financial reports and statements with various numbers, charts, and tables, or other reports that could not be accommodated in the sections above might fall under this.

The audience it serves can be likened to a reference section where the readers, who may want more depth information that you presented in the business plan, can turn to.

What Should Be in Your Appendix?

Some of these documents may be included in the appendix section of your business plan, depending on your needs as a business and who your plan is designed for.

1. Supplementary information

Documents that supplement and expound upon information discussed in earlier sections of your business plan may be included here.

Examples of additional information that can be provided are:

- Charts, graphs, and tables used in the analysis
- Sales and marketing material
- Website and social media documentation

- Raw data, research methods, and research protocols
- Questionnaires and survey instruments
- Product blueprints and images
- Technical and user documentation
- Detailed competitor analysis
- Property designs

2. Legal documents

Including legal and compliance documents in your appendix helps indicate that you follow all laws and legal requirements. You may gain the confidence of your stakeholders and possible investors by being transparent in this way.

These are just instances of the several legal documents you can include:

- Incorporation papers
- Licenses and Permits
- Intellectual properties, i.e., trademarks, copyrights, patents.
- Building permits and rental agreements
- Supplier and vendor contracts
- Equipment documentation
- Stock certificates

3. Organizational and personnel details

You will provide details in this area that will give readers an idea of how your business operates and the people who run it. Several of these documents consist of:

- Organizational chart
- Job descriptions and hiring procedures
- Resumes for executive positions
- Certifications and degrees

- Affiliates such as attorneys or accountants

4. Additional financial documents

Adequate financial data is already included in the major body of your financial plan. However, depending on your target audience, they may require access to extra information such as:

- List of assets within the business
- Credit history
- Business and personal tax returns
- Spreadsheets of financial projections
- Historical and current financial statements
- Equity structure and debt repayment plan
- SBA (Small Business Administration) loan agreements and business loans.

5. Achievements and testimonials

Finally, you can provide evidence of accomplishments that support the success and integrity of your brand. This is an excellent place to emphasize:

- Media and press clippings
- Testimonials and success stories
- Expert endorsements
- Awards and achievements

Tips to Make Your Appendix More Enriching

- *Make it scannable*

Ensure that the information which is provided in the appendix section of your paper is understandable and easily retrievable. If the reader is going to be accessing various documents, then when preparing the documents, ensure that you include the table of contents.

- ***Relate to the business plan***

Each thing that you include in the appendix should relate to the thoughts and data in the business plan.

Including footnotes to the supplemental papers and the facts described in the business plan, one can create a link.

- ***Don't forget to include the confidentiality statement***

Add a clause stating that certain information contained in the documents is privileged and confidential if you are sharing certain legally restricted documents such as the balance sheet. This is a practical way of ensuring that those individuals who are allowed privileged information do not pass it to a third party.

- ***Keep the appendix supplementary***

When writing your business plan, ensure that it can sustain itself and is not dependent on an appendix. It is unwise to risk having potentially low content in the main area as your viewers rarely will get to this part of the content.

NOTE: Thus, never attempt to put information in the appendix that the reader must be aware of in its totality; all information in the appendix should be additional only.

Chapter 6
Marketing Psychology

Knowing what customers want and what will draw them in is important when marketing to them, whether they are current or potential. If you don't get your client's attention right away, someone else will. Understanding your target audience's opinions is essential for effective marketing. You can better comprehend what motivates people to make decisions—especially purchases—if you are aware of how they think.

You can adjust your marketing strategy to fit every personality you wish to draw in and retain once you begin to understand this. It is important to understand that different customer bases may require different marketing strategies. Understanding a few marketing psychology concepts will help you produce eye-catching marketing materials targeted at your target market.

Let's first define marketing psychology before delving deeper into it.

What is Marketing Psychology?

Marketing psychology entails conducting research to ascertain the reasons behind people's thinking and actions. By integrating general psychological concepts into their strategies, marketers can be able to understand the consumer's perception of their communication. Marketing psychology, on the other hand, helps marketers to convince customers to purchase products or behave in a specific manner.

It is important to note that the brain operates in a certain manner and employs certain strategies to facilitate individuals' decision-making. Acquiring the knowledge of those shortcuts will assist you in increasing your followers. In short, being aware of the what, how, and why of people's behavior and thinking will help design a more effective marketing plan. In addition to this, this knowledge could help you to build another business identity.

Understanding Consumer Behavior

Consumer behavior can be defined as the actions and processes that people go through when they choose, use, and dispose of a product or a service. The consumers' behavior in the market is determined by numerous psychological, sociological and cultural factors.

The process is divided into several stages, which are problem-solving, data gathering, alternative assessment, choice of supplier, and evaluation after the purchase. In the course of these phases, there are several factors that may affect the consumers; these include the individual's perceived beliefs and values, societal standards, persuasion messages, product characteristics, and situational aspects.

Markets are a crucial factor that businesses need to understand in order to create proper marketing strategies and offer products that satisfy the customers' necessities and desires. The marketing personnel require understanding and interpreting consumer behavior data so as to make proper marketing decisions on trends and patterns of consumption and demand in order to influence product design, price, promotion and distribution.

The Psychology of Buying

Buyer psychology involves the cognitive and behavioral processes of buyers that lead to the decision to purchase a certain product. It focuses on the psychological, emotional, and cognitive factors that affect consumers' decision to buy a product or consume a service.

Assume that you are a watch seller in the premium category. Elements such as the influence of a friend's appeal to emotions and the popularity of the watch brand may have influenced this person to buy this watch.

REMEMBER: you may adjust your marketing and sales tactics to better suit the needs and wants of your target audience by learning what drives them to make a purchase. Let's examine some of the major variables that affect consumers' purchasing decisions and offer helpful advice on how businesses can apply these insights to increase profitability.

Factors Influencing Consumer Decisions

Consumers' decisions are impacted by psychological factors as well as personal, social, and cultural factors. Knowledge of these factors will enable one to use appropriate strategies to address the needs and wants of the customers.

1. Psychological Factors

The psychological factors that drive consumer decisions include

- *Perception*

Perception is the process through which an individual receives, organizes, and interprets their stimuli information to provide a meaningful configuration of the environment. Sensory marketing is how consumers visually, auditory, tactually, gustatory, and olfactory perceive products and brands. For instance, a consumer stops at a particular product due to the attractive packaging or a tease that accompanies an advert. Let's say there is a perfume, and it has a nice-looking bottle, and the company associates it with the feeling of luxury. In that case, the consumers might perceive the product as being elite, and therefore, they would wish to acquire one. Likewise, if a product is packaged ugly or if the packaging design of the product is complex, then it can lead. In that case, for a lot of people, it is going to be considered as low quality even if, when it comes to results, it is a lot more effective.

- ***Motivation***

Motivation is a phenomenon that describes the internal processes that consumers go through to achieve their needs and wants. Among the most popular theories of consumption motivation, it is possible to mention Maslow's hierarchy of needs. For instance, at the personality level of the need hierarchy, consumers need food and water, which are basic physiological needs. An example is a fast food restaurant that gains from it by offering quick, tasty meals. For instance, at the top of the pyramid, consumers may be driven by esteem products, whereby they are getting products that are socially recognized as being of high status, including cars and branded clothes. A brand like Rolex does not sell watches with a message that says they are watches, but instead says status symbols.

- ***Learning***

The general nature of learning is focused on the change of behavior among consumers as influenced by past events. For instance, a customer who has a particular brand of smartphone prefers to order from the same brand to avoid being disappointed and become loyal to the brand. This is why corporations spend their resources to deliver good customer relations and quality goods and services. Likewise, the situation where a customer experiences a negative value, say, through a low quality product or unsatisfactory services, will serve to eliminate the 'brand' from the list of preferred brands for the future. For instance, a consumer purchases a new electronic gadget but the gadget has a short life span and often has breakdowns. In that case, they will not buy from that specific brand again, and the worst, they will refer that brand to others.

- *Beliefs and Attitudes*

Perceptions are usually enduring psychological states of mind and are concepts that consumers hold in their minds with regard to products, brands, and services. These can greatly affect the buying decision. For instance, an individual with PVA who sees organic food as healthier will always order organic products as opposed to non-organic ones. This leads them to buy organic products even if the normal ones are cheaper in the market, as seen in the hypothesis. Likewise, perceptions related to the brand may be influenced by marketing communication, consumer and other people's talk, and consumption experiences. For instance, let a consumer has a favorable perception toward a given brand, say Apple, they will conceive it to be innovative and so reliable. In that case, it has every likelihood of making repeat sales of its product to the end consumer and even persuading other consumers to patronize its product.

2. Personal Factors

This has also been shown to mean that gender, culture, and a person's understanding of how a certain item could help fix a certain problem, for instance, how food containers that are microwave-safe could help with dinner preparation, affects the products and services that a person will pay for.

Some of the personal factors that drive consumer decisions are:

- *Age and Life Cycle Stage*

Selling targets, needs, brands, and consumers' financial abilities and preferences also differ depending on the age and life stage of the consumers. For instance, youths may consider fashionable apparel and devices as gadgets as their primary wants due to the urge to conform to the young generation's standards. Thus, luxury fruit vendors such as Apple and fashionable clothing brands such as H&M invest in this target market offering products and advertising campaigns appealing to hi-tech youth Penn, 2001. On the other hand, middle-aged consumers might consider more practical products; those that are long-lasting may be home appliances and family cars. For example, Toyota and Whirlpool corporations target this market segment with a focus on solidity and family-oriented characteristics. In contrast, older consumers might be interested in some healthcare products and services wherein Nestle's Ensure and Philips medical company focus on conveying healthy and positive images to this segment.

- *Occupation and Economic Situation*

Occupation and the overall economic situation of a consumer greatly affect the purchasing capability and expenditures that are spent on products. For example, an income-earning individual such as a corporate executive earning a good salary would be more disposed to spend on expensive prestige goods such as Rolex watches or holidays at five-star hotels. Their work may also involve wearing specific uniforms and accessories; therefore, they are forced to make further expenses on professional clothing of Hugo Boss or Brooks Brothers. On the other hand, a low-income earner, for instance, a student or a first-time employee, will most likely consider price shift and quality when choosing where to shop; they may prefer Walmart or Target, for example. Moreover, certain products may be relevant to their profession; a builder, for example, would probably buy sturdy and reliable working shoes from Timberland, and a graphic designer would get Apple or Dell laptops for efficient performance.

- *Lifestyle*

Another personal factor is the level of living, which defines the way of living of a person or group of people. Lifestyle captures how consumers invest their time and money in activities, interests, and opinions they hold. An example is the case of an active product segment where the consumer is likely to draw a balance in favor of sales that relate to products and services touching on health and fitness. Companies like Nike and Fitbit use this demographic by making sports wear, running shoes, and tracking devices, respectively. These consumers are characterized by their affinity to advertising that spears an appeal to performance, the health sector, membership of running clubs, and the like. Consequently, while a person living in the country-side may consider fun and quality as the most important factors, such as fun and quality, a person with a more intensive schedule associated with the life of big cities will prefer products that are exactly the same – the services of Blue Apron for the delivery of food or Uber for delivery from restaurants. Firms in business targeting this segment tend to focus on messages such as convenience and saving time from clients in their advertising strategies.

- *Personality and Self-Concept*

Consumer personality and self-image affect the kind of products that consumers are likely to get attached to since, for every consumer, this is an avenue through which they can portray their personality. For instance, a consumer whose personality is associated with creativity and self-directional will require items such as hand-crafted or Non-mainstream, and those that the consumer can specify their color and size. Such consumers are focused on web-based stores, for example, Etsy, which sells handmade and vintage items and therefore aims at the target audience interested in the uniqueness and customization of the products. However, a consumer who cares about nature is more likely a focus on ecologically friendly products and will give preference to some companies that pay attention to this problem, for example, Patagonia or The Body Shop. Sometimes, these brands promote the environ-mental-friendly initiatives and products they support as well as the ethical sources of their materials that will resonate with the self-image of this segment.

3. Social Factors

The products and services buyers choose to purchase may also be influenced by social factors such as their place of residence and family dynamics.

Under the social factors, we have the following:

- *Family*

Family is an important aspect that has a direct influence on consumer behavior. It was clearly indicated that the opinion of the family influenced customers' buying behavior, particularly for household products and services. For instance, the roles of caring for children are evident especially when the parents are deciding on their children's preferred cereals brands or the friendly vacation spots for a family. Thus, a family with children under 12 years might choose a minivan with comfortable space, for example, a Honda Odyssey, rather than a sports car. In the same manner, children can also cause shifts in the parents' consumption patterns by requesting specific toys, clothing, or food. When communicating the message to consumers, marketers focus on the aspects that are important to family members by appealing to their reasoned and emotional needs, needs relating to the children, and needs involving the parent's respect by pointing at aspects like the nutritional value of the foods or safety and entertainment aspects of cars among others.

• *Reference Groups*

Reference groups are people to which the consumers relate or wish to be like; they can be family members, co-workers, or movie stars. These groups Shape the consumers' attitudes, opinions, and behavior in a very big way. For instance, if all the people in a certain group are using a given brand of smartphone, then it will be because everyone wants to be identified with the group and, therefore, needs to conform with the rest by using the same brand as the rest of them. Reference groups are frequently used in regard to influencer marketing when celebrities or popular bloggers promote goods. An example of such a strategy is a beauty brand that might work with key beauty bloggers to popularize its lots, and the fans of those bloggers would buy those products by recommendation of their beloved influencers. Likewise, expert associations or people in the same working field may take part in the decisions concerning commodities, for instance, the business computer program or the corporate uniforms.

• *Roles and Status*

Another aspect that may be mentioned as influencing the purchases is the position in daily social and occupational interactions as well as the status one has. A person is mostly in a certain status as a parent, employee, student, or leader within the society, which determines their needs and wants. For instance, the youth may require the best clothing and accessories to wear in the workplace, especially when they have a corporate job, including a suit from Brooks Brothers or a Samsonite briefcase. At the same time, a college student might always look for cheap and use-oriented products like Acer cheap laptops or IKEA cheap furniture for the dorms. Companies also tend to set their products with specific roles and statuses, where marketers show how these commodities can be helpful and valuable for those positions. For instance, the social platform LinkedIn offers its superior services to the working class in their bid to further their careers; the platform's key selling point is the all-encompassing opportunity to network.

- *Social Class*

Purchasing power and standards of living, such as income, education, and occupation, create a bond between social class and consumer behavior. First of all, the brands, the products, and the services preferred could also vary considerably depending on the extent of social class. For instance, the high class will go for a brand like LV or BMW because these brands symbolize success in their eyes. These consumers are usually reached with messages that contain concepts such as scarcity, superiority, and prestige. On the other hand, lower-class citizens are likely to emphasize the values and use the brands such as Walmart or Ford. It may be the reason why marketing communication to this consumer segment is typically based on the economizing message of affordability, durability and functional utility.

The Role of Emotions in Marketing

Being a social being we humans are probably the most emotional of all living beings on earth. This is primarily because their capacity to convey their feelings to other people verbally, non-verbally, in writing or whatever other conceivable way that is available is what makes them the best. This element is well known by the marketers proper to their placement in the marketing industry and employs the use of emotional appeal. Though human minds create marketing strategies, there is always an emphasis put on the aspect of emotions. Feelings are effective marketing appeals because they can influence consumers' choices and build long-term associations with commercial companies. Thereby, specialists can design culture touchpoints that are even more engaging and appeal to people's emotions.

Below are key elements of utilizing emotions in marketing to create strong and long-lasting connections with the target consumers.

David Whitehead

How to Incorporate Emotions Into Marketing to Build Deep Emotional Connections With Consumers

1. Understand customer emotions

Any effective marketer tries to understand the cue of and feel to which his market is susceptible. Research is a way that allows marketers to discover the necessities, concerns, and aims of the target consumers by means of market investigations, customer data assessment, and application of such techniques as focus groups and surveys. From this information, they are ready to adjust their strategies of marketing and use particular stimuli to wake up certain emotions in their target audience.

2. Master the art of storytelling

Marketers are likely to create an understanding with consumers via the use of stories that embrace the lives, beliefs, and aspirations of all people. A good story can make the listener or reader feel happy, empathetic, nostalgic, or feel that they belong to a certain group. The potential of storytelling marketing communication tools can help marketers create a bond between their business and its consumers by appealing to the latter's belief system by telling the story of why the business is important.

3. Provide personalized content

Individuals' emotional processes can be appealed from the side of marketing communications and experiences regarding what the person likes. Marketers might develop content that reflects the characteristics of the customers for this reason to be directed towards the needs of the customers. Employees who remember their customers, showing them that the company values them and that the company respects customer individuality, stand a good chance of making those customers do business with the company.

4. Make use of visual and sensory elements

The visual and sensory aspects have the ability to emotionally trigger people. It is possible to stir up specific emotions using such things as colors, captured pictures, sounds and even smells. To achieve arousal in consumers, these components can be put intentionally by the marketers in branding, packaging, ads as well as in-store experience. For instance, warm colors and soft lighting used in a retail store will create the perception of comfort, thus making the customer spend a lot of time with the business, hence creating a positive rapport.

5. Use emotional appeals to create emotional connections

The Advertisement, which employs appeals to emotions, can be very effective as consumers are likely to be moved by it. Very often, marketers use humor, appeal to past experiences, fear, or empathy to establish a particular emotional connection with the audience. The observers' perceptions of a brand can be influenced and the customers receive a powerful brand image in the shape of lust commercials.

6. Prioritize trust and authenticity

Consumers have an emotional connection with the brands they perceive as trustworthy, honest, and transparent. Responding to clients' comments and interacting with them also promotes trust together with emotional relationships.

Navigating Cognitive Biases

The human mind, when processing information from its environment, can systematically err in its cognitive processes, and this affects its decision-making. This is a psychological error termed cognitive bias.

Thus, it can be described as errors in judgment, the irrationality of rationality, and limitations of decision-making. Everyone has prejudices, and denying it means the person is in denial, which is another type of prejudice.

Cognitive biases are real, and they influence how customers receive and process information about products and services, which is an aspect of marketing that may influence the customers' decision to buy. For instance, the Anchoring bias explains the tendency to overweight initial information received and underweight subsequent information in the decision-making process. Marketers who give information that can serve as an anchor will be in a vantage position; for instance, setting a higher price than offering a discount.

Common Cognitive Biases in Marketing and How to Leverage Them for Success

1. Anchoring Bias

Anchoring bias is a common phenomenon where people rely on the initial information provided to make decisions. If you are looking for a used car, for instance, the first price that you come across that you like will act as your base price; any price below that is considered cheap, and anything above it is expensive.

To benefit from this type of advertising bias, you have to be the first brand that comes to the minds of consumers. Of course, regular consumers who are already acquainted with your brand will be able to do it more easily.

- During big retail holidays like Black Friday, make sure to start advertising early.
- When displaying a discount, always put the crossed-out info first in order to put the size of the discount into perspective.
- In search menus, always put highlighted deals at the top.

NOTE: If someone is a member of your loyalty program, they probably check out your discounts first since they have unused points or coupons in their account. This makes a rewards program an excellent tool to promote the anchoring bias.

- Put the main selling points at the top of the program's landing page
- If you have a subscription program, always showcase the annual membership first, especially if the monthly price is lower
- Offer double point campaigns during the holidays to make your loyalty offerings more enticing than the competitors'

2. Confirmation Bias

Confirmation bias is a cognitive bias where a person will seek out and interpret information in a way that supports their existing beliefs while disregarding or dismissing information that does not. It is for this reason that such bias can greatly affect both the marketers as well as the consumers. For example, marketers may not pay much attention to the data collected related to the marketing plan and the feedback that they receive, thus missing out on important information that could restrict the need for change. On the other hand, consumers may stick to brands and products that reflect their own inclinations and values, thereby ignoring other similar brands and products that do not share the same concept.

This bias can cause people to have a limited view of the world and focus only on a particular aspect that they deem important. To marketers, this could mean that they do not seize the right moment to alter or create new strategies for the market because they are too occupied with cementing their ways. As for consumers, it may entail a rather constrained assessment of the options because consumers usually do not stray too far from the brands and products they already know and support.

NOTE: To make use of confirmation bias, marketers should create campaigns that are in congruence with the target market's existing beliefs and philosophy. Here are some strategies to consider:

- Segment the market based on consumer preferences. By segmenting the market based on consumer preferences and behaviors, you can create personalized messages that resonate with specific groups. This involves tailoring content to echo the values, beliefs, and interests of the target audience, making the marketing message more relatable and convincing.
- User-generated content and reviews. Encouraging satisfied customers to share their positive experiences can reinforce the beliefs of potential consumers who already lean toward the brand. Displaying testimonials, reviews, and user-generated content prominently on marketing channels can create a sense of validation and trust for new consumers, confirming their inclination to choose the brand.
- Use social proof and influencer endorsements. Collaborating with influencers and leveraging social proof can amplify the effect of confirmation bias. When consumers see their favorite influencers endorsing a product or service, it reinforces their existing beliefs about the brand's quality and relevance. Highlighting the popularity and widespread acceptance of a product can further convince potential customers who are seeking validation from others.
- Engage in consistent branding and messaging. Maintaining a consistent brand image and message across all marketing channels helps reinforce consumer beliefs. Consistency builds familiarity and trust, making it easier for consumers to justify their loyalty to the brand. You should ensure that your messaging aligns with the core values and identity that your audience associates with the brand.
- Use feedback and adaptation: While leveraging confirmation bias, it's also important that you remain open to feedback and continuously adapt. Regularly collecting and analyzing customer feedback can provide insights into evolving

consumer preferences and help you adjust your strategies accordingly. Balancing confirmation bias with a willingness to embrace constructive criticism can lead to more effective and dynamic marketing efforts.

TIP: Applying these strategies, it will be helpful to start with market research to realize the basic values and tastes of consumers. This study should, therefore, guide the creation of messaging that is targeted at these assumptions in an effort to change their perceptions. It is also possible to develop certain spaces for interaction, including social media profiles or feedback websites, in which enamored customers can leave their feedback and, therefore, contribute to the positive perception of the brand.

Moreover, the integration of data analytics will assist in tracking the success of these strategies and, therefore, enable the organization to make changes to the strategies implemented based on the output from the data collected.

3. Scarcity Bias

Scarcity bias is one of the psychological factors that works in a way that people give higher value to the things that are rare or difficult to get. This is because it is influenced by the Fear Of Missing Out which is a phenomenon that makes people make quick decisions to ensure that they do not miss out on a certain opportunity for acquiring something deemed to be desirable. Lack can make people feel that they are running out of time and can increase the value of a product or a service. In marketing, this bias is rather effective in creating the demand and encouraging the consumers to act right away.

If a consumer thinks that a certain product is limited, they may have the desire for it increased. This reaction stems from the idea that when the availability of a certain commodity increases, then its value decreases. The more scarce the item is, the more people will desire it. The different ways through which scarcity can be presented include offering products on a limited-time basis, informing customers that the stock of a certain product is low, even going out of stock, or making products available only for a limited period.

NOTE: Scarcity bias can now be used in your marketing strategy in the following ways to help you achieve your goals.

- Come up with offers that are time-sensitive and thus compel the customers to make a purchase. This includes flash sales, holiday offers/sales, or weekend sales to help create a sense of urgency. Ensure that the consumers are well aware of the time limitation through countdown timers on your website, emails, and social media platforms. This urgency can force the potential buyer to make a decision quickly so as not to lose the opportunity to get the deal.
- Messages that inform the customer that a certain product is nearly out of stock should be shown. Terms such as "Only three left in stock!" or "Hurry, selling fast!" are found to appeal to consumer's FOMO. This is because people are likely to buy popular or common products which are easily found in the market. It is necessary to have correct inventory levels and update these notifications in a real-time manner to gain credibility.
- Provide unique items or give the first shot at new products to a certain number of consumers. This could be done by using pre-orders, members only offers, or by introducing limited stock products. Ensure that the customers understand that these are limited offers to give them a feeling of privilege and that they need to grab the opportunity.
- Sustain the product availability by linking it to certain seasons or events. For instance, coming up with a product that is only available for a certain period, like during a holiday or an event, can generate much-needed interest and rush. Ensure that these items are well displayed, and do not forget to include the fact that they are seasonal products.

- Increase the perceived value by giving the customers special packages or features that are limited in time. For example, you could include a famous product with another new product or give a gift with a purchase, but for a limited time only. This way, not only the scarcity is used but also the value of the purchase is increased, which leads to faster decisions.

TIP: To effectively incorporate scarcity bias into your marketing strategies you have to first determine which products and or services can be marketed using scarcity themes. First, consider the items that you sell and the trends in sales and customer behavior to establish which of them can be offered at a limited time or when the stock is low. Roll out these scarcity messages through all your marketing mediums (email, social media, and your website).

Ensure that the scarcity aspect is well captured in your communications. Make sure the language and images are active and forceful and communicate a sense of emergency. For instance, add countdown timers in your emails or in your website banners and inform your customers of the time they have left to buy your products. Also, measure the results of your scarcity marketing initiatives and assess the effectiveness of your tactics by collecting data. Track metrics like the conversion rate, sales volume, and customer interaction to determine the success of your strategies and changes that need to be made.

4. Loss Aversion

Loss aversion postulates that a person's emotional state is more negatively affected by the loss of something than the gain of something else of similar value. This can be attributed to a concept that states that losses are felt to be twice as powerful as gains in the human psyche, thus making fear of loss a significant factor. In marketing, it is crucial to know the consumers' psychology, especially loss aversion, to effectively control their behavior and choices.

The desire to avoid loss can also be evidenced by consumers' reluctance to change brands, their reluctance to experiment with new products, and their inclination toward the existing state. This bias is useful to marketers because it underlines the fact that messages should be constructed in a manner that focuses on the possible consequences of inactivity or the lack of utilization of a specific product or service rather than the gains that can be obtained from the usage of the product or service.

NOTE: Here are the ways through which you can use this bias in your marketing strategies:

- Offer free trials or samples. This helps the consumer to get a taste of your product without them having to make a purchase first. After some time of using the product and incorporating it into one's daily routine, the consumers may experience a form of loss when they are forced to stop using the product. This strategy helps in lowering the perceived risk, and hence, the chances of the client backing out at the end of the trial period are low.
- Promise a money-back guarantee. It is one of the ways through which the perceived risk of buying a given product is lowered. It puts the consumer in a state of mind where, in case they do not like the product, they could get their money back, hence enabling them to be more comfortable in trying your product. To further assure the customers, it is advisable to highlight how hassle-free and guaranteed the process of getting a refund is.
- Highlight opportunity costs. Enumerate the consequences that your consumers will face if they do not patronize your product. For instance, if your product is a time or money savior, you should explain the amount of time or money the client will lose in the long run if they do not buy. Illustrate these possible losses in more detailed and real-life situations so that it is not just an abstract idea.

- To make the customers feel like they need to buy the product as soon as possible, give them special offers or promotions available only for a limited time. Ensure that the message passes across the implication of not grabbing these deals; it means the consumer is missing out on saving or getting more value. Words and phrases such as "Don't miss out," "This is your last chance," or "Hurry up, the offer is valid only for a short period" stimulate panic about losing a good deal.
- Show through pictures and reviews how your product has helped other people and what they could have lost if they had not used your product. Using the actual real life experiences of people who have been helped and who have benefited from the treatment can help to put a face on the potential losses.
- Implement subscription models or loyalty programs. This can be achieved through the loss aversion theory since the company can create a continuity of business relations with the customers. The more time consumers spend as members or clients of a loyalty program, the more they are likely to worry about such factors as the loss of earned perks, bonuses, or ease of access if they stop engaging with your service.

5. Recency Bias

Recency bias is defined as the cognitive predisposition whereby people assign higher weights to recent events and information compared to those that occurred in the past. This bias plays a crucial role in decision-making since the last events and information are easier for an individual to recall from memory. Recency bias in marketing refers to the consumers' sensitivity to the most recent information they receive regarding products and services they need to buy.

The phenomenon of recency bias is due to the fact that human memory mechanisms work in a certain way. Recent events are easily remembered compared to past events; thus, they tend to have a great impact on the way things are perceived and done. From the marketers' perspective, this bias presents a chance to regularly interact with consumers, thus keeping the brand relevant.

To leverage recency bias in your marketing strategy, employ the following strategy:

- Strive to display new customer reviews and success stories on your website, social media, and advertising campaigns. Recent customers' positive comments can be very influential to other consumers as they represent the current state of satisfaction.
- Ensure that you post new content to your website, blog and your social media account frequently. This could be anything from new posts to the blog, new products that the company offers, news on the company, or information that is related to the industry. Thus, maintaining content freshness helps to provide consumers with fresh material on a regular basis, thus strengthening their awareness of your business.
- Ensure that your marketing strategies are relevant to the season and other celebrations happening around the world. For instance, coming up with a promo calendar, which includes the creation of product content related to seasons, holidays, or events, can help make the brand more timely and thus appealing to consumers.
- You should use email marketing to send reminders of new products or services, promotions, offers, and or recommendations to the subscribers. Retargeting campaigns can bring back people who have visited your site and engaged with it but have not made a purchase with new products or offers to make another purchase.
- Continuously post, like, and comment on social media accounts and join the conversation of trending topics. Social media is by its nature a real-time communication medium, and therefore is a perfect environment to apply the phenomenon of recency bias. Share stories, go live, and use live posts to ensure that your audience remains interested and up to date.

- Come up with flash sales and limited-time products to help the consumers act due to the recency effect.

6. Framing Effect

This is the level at which people's choices are swayed by the way that the information is framed rather than the information itself. It is not uncommon for a message to be presented in a positive or negative light, and the latter can come with a major influence on the audience's decision-making. For instance, a product being described as having 90% less fat will be more persuasive than saying that it has 10% fat in it, even though both convey the same message. This phenomenon underlines the significance of the presentation in determining the consumer's behavior and choice.

The framing effect arises due to the differential risk-taking tendency of a person when the frame is negative and when it is positive. One of the factors that can be used in marketing to increase the attractiveness of products and services is the known psychological bias that can be utilized to create more effective messages for the target audience.

Do the following to leverage it for your marketing success:

- Emphasize the positive features of your product/service that you are going to offer. For instance, rather than saying, 'Our product cuts down on defects to the tune of 20%,' one can say, 'Our product eliminates 80% of defects. ' This positive construction gives the impression that the product is more reliable and desirable.
- However, focusing on the possible negative consequences can also work in some situations, especially when you want to establish a sense of crisis or stress the relevance of your product. For instance, "Hurry up and don't miss the chance to get it limited time offer" or "Avoid the failure of the repair, which will cost you a lot of money by using our service"

appeals to consumer's fear of losing out or facing negative consequences.

- Describe your product's features in terms of what they can do for the consumer. Instead of using the statement, "Our fitness program includes ten workout routines," you could say, "Get fit with our ten workout routines," here, the emphasis is on the positive result that can be obtained.

- It is recommended that you use comparisons to present your product as better than the others in the market. For example, "Our product uses 50% less energy than the other brands" positively puts the benefit. This comparison can make your product more appealing by directly highlighting how superior it is to the competitors' products.

- If possible, wrap numerical data up in productive terms or paint the picture in the light. For instance, instead of stating that 'Only seventy percent of the customers are satisfied,' one can come up with 'Seventy percent of our customers are satisfied. ' This just shows that even the tone of the language used can make a big difference.

- Capitalize on the loss aversion by conveying the possible consequences of not using the product that you are offering. For example, 'Don't let pass by the opportunity to save 20% with our discount' or 'Don't let this pass you by; our exclusive offer ends soon' could be more effective than just stating the discount.

TIP: To make these strategies more effective, here is what you can do: Begin with the assessment of your existing message and determine which segments need a framing enhancement. Review your product descriptions, ad copy, website, and social media content, and make sure that it is written in a way that will attract and influence your audience the most.

Carry out A/B testing to establish the frames that are likely to work best for your audience. For instance, develop a positive and negative version of an advert and compare the performance in relation to engagement and conversions.

When creating your messages, remember the environment and the patient's preference as the audience. Thus, positive framing may be suitable for a healthy-minded public, and negative framing for products associated with security or risk. Adapt the framing strategy to the target audience's desires and fears because certain framing strategies are more effective for certain audiences.

Also, use visual elements to support the framing of the communication to the target audience. Graphics, colors, and the design of the product normally go a long way in how the consumers perceive the product. For instance, to make use of the framing effect, green should be used for positive messages and red for warning messages.

7. Authority Bias

The authority bias is a cognitive bias that results in people being more willing to act upon the words of an authority figure. This bias is a result of the attitude of giving more credibility and trust to the words of experts, celebrities, or those who have authority in society. It has been observed that using authority bias in marketing can help boost the persuasiveness of your messages and gain consumers' trust and attention.

In this case, when consumers witness endorsements from authorities, then they shall be convinced of the credibility of the product or service in question. This is because authority figures are usually perceived to have knowledge and or high status in society, and so their opinions and recommendations are trusted.

How to leverage this for marketing success:

- Engage other people in the business or those who have a good standing in your area of practice. For instance, if you are promoting a health product, then make sure to get the recommendation of doctors or other health personnel. It gives credence to your product, and because of this, consumers can be swayed to trust the brand.

- Choose the celebrities that support your brand and its principles and objectives, as well as the target consumers. Celebrities are a very extensive audience, and you can draw more attention to your product with their help. They can lend a star power to your brand, which makes it attractive to many people.
- Put your efforts in with people who have large numbers of followers and clout within your niche. Influencers are usually in a good relationship with their followers and can give sincere and personal recommendations. It is, therefore, advisable to use influencers whose values are similar to those of your brand together with the right target audience.
- Emphasize the achievements of the product or the company, whether it is an award, a certification, or a recognition. This is because one can place badges, seals, or certificates which are from accredited institutions or bodies to give the product a boost on the credibility front.
- Include such as having some of the industry or community leaders give a testimony on the product or service. Such endorsements are useful to establish social proof and convince the user about the authority bias. It is recommended to confirm that the testimonials are real and the sources can be trusted.
- Create content that substantiates your knowledge in the industry you are in. Specifically, it might encompass white papers, research papers, articles from industry specialists, and comprehensive step-by-step instructions. Thus, sharing useful and reliable content can help your brand become a thought leader and gain the audience's trust.

TIP: Perhaps the only way to increase the impact is to start identifying the authority figures that can help endorse your brand. Identify opinion leaders, famous people, and public figures who have a positive image and whose beliefs and ideals are in accordance with your brand's identity. Approach them with a proposal that would be mutually beneficial and explain how their support can be advantageous to both of you.

Develop marketing collateral that includes these endorsements as part of your marketing collateral. Quote, picture, or video of the authority figures talking about your product or service for sale. It is necessary to place these materials on the website, social networks, advertising, and other promotional resources.

Ensure that any certifications and awards that you have are well placed on the product packaging, website and any other channel that you intend to market the product. Add logos and badges of known organizations to the design of your materials to make them look professional and trustworthy.

Create content that commands respect and makes the reader trust you and benefit in some way from what you wrote. Repost this content on your blog, social networks, email newsletter, and other appropriate media. Interact with your audience by organizing webinars, live questions, and answers, or interviews with specialists in the field.

8. Halo Effect

The halo effect means that the general perception of a brand or product affects the reception of certain characteristics that it possesses. Positive experiences with one product from the brand lead to the consumers' expectations of the other products from the same brand to offer the same quality and satisfaction. This bias suggests that a favorable attitude towards one product can increase the perceived quality of the overall brand and influence consumer judgments and behaviors concerning the other products in the brand's portfolio.

It is especially effective in marketing as it focuses on the consumers' perception that is based on their feelings and beliefs about the brand. A positive attitude towards one product may transfer to other products of the same brand and enhance the consumers' confidence, commitment, and willingness to experiment with the same brand products.

To use this to its full effectiveness, practice the following:

- Concentrate on developing a high-quality deliverable that can act as the cornerstone of your brand. This product should meet high quality standards and the level of performance and garner immense customer satisfaction. Thus, a strong core product may help to adopt a positive image of the brand and create a basis for the halo effect when it comes to other products.
- Link your products and advertise them as one package. For instance, if you sell smartphones, and consumers like them, then you should market other items, such as smartwatches or headphones that are compatible with the smartphones. This will make the consumers associate something positive with your product; for instance, using statements such as 'From the makers of [popular product].'
- It is important that every one of your products is of the same quality and has the same branding. Consistency builds on the positive perception that results from the halo effect. Coherent packaging, graphic design, and copy in your product catalog will help to enhance the brand's image and identity.
- Share customer feedback for one product and apply it to the rest of the products to create trust. Then, use these testimonials across your marketing platforms to paint a consistent and good image of the brand. Incorporate the level of satisfaction of customers on the different products in the market from your brand.
- Use influencers and brand ambassadors that can testify to the quality of different products by your brand. It means their endorsements can rule out the halo effect by sharing positive experiences with a number of products. Pick real fans of your product who would be able to give a word-of-mouth recommendation.

- Introduce programs that will make the customer purchase other products within your brand. Give buyers motivation; for instance, when they buy more than one product, they get a discount or a prize. Combining several products and selling them at a lower price than the individual price of the products also influences the consumer to try other products, and thus, the positive halo effect is extended.
- Ensure that your brand's values, mission and quality are well highlighted and marketed in all the marketing activities. When consumers have positive attitudes towards the brand's core values and mission, they are likely to generalize this perception to other products of the brand, thus increasing the halo effect.

TIP: Another positive side of the halo effect can be used to determine your key product – the product that is most praised by consumers and occupies the leading position in the market. Emphasizes the marketing of this product, guaranteeing its quality and, specifically, the satisfaction of its consumers.

Then, develop other marketing strategies that associate this flagship product with the other products you are offering. Connect them using visual and verbal associations and stress the common element and brand values. For instance, if your principal product is a quality kitchen appliance, then you can offer other kitchen utensils and accessories from the same brand.

Gather and use the actual word of the customers for your best-selling product and other products you are offering. Use these reviews on your website, social media, and in your advertisements. You can also create videos that include the customers giving testimonies of the satisfaction that they have realized from using different products of your brand.

Having influencers and brand advocates promote your products. Make sure that these influencers are really fond of your products and actually use them as the trust of an audience is very important. Promote them to tell about their experiences with different products of your brand, thus forming a generally positive impression of your brand.

Incorporate a reward system that will encourage customers to buy more than one item at a time. Give the customers special offers, discounts, or sets that will make them purchase other products.

9. Decoy Effect

The decoy effect or asymmetric dominance effect is a persuasion technique that modifies consumers' choices between two options when a third, less preferable option is presented to them. This third decision, or as it is more commonly referred to as the decoy, is, in fact, developed to enhance the attractiveness of one of the initial options. The decoy is either priced or positioned in a manner that draws attention to one of the other options' values or attributes, thus leading consumers toward the favored choice.

The decoy effect capitalizes on the fact that people tend to compare options in relation to each other. Thus, when marketers strategically create the decoy, they can steer consumers toward the product they wish to sell, which can be a product with higher margins or strategic significance. This bias is useful in the field of marketing due to the fact that it makes decision making easier for the consumer and raises the probability of choosing the desired item.

How to leverage it for marketing success:

- Add a new pricing plan that is deliberately worse than the other two. For instance, if you have two packages, the standard, and the pro packages, create a package that costs slightly more than the standard package but has less value. This gives the premium option an appealing look as compared to the free one.
- Emphasize those factors of the decoy option so that the choice meant to be chosen would be more appealing. For instance, if

the decoy product has fewer features than the premium product, yet it is offered at a close price to that of the premium product, then the premium product will be perceived as the better proposition. It is crucial to make the differences distinguishable; thus, one should employ comparison charts.

- Apply the decoy effect in product bundling. Introduce a variant that consists of several goods at a price that would seem more beneficial than purchasing the products separately. Suggest a third bundle that has one or two fewer products or features than the first and is slightly cheaper than the first bundle to make the first bundle more appealing.
- Apply the decoy effect in subscription models by providing three options for membership. The middle tier should be made in a way that consumers would be inclined to take the higher tier service since the middle tier is not as valuable but priced almost the same as the higher tier. This makes the highest package look like the most preferred one among the rest.
- When extending the product line, provide a product that has lower performance compared to the other products. For instance, if you have software for sale, it is advised to provide a product with fewer options at a price that will make the full version seem like a better deal.
- When on sales promotions, apply the decoy effect to draw the attention of the consumers to the value of the promoted product. Something that could be done is to present another product that is either cheaper or has fewer aspects than the sale item to create a sense of value for money.

TIP: To begin implementing these strategies, it is crucial to know the items or services to be marketed. Consider your pricing model and options and decide in what way a decoy should be offered to the customers. Analyzing your target audience will help you come up with a decoy design that will help change their decisions.

Develop promotional materials that will explain the three options and make it clear why the planned option is the best one. Utilize comparison tables, features and benefits, and price comparison tables so that it would be easy to distinguish the differences. Make sure that the decoy option is highlighted together with the other options.

Also, split the traffic and compare the results of the implemented decoy strategy with the control group. It is possible to exhibit different groups of consumers to different configurations of options and compare their decisions. Apply this data to the decoy option and compare the price to find the best strategy.

Apply the decoy effect in all the marketing mediums that are available to you, such as your website, your emails and even the physical displays in your store. Direct the sales team on the decoy effect, its meaning, and ways of applying it to the customers. This will help reinforce the desired choice and, therefore, lead to better outcomes all through the touchpoints.

A good example scenario is: suppose you are a marketer of a variety of coffee makers:

1. Basic Model: Priced at $50, offering essential features.
2. Premium Model: Priced at $120, offering advanced features and better build quality.
3. Decoy Model: Priced at $100, offering slightly better features than the basic model but not as many as the premium model.

In the given practical example, the decoy model costs slightly more than the premium model but has certain important functionalities absent. The consumers are likely to view the premium model as providing much better value for an additional $20 and thus choose the premium variant.

Building Brand Loyalty and Trust

Brand loyalty is a situation where consumers prefer to purchase the same brand in the market even if there are other similar brands in the market. It does not only make the customers continue to engage with the same brand and purchase from it, but they also form positive attitudes towards the brand in question. The perception that the customers have towards a certain brand, behaviors and the values that it portrays definitely affect brand loyalty. Moreover, it is a vital tactic for increasing the customer's repurchase rates and ensuring loyalty to the brand.

Establishing Brand Identity and Values

The part of your branding, which includes what your brand communicates, the mission and vision, the ways in which you promote your product, and the emotions you wish your clients to associate with your company, falls under the brand identity. Brand identity, therefore, could be seen as the heart of the business and the commitment to the clients.

NOTE: Brand identity can also encourage consumers and make them create the feeling of brand loyalty since it captures the image and essence of your business in almost every aspect. Hence, brand identity is crucial in the progression of your business in the future.

Thus, if your brand is more than just your logo, how can you attain the same as Coca-Cola and other companies and put other unique features in the identification of your business?

Let's examine the elements of strong brand identity and the reasons you must create them:

- *The "Face" of Your Business.* Your brand's logo serves as the "face" of your company. However, a logo should do more for the company than just having an eye-catching appearance; it also has an associative function. It explains to the public that [this image] represents [your company name].

- ***Credibility and Trust.*** Having a distinct brand helps to make your product easily recognizable and creates your company as the leading brand in the market. It gives a brand a competitive advantage over its competitors and customer trust when it defines and does not change its identity face throughout the years.

- ***Impressions From Advertising.*** A brand identity acts as a template for each aspect of an advertisement for your company, regardless if it is online, in print, or in a YouTube preroll ad. A brand that has a face and is known in the industry is in a position to promote itself and create an impression on potential clients.

- ***Your Company's Mission.*** Your brand gains a sense of purpose and meaning when you give it an identity. This, in turn, provides a purpose for your business. Companies do, after all, have mission statements, right? You see, you can't have one without first establishing the identity of your brand.

Below is how you can create brand identity and values:

1. Understand Your Market and Audience

The process of conducting market research is the first and the most important step to building a strong brand image and identifying brand values. Market research entails the identification and collection of information concerning the market environment, its competitors, trends, and consumers. This process enables you to comprehend the rivalry and discover how to stand out from the competition.

The first step you should take is to assess your rivals. Examine their products, prices, promotions, SWOT analysis, and many more. This will assist you in identifying what is already present in the market and possibilities on how you can differentiate your logo. For instance, if your business idea is to produce fitness apparel, it will be useful to look at successful firms such as Nike, Lululemon, or Under Armour. Examine their products, audiences, advertisements, and consumers' opinions. Determine the missing products or services that your brand can provide or where your brand can differ.

Then, ensure you are up-to-date with the trends that exist in the market. According to industry literature, trade shows, and blogs, and news feeds. Knowing the trends in the market, like technology change, consumer behavior change, and policy change, will enable you to know the next direction the market will take and adjust your brand strategy to meet the market needs. For instance, you are in the tech industry. Therefore, knowing the trends such as Artificial Intelligence, the Internet of things and cybersecurity can be a way of positioning your products as the new age solution.

Acquiring the preferences of the customer is also crucial. Carry out questionnaires, group discussions, and interviews to establish what the customers for products like yours desire. Engage the use of online tools and social media listening to track conversations made by the customers. This information that comes directly from your target audience will help you to understand their requirements, challenges, and wants which in turn will help you formulate your product and marketing strategies.

For your target audience, it has to do with identifying who the target audience is and what influences them to make a purchase. This calls for the analysis of both demographic and psychographic characteristics of the consumer. Demographics consist of age, sex, income, education, and place of residence, whereas psychographics encompasses lifestyle, attitude, interest, and consumption behavior.

It is suggested to start with the creation of detailed customer personas. These are just your perfect customers, created on the basis of actual customers' data and research. For instance, if your business is to introduce a new range of green skincare products. In such a case, your target market may be women, 25-45 years of age, who are green consumers, living in urban areas with disposable income, and who are concerned with natural products and production. Understanding this persona better will ease your work as a marketer since you will be able to market your products and services in a way that will be appealing to this particular group.

In the same way, the needs and the problems of the target audience should not be forgotten either. Using interviews and focus groups as methods of qualitative research, it is possible to get more detailed information about their difficulties and wishes. For instance, when creating a new productivity app, you might find that the audience you want to reach has a problem with time management and needs tools that are easy to use and compatible with other programs. This knowledge can be useful in designing your app, its features, and the user interface.

Psychographic data is useful for understanding the personality of the consumer. Determine what factors affect the consumers' decision-making process, including brand preference, social pressure, or ethical concerns. For instance, if your products are organic food items, then the consumer might be interested in the health benefits of the product, sustainability, and the sources of the product. This is useful to understand because you can then focus on these aspects in your brand and advertising.

2. Define Your Brand Core

The brand core includes the mission, vision, and values of a brand. Let's take a look at how each forms your brand core:

- *Mission statement*

The mission statement is the foundation of any company's brand identity. It outlines its core business and the need for its existence in the society. It tells the answer to the question, "Why does the brand you work for exist?" A good mission statement is simple, coherent, and motivational. It acts as a compass that defines the direction of all your brand's activities and choices. It should explain the focus of your brand, the problem it addresses in customers' lives, and the value it offers.

Thus, the process of coming up with an effective mission statement requires the identification of what makes one's brand different from others in the market. For instance, if you are launching a sustainable fashion brand, then you will be requiring some of the following steps. In this case, your mission may be to "provide fashionable and quality apparel that has minimal adverse effects on the environment and espouses social responsibility in production. " This is your way of communicating to the consumers that you are a company that is conscious of the impact of our actions on the environment.

Also, a mission statement could be useful for ensuring everyone engaged with your project is on the same page. It helps to set the goals and objectives that are to be achieved in your organization, and hence, every member of the organization will be working towards achieving the same goals. For example, Patagonia Company's mission is to make the best quality products with the philosophy of preserving the environment, which shapes its business approach and employees' behavior.

- *Vision statement*

The vision statement defines the future objectives and desires of your brand, answering the query of where the brand wants to be in the future. It describes the desired future state and acts as a motivational tool to guide and encourage the team and other stakeholders. A good vision statement should be challenging and strategic, focusing on the future and the organization's direction.

When coming up with a vision statement, it is preferable to consider the result that you wish to achieve in the future. Think about what you envision for your brand in the future and what you want your brand to contribute. For instance, the vision statement of Tesla Motors, "To become the world's best and most innovative car company by popularizing electric cars and clean transport," is specific, inspiring, and focuses on the company's long-term mission.

Your vision statement should also be something to which your target audience can relate and thus encourage them to join your brand's journey. For instance, own a healthy and fitness products company. This may be your vision: "To make the world a healthier place and equip every person to live the best life possible." This way, your vision statement defines the future of your brand, as well as speaks to the hearts of the audience who share the same vision.

- *Core values*

Core values refer to the principles that define your brand's behavior, its choices, and its relationship with its customers. These values should depict what your brand is all about and what it aims to portray. These are the people who guide the ethics and morality of your brand; thus, they affect all aspects of the business, from the products to the services, marketing to the organizational culture.

This process of identifying the core values involves self-reflection and understanding of the brand's essence and mission. Think about those values that you are not willing to compromise for your brand and the behavior that you wish to see in your organization. For instance, in a tech startup company, the organizational values might be innovation, customer orientation, ethics, and teamwork. These are some of the corporate cultures that determine how you create your products, serve the customers, and behave as a team.

Core values also play a useful role in branding and establishing a brand identity that would enable the brand to stand out from others. These tell your customers what sets you apart from the competitors and why you should be their preferred choice. For instance, Ben & Jerry's has the core values of social justice, high-quality products, and sound financial management which not only inform its operations but also form a connection with the consumer, making them a loyal fan base.

REMEMBER: The proper identification and consistent application of the core values may help to gain the trust of the consumers. It reveals that your brand has values and beliefs that are important and not just the growth and earnings. This can result in the development of closer relationships with the target audience and their loyalty to the brand in the future.

3. Develop Your Brand Personality

It defines what your brand personality is, that is, the attributes and the tone of voice of the brand. Brand attributes are defined by the process of visualizing the brand as a person and deciding on the characteristics you wish the brand to possess. It is advisable to make these attributes reflect your brand's mission, vision, and values and appeal to your target market. For example, suppose your brand is built on the concept of technology. In that case, you may desire your brand to be associated with innovation, daring, and progressive. On the other hand, if your brand is in the luxury skincare products niche, then your brand's personality might include elegance, class, and trust. These attributes assist in the generation of a brand identity that will differentiate your brand from the competitors and make it recognizable by consumers.

Take the case of Apple, for instance. The various brand attributes that describe Apple are innovation, stylish, and easy to use. These traits are evident in the company's products, advertisements, and how they handle their consumers. One can also notice the innovative aspect of the company as it constantly develops innovative new products; the sleek and user-friendly characteristic is seen by its products' design, which is simple and easy to use.

However, the tone of voice is the manner through which the brand speaks to the audience. It portrays its character and influences people's perceptions. It has to be unified and apply to all the aspects of a company: advertising, social media, customer service, and even internal communication. The tone varies from being warm and welcoming, formal and informative, confident, relaxed, and even funny, and it will largely depend on the kind of image that a company wants to portray and what kind of audience it wants to attract. To illustrate this, a financial services company might use formal and informative language to build credibility, while a fashion company might use relaxed and entertaining language to appeal to the youth.

For instance, the brand name Innocent Drinks. Their language is informal, they use humor, and they talk to the viewers as friends, which makes them easy to connect with. This tone is present in their products' packaging, social media profiles, and advertising strategies. Thus, Innocent Drinks, employing a light and humorous tone, stands out from the numerous beverage brands on the market and engages consumers who are drawn to the brand's character. This consistent tone of voice not only fosters brand awareness but also strengthens the customer's bond to the brand as if the brand personally contacts them.

4. Create Visual Identity

Your visual identity consists of the logo, color scheme, font, and images. Now, let's see how each contributes to the formation of an appealing visual identity.

- ### Logo

Your logo is the embodiment of your brand's unique characteristics; it is the face of your brand and what people can identify with. A good logo should be easily remembered, flexible, and can be used for many years. It should embody the DNA of your brand in the simplest and most powerful way possible. Thus, while designing a logo, it is useful to incorporate shapes, symbols, and typography that are in harmony with the brand and familiar to the target audience. For instance, Nike uses a check mark as its logo and it represents movement and swiftness. It complements the athletic brand very well. It is recommended to design a logo that can be well identified and can be used in various sizes and on various media.

- *Color Palette*

The color palette makes it easier to establish a brand's identity and makes sure it is recognized easily. Colors are powerful in stirring up feelings and can also communicate the intended information about your brand. Choose the color that reflects your brand attributes and which will be appropriate for your target market. Remember cultural symbolism and how colors affect people's moods and feelings as you make your decisions. For example, the blue color is associated with the concepts of trust and reliability, which is why it is often used in the spheres of banking and financial services, while red and orange colors are bright and energetic, which is perfect for brands targeting the young population. To enhance brand recognition, it is recommended to use colors consistently on all the brand elements that are both print and digital.

- *Typography*

Typography helps to convey your brand and make the text easy to read. Identify the fonts that are most suitable for the personality of the brand and that are readable regardless of the device or scale. These are the serif fonts that give the traditional and reliable look, while the sans-serif fonts are preferred when one wants to give a modern touch. Try to use the primary font for the headings and the secondary font for the body text to help with hierarchy and visual contrast. For instance, a company that deals in luxurious products will choose to use serif fonts in their logo, while a tech company will use simple and sleek sans-serif fonts. REMEMBER: Thus, the use of typography maintains the unity of the brand and enhances the general perception of the brand.

- *Imagery*

Imagery also helps in coming up with a consistent theme that helps in creating the right and unified image. It is necessary to understand if a brand will focus on images or drawings, symbols, or their combination. As with any other style, it is advisable to ensure that the imagery style you are using is in harmony with your brand's personality and the interests of your target audience. For instance, lifestyle brands utilize high-quality photographs to create emotions and depict the products in actual contexts. On the other hand, Tech firms might employ pictures or symbols to make the information presented easily understandable and more presentable. Regardless of the style you go for, it should enhance your brand's story and evoke an emotional response from your consumers.

5. Craft Your Brand Messaging

Brand story, tagline/slogan, and key messages should be viewed as the core of your brand communication.

- *Brand Story*

Your brand story is a highly effective way of speaking directly to your audience's feelings and values and describing what your brand is all about. This part has to tell your brand's story, its history, purpose, goals, and principles persuasively and genuinely. Begin with the origin of your brand, what prompted the creation of the brand, and the challenge it seeks to address. Emphasize the values that define your brand and the decisions it makes, in addition to the brand's goals for the future. To come up with a brand story that will appeal to your target audience, the following guidelines may be of help.

For instance, the brand Patagonia presents a great narrative of the owner's love for rock climbing and the company's mission concerning environmental conservation. Their brand story is to "build the best product, cause no unnecessary harm, and use business to inspire and implement solutions to the environmental crisis. " This story is not only about the company's values but also targets the audience who are passionate about the environment and outdoor activities.

- *Tagline/Slogan*

A tagline or slogan is a short, catchy phrase that aptly sums up your brand and what it offers. It should be unique and catchy and should tell the consumers what your brand can offer for them. Before developing a tagline, one must identify the brand's positioning, the target audience, and the major brand messages. It should inspire an emotional response and curiosity while, at the same time, distinguishing your brand from the rest.

For example, Nike has "Just Do It" as its slogan, which reflects the spirit of Nike which is to encourage people and be the best. It has become the imagery of Nike's brand and appeals to consumers who want to be encouraged to accomplish their purpose.

- *Key Messages*

Your key messages help to maintain the consistency of the conversation your brand has with its audience at all the touchpoints. These messages should be in accordance with your brand's values,' and they should be relevant to the target audience and their wants and desires. Think about the values of your products and services and the consumers' psyche to influence their buying decisions. Your key messages should be the things that set your brand apart why consumers should select you, and how your products will benefit them.

For instance, the brand under consideration is a skincare brand. A skincare brand that is based on natural products and environmentally friendly approaches might use slogans like "Achieve your glow with our green beauty products" and "Nurture your skin and the world with our vegan and cruelty-free products. " These statements would help to support the brand's image and its goals of providing high-quality products that do not harm the environment and animals.

6. Consistency and Integration

You need to develop a brand guideline that will help in the provision of consistency. It is an assurance that everyone is on the same page about your brand and what it stands for. These are your brand guidelines, internal alignment, and external communication to ensure the attainment of consistency and integration.

- **Brand Guidelines**

The brand guidelines act as a reference to ensure that the brand is depicted in the right way in all the advertising materials and channels. This guide should define the guidelines and recommendations for brand logos, colors, typography, images, and voice. It makes sure that every message, may it be a social media post or a package, has the same brand personality and voice. Give concrete recommendations as to how much space should be left between different elements, what sizes are optimal, which colors should be combined, and when it is most appropriate to use the logo, typography, and other elements of the visual identity so your team, as well as your partners, can follow the rules and ensure that your brand's verbal and visual identity is consistent.

For instance, some of the items that your brand style guide may contain include the specific color codes of your brand in Pantone, RGB, as well as CMYK codes, guidelines on the use of logos including size, typography, rules regarding the use of images such as photography styles or icons and the right tone and language to use for certain audiences.

- *Internal Alignment*

Internal alignment means that all employees of the organization know the organization's values and contours and act in accordance with the brand. This means that the employees, ranging from those who interact with customers to the senior management, are put through seminars to understand and convey the brand image. Organize sessions, develop documents, and have frequent team meetings to share with employees the brand's mission, vision, values, and messages. Remind the team about the brand story and their part in the whole process of delivering the brand message.

Employees can be incorporated in the process of creating brand guidelines, and then you can ask for their opinion to make sure that they will follow the guidelines religiously. Equip them to become brand advocates by equipping them with the necessary information and resources on how to take the brand's message to the general public, customers, business affiliates, and other stakeholders.

- *External Communication*

Use your brand identity and message in all the external communication channels and make sure that the target audience identifies with your brand. This includes your website, your social media pages, packaging, advertisements, and even the interactions between your company and the clients. To achieve this, your brand's visual identity, including the logo, color, typeface, and images, should be well utilized on these platforms to create brand consistency.

An example of this is when you are creating your website; it is recommended to use the same colors and fonts as defined in your brand style guide to ensure the look and feel are cohesive. Ensure that you incorporate your brand's tone of voice as well as important brand messages into your social media posts and adverts so that your target audience will be able to relate. That means that the packaging should also reflect your brand's identity through the design that matches the personality and values of your brand.

7. Monitor Your Brand and Evolve

It is recommended to use feedback for tracking the brand. It also assists in assessing the extent of the match between the brand and the audience, employees, and stakeholders. Get information from surveys, customer feedback, social media, and employees to find out how your brand is viewed. This means do not only look at the quantitative data (sentiments, anecdotes, satisfaction ratings, sales, etc.) but the quantitative data as well. Here are some tips to help you analyze the feedback that you received with regard to your brand strategy.

For instance, the customers may have a positive perception of your brand concerning sustainable initiatives but cannot make sense of your products. In that case, you may be required to readjust your message or perhaps focus on your products. Likewise, if employees are unable to communicate the brand's values to customers, ensure that they are adequately educated and supported regarding the brand.

NOTE: Always remember this: always be updated. In order to remain competitive in a particular market, it is crucial to be aware of the changes taking place in the market place, changes in technology, and changes in the consumers' behavior. Watch the competitors and changes in the market to determine the new trends and potential risks and opportunities. Check your brand strategy and elements of visual identity, communication, and brand values as often as necessary to meet the current market and customers' expectations.

For instance, if the consumer is now more concerned with the environment, changes such as packaging to embrace the environmental conservation agenda may be considered. Technological innovations that are emerging are likely to generate new approaches for engaging customers; thus, identify how these advances can be incorporated into your brand's digital marketing plan. Ensure that the brand transformation is in line with the changing market trends but at the same time sticking to the corporate identity and values.

Tips for Creating Emotional Connections With Customers

People will buy products and services from companies they have confidence in, and this confidence is often emotional. It has been noted that people are likely to stand for a brand which they can associate with. To give the customers the feeling that they are part of the brand's success, marketers try to establish and maintain emotional attachment.

Suppose your message targets the basic values of your audience. In that case, your message will create lasting and positive opinions about your brand. Below are tips that can assist in developing this critical relationship between your business and the customers.

1. Tell a compelling brand story

Create a brand story that can be real, simple, and touching. Your story must tell how your brand came to be, what it stands for, and the processes that were taken in developing it. Talk about your brand stories and the issues it has faced. A story that captures the audience's attention builds a bond and makes your brand stand out and be easily recalled.

2. Make use of emotional branding

Brand your logo and message to make people feel happy, recall pleasant memories, trust you, or get inspired. This can be done through visuals, colors, and messages that would appeal to the emotions of your target audience. It is the use of words, pictures, and music to create specific moods that will help in persuading customers.

For instance, Coca-Cola's "Share a Coke" campaign, in which the brand name was replaced with the most popular names in different countries, appealed to people's emotions, specifically joy and connectedness. Coca-Cola launched a very successful campaign that encouraged consumers to enjoy a Coke with loved ones. This, in turn, fostered unity and happiness since people were able to bond.

3. Offer exceptional customer service

Emotional appeal can be greatly boosted by special customer service. To sum up, make sure every contact with the customers is positive, solutions-providing, and unforgettable. Teach your customer service personnel to be sensitive to the customers' needs, attend to them promptly, and initiate actions to meet their needs.

4. Build a sense of community and engagement

Develop loyalty and encourage consumers' participation by responding to the customers' comments on social networks, organizing events, and creating opportunities for consumers to communicate with each other. Promote user reviews, ratings, and testimonials to capture the issues of the customers. Display the testimonies and experiences of your customers to show appreciation to them.

5. Personalized customer interactions

This enhances the customer experience by making it more personal and relevant to them. Segment your customers and use this data to craft messages, offers, and advertising that speak directly to each recipient's interests and actions. This makes the customer feel that they are unique and that the company has taken time to know them.

6. Be authentic and transparent

It is recommended to be honest and open in the interactions and decisions made. Customers appreciate brands that are truthful and forthcoming about their operations, beliefs, and problems, as these aspects of the brand are critical to the customer's purchase decision-making process. More often, transparent organizations are believed to be more credible and develop a close bond with clients.

7. Create memorable experiences

Learn to create experiences that can be described as memorable as well as emotional in form so that the targeting customer can be able to feel and enjoy. It could be through gifts, sales, coupons, membership clubs, or special educational promotional coupons. This gives your brand exposure, and the customers always come to you whenever they need a similar product because of the memorable experiences they had with it.

Strategies for Building Trust and Credibility

Any entrepreneur, and especially professionals involved in sales, is very familiar with how important it is to gain the trust of prospective buyers. Some would even argue that two of these variables are as critical as any other in the sales process. Lastly, it is impossible to convince a customer who does not have confidence in you to engage with your business. Besides, they are not very likely to follow your ideas or to be advised by your opinion if you do not seem credible to them.

No matter if you're employed in the call center, have your own business, or are a sales representative, you need to understand how to gain the client's trust. Here are some pointers to get you going:

1. Be honest and transparent

This one should be considered as rather obvious, still, it requires a mention. Customers are quite clever and can easily tell when you are trying to pull a fast one on them. Ensure that the clients are informed of your policies, prices, and other aspects of the goods and services you offer.

In addition to that, make sure to be punctual and adhere to the schedule as well. It is important that once you have agreed to do something then you do it. It is recommended that if someone is not in a position to meet the request, then it is better to be honest with the customer. Hyping something you know you cannot deliver is one of the easiest ways to sabotage yourself.

2. Establish yourself as an authority in your field

It is crucial to build credibility in the eyes of your customers, which is why it is one of the most effective strategies. Consumers expect the business and the salespeople to have adequate knowledge and information concerning the products and services that they offer; therefore, you should be in a position to address the consumers' concerns.

In this manner, you will be able to build your company's credibility and that of your industry as a whole, thus ensuring that people will continuously patronize your services. It is recommended that you utilize every chance you have to gain more knowledge about your area of business by reading trade publications, going to trade conferences and trade shows, and attending trade fairs.

3. Be passionate about your work

Customer service is a passion that one has to have in order to provide excellent service to clients. It would be quite hard for you to convince your clients that they should trust you if you lack passion for what you are selling. As a result of this, confident and passionate employee will perform their duties in a certain way, including how they move their body and how they relate to customers.

Some people in the sales field may think that all one has to do is act the part until one can actually be the part, but the client is not stupid and will know that the interest being shown is not genuine. Instead of pushing for the sale of something that does not have the backing of your conviction, it is advisable to consider a completely different business.

4. Get customer testimonials and online reviews

The happiest customer is the one who will ensure your business is recommended to many people. To acquire some credibility and trust with the potential customers it is very important to have testimonies from other customers who have been served before.

Ensure you get great reviews from past clients and post them on your website, GMB listing, or even other places the potential clients may find them. Always remind the clients to leave feedback on popular review sites such as Google Reviews, Yelp, and Angie's List. A prospective client has to be convinced that you are not blowing hot air; other people have had good experiences working with your company.

5. Offer exceptional customer service

Suppose you want to gain the confidence and reputation of your clients quickly. In that case, you need to have an effective customer care team that will always look for the interest of the clients even after the sale. New customers are not easy to come by, but the ones that are there are even harder to stick around.

This is why it is paramount to cultivate good relations with your customers since they are the life blood of business. They are likely to do business with you again in the future if they think they can turn to you for help.

Chapter 7
Developing a Marketing Strategy: A 7-Step Process

Getting your goods or services in front of consumers may be an exciting challenge, regardless of whether you work for a huge marketing company or are a small business owner. To appeal to your target market, you need a broad range of abilities and information, and developing a marketing strategy can be essential.

Let's examine what a marketing strategy is in more detail, as well as the steps you must take to implement one.

What is a Marketing Strategy?

A marketing strategy is a comprehensive plan devised by a business to reach its target audience and achieve specific goals, such as increasing sales, brand awareness, or market share. It involves identifying target markets, analyzing competitors, and determining the best marketing mix (product, price, place, and promotion) to effectively communicate the brand's value proposition. NOTE: a successful marketing strategy aligns with the overall business objectives and leverages various channels and tactics to engage and convert potential customers, ensuring a cohesive and consistent brand message across all touchpoints.

Let's now look at the various steps to develop a marketing strategy.

Step 1: Defining Your Target Audience

Any successful marketing strategy must start with defining your target audience. Once you know who your ideal clients are, you can better cater your messaging, goods, and services to suit their demands.

These days, identifying your target market entails more than just knowing your prospective clients' demographics. Two people are not always going to be interested in the same goods and services just because they are of the same age. Since every customer is different, it is impossible to categorize them all perfectly. To target the right population without limiting your audience reach, you should, however, take into account as many traits as you can and the fact that your target audience will be diverse.

NOTE: You can use the following methods to identify your target audience:

1. Carry out market research

In order to narrow down your precise target population, you may use the customer profiles you generate in this initial phase to find commonalities among your possible audience.

Start by examining demographic information, like income, location, gender, and age, to ascertain who is considering your goods and services. This information can be gathered by reading industry publications, conducting consumer interviews, or completing surveys. In your research, you should also take into account psychographics and behavioral elements, including interests, motivations, lifestyle choices, and hobbies. While buyer behavior may be influenced by demographic information like age and region, psychographic and behavioral traits like interests, values, and aspirations will truly identify your target customer. These look beyond the general characteristics of purchasers to examine their personalities in greater detail. This will assist you in more precisely defining your target audience.

2. Analyze existing customers

By attentively examining your current clientele, you can spot trends, patterns, and shared interests among your most devoted supporters. Gaining an understanding of your current clientele will enable you to identify the kinds of people who are most likely to find your offerings appealing or advantageous. You can then target your audience further with this information.

It's important to keep in mind that these clients have already done business with you, so the input you can get from them will be quite helpful in determining which of them are your best prospects.

3. Identify needs and pain points

It is essential to comprehend the needs, wants, and pain points of your ideal target audience in order to identify them successfully. This means you can better focus your marketing message to appeal to them, and it also helps you identify who your offer is most fit for.

To learn more about the problems and solutions your potential clients are looking for, you can perform questionnaires, surveys, and customer interviews. After you have this knowledge, you can use it to position your product or service as the answer to their issue and create an offer that the market will want to buy.

4. Study competitors

You can learn more about your target audience and assess what approaches to use when attempting to contact them by examining the marketing techniques of your competitors.

Examine their branding, messaging, channels, and any strategies they utilize. Find out which market categories they are aiming for and how they set themselves apart from competitors. In a market that is growing quickly, it is crucial to stand out, but researching your competition may also inspire you and help you find gaps in the market that you can close by focusing on underrepresented groups.

5. Create buyer personas

You can use the information you have acquired about your current and future audience to develop buyer personas. The fictionalized versions of your ideal customers are called buyer personas. By taking this step, you can more easily humanize your target demographic and adjust your marketing to suit their tastes.

Names, demographic information, goals, challenges, and a brief section on interests and hobbies should all be included for each customer persona.

To account for the diversity of their target population, businesses frequently need to develop different buyer personas. The total customer experience can then be enhanced by utilizing these customer personas. Because each customer will uniquely interact with your business, it can be helpful to walk each persona through the purchase process in order to identify any obstacles or pain spots they might encounter. After that, you can use this data to better focus your message, product, or service and enhance the whole customer experience.

Step 2: Setting Clear Marketing Objectives

Setting goals is a crucial part of your marketing plan. They are frequently where you begin. Objectives are the cornerstone of any strategy you create to achieve your goals and provide guidance for what must occur for your good or service to succeed in the marketplace.

Reaching out to your target market and explaining the advantages of your good or service is the goal of marketing, which will help you successfully attract, retain, and expand your customer base. Therefore, your marketing objectives ought to align with the particular business goals that your organization hopes to accomplish. Your marketing plan will remain in line with the business strategy and demonstrate the marketing's impact if it follows a top-down hierarchy of goals.

Your marketing efforts will have a true north when you set focused, realistic, and quantifiable goals early on. This gives you the opportunity to convince leadership that your marketing plan is the best course of action and highlights the strategic significance of the job the team is doing.

Below is how to set clear marketing objectives.

SMART Goals Framework

The SMART Goals framework is a widely used method for setting clear, achievable, and meaningful goals. SMART is an acronym that stands for Specific, Measurable, Achievable, Relevant, and Time-bound.

Let's consider a goal: "I want to increase the sales revenue of our online store." Let's see how this goal can be SMART.

- *Specific*

Goals should be clear and specific, answering the questions: Who, What, Where, When, and Why. This helps focus your efforts and clearly define what you are working towards.

For example: "I want to increase the sales revenue of our online store by expanding our product range and improving our marketing efforts."

- *Measurable*

Goals should have criteria for measuring progress and success. This could involve quantitative metrics or other indicators of progress.

For example: "I aim to increase our monthly sales revenue by 20%."

- *Achievable*

Goals should be realistic and attainable, given your current resources and constraints. This involves assessing what is possible and setting challenging yet achievable objectives.

For example: "I will achieve this by adding five new product lines, optimizing our website for better user experience, and running targeted marketing campaigns."

- *Relevant*

Goals should align with your broader objectives, values, and long-term ambitions. This ensures that the goals matter to you and are worth pursuing.

For example: "Increasing sales revenue aligns with our business objective of growing our market share and expanding our customer base."

- *Time-bound*

Goals should have a clear timeline, with a start and end date, creating a sense of urgency and prompting action.

For example: "I will achieve this goal within the next six months."

Aligning Objectives With Business Goals

Aligning objectives with business goals is essential to ensure that all efforts within an organization are contributing towards the same overall mission and vision. This alignment helps in resource optimization, improving efficiency, and achieving strategic outcomes.

1. Understand the business goals

Overarching business goals are high-level objectives that guide a company's strategic direction and decision-making. These goals can include:

- Growth: focuses on increasing the company's size and market presence.
- Profitability: aimed at maximizing revenue and reducing costs to enhance financial performance.
- Market expansion: seeks to enter new geographic regions or market segments.
- Customer satisfaction: emphasizing the improvement of customer experiences and loyalty.
- Innovation: drives the development of new products, services, or processes.
- Sustainability: aimed at ensuring long-term viability and minimizing environmental impact.

These goals serve as the foundation for setting more specific, actionable objectives across the organization.

2. Break down the goals

Break broad business goals into specific, actionable objectives. This has to do with breaking down overarching goals into smaller, detailed tasks that can be assigned to various departments or teams. For example, a goal of increasing market share might lead to the marketing team launching targeted campaigns, the sales team expanding its outreach efforts, the product development team enhancing product features based on customer feedback, and the customer service team improving response times. Each objective is designed to directly contribute to the larger goal, ensuring that all parts of the organization work in a coordinated and focused manner toward achieving the business's strategic aims.

3. Communicate clearly

Effective communication is important for ensuring that all team members understand the business goals and how their individual and team objectives contribute to these overarching aims. This involves clearly articulating the goals and breaking them down into specific, actionable objectives for each team. Regular updates, meetings, and transparent discussions help maintain alignment and foster a collaborative environment. When team members see the direct connection between their efforts and the company's strategic goals, it enhances motivation, accountability, and a unified drive toward achieving the business's success.

4. Align resources and capabilities

This involves strategically allocating time, budget, and personnel to ensure that objectives are achievable. This includes providing the necessary tools, technology, and training to enhance team skills and capabilities. When you ensure that each department has the resources it needs, such as a sufficient budget for marketing campaigns or skilled personnel for product development, the organization can effectively work towards its goals. Proper alignment ensures that all teams are equipped to meet their objectives, thereby driving the overall success of the business.

5. Monitor and review progress

You've to regularly assess how well your team is advancing towards their specific goals and how these contribute to the broader business objectives. This process includes setting key performance indicators (KPIs) to measure success, conducting periodic reviews to evaluate performance against these metrics, and identifying any deviations or areas needing improvement.

6. Encourage feedback and adaptation

Feedback and adaptation help maintain agility and responsiveness within an organization. Establishing a feedback loop where team members can freely provide input on objectives fosters a culture of openness and continuous improvement. This feedback can offer valuable insights into the effectiveness of current strategies, potential obstacles, and emerging opportunities. Being flexible allows the organization to adjust objectives in response to evolving business conditions, customer feedback, or new market trends. This adaptability ensures that the organization remains proactive and capable of seizing opportunities while mitigating risks. It further enhances its ability to achieve long-term success.

Step 3: Analyzing Your Competitive Landscape

When your competitors are outpacing you in business, and you're not sure why, it can be one of the most aggravating circumstances in the industry. Even if you provide excellent products, outstanding customer service, and intelligent educational marketing, you nevertheless watch your market share decline. You can't just watch your rivals with interest and wonder what they're doing well in order to unravel this riddle. You must systematically create a competitive landscape study.

One proactive method to learn how you compete with other companies in your field is to do a competitive landscape analysis. You can close the gap with your rivals by capitalizing on the strengths of your business rather than taking a purely reactive strategy. Doing it well requires preparation and work, but the rewards can be substantial.

Before we go further into how to analyze your competitive landscape, let's first understand what it means.

A competitive landscape analysis is a systematic approach to identifying and researching your competitors. You do a thorough examination of their methods for developing new products, marketing, selling, and carrying out other crucial tasks. Rather than speculating about why you are not performing as well as you could, the research enables you to create counterstrategies based on precise and trustworthy data.

The following five subjects should be included in a competitive landscape analysis:

- Who your company's competitors are
- The products and services your competitors offer
- Your competitors' strengths and weaknesses
- The strategies your competitors are using to achieve their objectives
- The overall market outlook

Competitive landscape analysis can assist any business, from the smallest startup challengers to the industry's dominant players. Gaining insight into the strategies used by your rivals to increase their profits can help you increase your own.

Conducting Competitor Analysis

1. Identify your competitors and categorize them

The first step is straightforward yet well-thought-out. You must ascertain every potential rival in your sector, including the less well-known ones. Being aware of every player in the market is the aim here, as opposed to picking and choosing to ignore some.

As you find additional competitors, categorize them into the following groups:

- Direct competitors. These companies cater to the same target market as you and offer the same goods or services.

Consumers frequently use these brands as a point of comparison when choosing what to buy. For instance, in the demo automation space, Arcade and Storylane are direct rivals.

- Indirect competitors. These companies provide distinct solutions to the same problem. They give you chances to increase the scope of what you provide. For instance, Scribe and Whatfix address the issue of internal training plus documentation, but in different ways.
- Legacy competitors. These are well-known businesses that have been in your sector for a while. Customers regard their name as trustworthy, and they enjoy a strong reputation in the industry. Ahrefs, for instance, is a well-known rival in the SEO sector.
- Emerging competitors. These are fresh competitors for established companies, offering distinctive value propositions and an inventive business strategy. For instance, ChatGPT surpassed multiple brands and entered the conversational AI industry as a disruptor.

2. Find out where each competitor stands in the market

As soon as you are aware of every competitor, begin assessing where they stand in the industry. This stage will assist you in determining your existing market share and client satisfaction levels. It will also highlight the top competitors in your field, whom you should give priority in your analysis report.

Additionally, you can identify what's lacking in the existing situation by analyzing the market landscape. Even in a saturated market, there are still openings and possibilities for your business to succeed.

Make a graph with the market presence (Y-axis) and customer happiness (X-axis) as the two parameters to map the market positions of competitors. Next, group competitors in every one of these quadrants:

- *Niche*. These are low-market-share brands that have high customer satisfaction ratings. They're probably successfully aiming for a particular audience niche.
- *Contenders*. Despite having a strong market presence, these brands have low consumer satisfaction ratings. They could be recent competitors with a potent sales and marketing plan.
- *Leaders*. These companies have a significant market share and very happy clients. They are the main participants and well-liked by your audience.
- *High performers*. These are yet another group of new entrants that have a low market share yet strong customer satisfaction ratings. They provide a good substitute for those who don't want to purchase from well-known businesses.

This visualization will show you the precise level of market saturation. However, it will also demonstrate strategies for gaining traction and taking on established businesses.

3. Thorough benchmarking of important competitors

Step 2 will help you focus on the handful of most crucial competitors to target out of dozens of others. It's time to create a benchmarking study and conduct a detailed analysis of each rival.

Recall that the goal of this exercise is not to expose every competitor's flaws. You must unbiasedly identify each brand's advantages and disadvantages.

The following are the main things to think about when comparing competitors:

- *Quality*. Evaluate the caliber of each competitor's goods and services. Compare the features of their products to determine what gives them the advantage over you. To learn what customers think about the caliber of their offering, you can also assess customer reviews.

- *Price*. To comprehend the pricing strategies used by your competitors, note their price points. To learn about value for money from users' viewpoints, you can also conduct interviews with their clients.
- *Customer service*. Examine the support channels they offer, including chat, phone, email, knowledge base, and more. Customer ratings are also available on several third-party platforms.
- *Brand reputation*. In order to ascertain how consumers view the brand, you should also evaluate the standing of each rival in the marketplace. Keep an eye out for any negative remarks made about certain competitors.
- *Financial health*. If at all feasible, seek out performance metrics to evaluate a brand's financial development. Data on indicators like profit margins and sales growth are available.

Primary and secondary research will also be used in this benchmarking project. Give this stage enough time to make sure your competitive analysis is flawless.

4. Extensive analysis of their marketing approach

Although the first few steps will help you identify areas for improvement in your main offering, you also need to research the product marketing strategies of your competitors.

To understand how they approach customers, you must go deeply into their marketing tactics. You can examine each marketing channel and make a note of your findings regarding how they appeal to their target market and accentuate their unique brand identity.

Here are a few important marketing channels to consider:

- Website. Examine the copy and structure of the website to determine the positioning and brand voice.

- Email. Sign up for newsletters to find out more about their tone, copywriting, topics they cover, and more.
- Paid ads. To determine whether any competitors are running paid search engine advertisements, use tools such as Ahrefs and Semrush.
- Thought leadership. Utilize digital assets such as podcasts, webinars, courses, and more to track a brand's thought leadership initiatives.
- Digital PR. Explore whether a brand is spending money on digital PR to generate awareness about its brand and evaluate its approach.
- Social media. See how frequently brands utilize various social media platforms and what kinds of material generate the most interest for them.
- Partnerships. Analyze high-value partnerships to determine whether brands collaborate closely and provide mutual benefits to any businesses.

It is possible to compile a comprehensive report that covers every aspect of a rival's advertising plan. This will point your marketing strategy in the correct direction.

5. Carry out SWOT analysis

In a competitive analysis activity, producing a SWOT analysis matrix for every company is the last stage. SWOT is an acronym for Opportunities, Weaknesses, Threats, and Strengths. For small business owners who wish to grow their firm, advance in general, or even take on a new project, a SWOT analysis is a helpful tool.

Also, consider the SWOT analysis to be the last phase in compiling all of your information to address the following questions:

- What is your competitor doing well?
- Where do they have an advantage over your brand?

- What is the weakest area for your competitor?
- Where does your brand have the advantage over your competitor?
- In what areas would you consider this competitor a threat?
- Are there opportunities in the market that your competitor has identified?

Let's look in detail at how to perform a SWOT analysis.

- *Identify Competitor's Strengths*

To effectively identify and evaluate a competitor's strengths, start with thorough research and observation. Assess their brand recognition through market surveys, consumer reviews, and industry analyses to understand how prominently their brand stands out in the market. Evaluate their product offerings by visiting their stores or online platforms, reading customer feedback, and comparing features to gauge innovation and customer appeal. Analyze their marketing strategies by reviewing advertising campaigns, social media presence, and promotional efforts to determine how well they engage and influence their target audience. Additionally, study their customer service reputation by examining online reviews, customer testimonials, and feedback channels to assess satisfaction levels and responsiveness. Lastly, explore their distribution channels to ascertain the extent and efficiency of their product accessibility across different markets and platforms.

After gathering this information, compare and analyze the competitor's strengths against industry benchmarks and your business capabilities. Identify specific areas where they excel, such as brand reputation, innovative products, effective marketing, superior customer service, and extensive distribution networks. Consider how these strengths contribute to their competitive advantage, customer loyalty, and overall market positioning. This comprehensive analysis provides insights into what makes your competitor successful and can guide strategic decisions for your own business, helping to enhance competitiveness, innovate product offerings, improve customer engagement, and optimize distribution strategies accordingly.

- *Assess Competitor's Advantages*

Assessing where your competitor holds advantages over your brand involves a systematic analysis of key factors that contribute to their competitive edge. Start by researching and comparing production costs —this can be done through industry reports, supplier relationships, and publicly available financial data. Look into economies of scale, operational efficiencies, or technological advantages that enable them to produce goods or services at lower costs compared to your business.

After that, examine their market share and market penetration strategies. Analyze market research data, sales figures, and industry reports to understand their share of the market relative to yours. Consider their distribution networks, brand loyalty programs, and customer retention strategies that contribute to their broader customer base and market dominance. Assess their established relationships with key stakeholders such as suppliers, distributors, and strategic partners—this can provide insights into their ability to secure favorable terms, access exclusive resources, or collaborate effectively within the industry.

After gathering this information, compare these advantages against your own business capabilities and market position. This analysis helps identify specific areas where your competitor outperforms, allowing you to strategize on how to mitigate these advantages through targeted improvements in operational efficiency, market expansion efforts, strategic partnerships, or innovation in product offerings.

- *Identify Competitor's Weaknesses*

Conduct a thorough assessment of areas where your competitors fall short relative to industry standards or compared to your own business. This can be achieved by analyzing customer reviews, industry reports, and market research data to pinpoint issues such as product quality concerns, inadequate customer service, or inefficient processes.

Evaluate their geographic presence and distribution capabilities to understand any limitations in reaching potential markets or serving existing customers effectively. Assess their technological infrastructure to identify outdated systems or lack of innovation that may hinder their ability to adapt to market changes or meet customer expectations.

REMEMBER: Identifying these weaknesses enables businesses to capitalize on opportunities to differentiate themselves and strategically position their offerings more effectively in the marketplace.

- *Highlight Your Brand's Advantages*

This step requires you to identify specific strengths that set your business apart from competitors. You can do this by examining your unique product features or proprietary technology that differentiates your offerings in the market. Analyze customer retention rates and satisfaction surveys to gauge higher levels of loyalty compared to competitors. Evaluate your brand's reputation, whether it's for reliability, innovation, or superior customer service, based on customer testimonials, industry awards, or market perception studies.

Also, consider your pricing strategies and competitive pricing analysis to understand how effectively you position your products relative to similar offerings in the market. All these help businesses strengthen their market position, attract new customers, and foster long-term growth and profitability.

- *Evaluate Competitor as a Threat*

Carry out a strategic analysis of your competitors' actions and capabilities that directly impact your business's market position. Begin by monitoring their pricing strategies through market research and comparative analysis to identify any aggressive pricing tactics that could undercut your pricing structure or diminish your market share.

Track their new product launches and innovations by studying industry news, trade publications, and patent filings to anticipate how these offerings might attract your customer base or set new industry standards. Assess their efforts to expand market reach through geographic expansion, online platforms, or strategic partnerships, considering how this could potentially increase competition in key markets.

Analyze their brand positioning and marketing campaigns to understand how they communicate value propositions and differentiate themselves, which may influence consumer perceptions and purchasing decisions.

Lastly, evaluate their customer acquisition strategies, such as promotions, loyalty programs, or targeted advertising, to gauge their effectiveness in attracting and retaining customers who could otherwise patronize your business.

REMEMBER: All these are to proactively respond to competitive threats and refine your strategies to maintain or enhance your competitive advantage in the marketplace.

- *Identify Market Opportunities Recognized by Competitor*

This is all about researching your competitors' strategic initiatives and market actions to uncover areas where they are capitalizing on emerging trends and consumer preferences.

Analyze their product launches and expansions to identify new market segments they are targeting, which may indicate untapped opportunities or gaps in the market not yet served. Study industry reports, trade publications, and patent filings to track technological advancements they are leveraging, as these innovations may open up new markets or improve operational efficiencies.

Additionally, monitor any regulatory changes they are adapting to, as these shifts could create opportunities for growth or competitive advantage. When you effectively do this, you gain insights into potential market opportunities and adjust your strategies to capitalize on them effectively.

Step 4: Crafting Your Unique Value Proposition (UVP)

Determining your unique value proposition (UVP) is essential for small business owners looking to draw in their desired clientele. Your unique value proposition (UVP) is what sets your company apart from the competition and entices potential customers to select your offerings.

A strong UVP explains to potential customers why your business is the best fit for their needs. Your website, landing pages, and social media profiles will all benefit from having an efficient UVP to increase traffic to your site and boost sales.

UVP Essentials and Examples to Effectively Communicate Your UVP

In marketing, your Unique Value Proposition (UVP) must have certain requirements to effectively attract your ideal customers. Some of the essentials of your UVP are:

1. Clear and concise statement

Your UVP should be a clear, concise statement that communicates the unique benefits of your product or service. Avoid jargon and focus on delivering a straightforward message that is easy to understand.

For example, run an online grocery delivery service. Your UVP might be: "Fresh groceries delivered to your doorstep in under an hour." This statement avoids jargon and directly highlights the unique benefits: the freshness of the groceries and the quick delivery time. It's easy for potential customers to understand and immediately see the value your service offers.

2. Target audience focus

Tailor your UVP to address the specific needs and desires of your target audience. Understand their pain points, preferences, and what they value most to ensure your proposition resonates with them.

For instance, if you offer fitness training programs for busy professionals, your UVP could be: "Achieve your fitness goals with personalized, time-efficient workouts designed for your busy schedule." This statement addresses the pain point of limited time and the desire for personalized solutions, directly appealing to professionals who need effective, flexible fitness options that fit into their demanding lifestyles.

3. Highlight unique benefits

Emphasize what sets your product or service apart from competitors. This could be unique features, superior quality, exceptional customer service, innovative technology, or exclusive offerings.

For example, sell a meal kit subscription service. Your UVP might be: "Experience gourmet meals at home with our chef-curated recipes and farm-fresh ingredients delivered weekly." This statement emphasizes the unique benefits of chef-curated recipes and the use of farm-fresh ingredients, which sets your service apart from standard meal kits.

4. Value delivery

Clearly articulate the value you deliver to your customers. Explain how your product or service solves their problems, improves their situation, or offers benefits they can't find elsewhere.

For example, if you offer a cloud storage service, your UVP could read: "Securely store and access your files anytime, anywhere, with our user-friendly cloud storage solution that offers 24/7 support and 99.9% uptime." This UVP clearly communicates the value delivered—secure, reliable access to files from any location, coupled with round-the-clock support and exceptional uptime. It highlights how your service solves the problem of file accessibility and security while providing benefits like ease of use and dependable performance that customers may not find with other providers.

5. Emotional appeal

Incorporate emotional elements that connect with your audience on a deeper level. Consider how your offering makes them feel, enhances their lifestyle, or fulfills their aspirations.

Let's say you run a travel agency specializing in adventure tours; your UVP might be: "Unleash your inner explorer with our unforgettable adventure tours, designed to create lifelong memories and ignite your sense of wonder." This statement taps into the emotions of excitement and fulfillment. It emphasizes how the tours make customers feel adventurous and inspired.

6. Credibility and trust

Build credibility by including elements that reinforce trust, such as testimonials, case studies, awards, or guarantees. Demonstrating reliability and proven results can strengthen your UVP.

A good example is if you offer a financial advisory service, your UVP could read: "Achieve your financial goals with our expert advisors, trusted by over 10,000 clients and recognized with multiple industry awards for excellence." This reinforces trust by mentioning a large number of satisfied clients and highlighting industry awards, which serve as third-party validation of your expertise and quality.

NOTE: including such credibility elements reassures potential customers of your proven track record and reliability. It further strengthens your UVP by demonstrating that your service is both trust-worthy and highly regarded.

7. Consistency across channels

Ensure your UVP is consistently communicated across all marketing channels and touchpoints. From your website and social media to advertisements and sales pitches, maintain a unified message.

A perfect example to illustrate this could be if your UVP for an eco-friendly clothing brand is "Stylish, sustainable fashion that cares for the planet," this message should be consistently presented on your website, social media profiles, email newsletters, advertisements, and even in sales pitches and customer service communications. Whether a customer visits your website, sees an ad on social media, or speaks to a sales representative, they should encounter the same core message about your commitment to stylish and sustainable fashion. This unifor-mity reinforces your brand identity, builds trust, and ensures a cohesive customer experience.

Step 5: Selecting Marketing Channels and Tactics

Choosing the appropriate marketing channel involves more than just reaching as many people as possible; it also involves putting your brand in front of them when they are most responsive. Choosing the best marketing channel can have a big impact on brand visibility, customer acquisition, and business success.

The Importance of Marketing Channel Strategy

Businesses need to have a solid marketing channel plan since it dictates how they will connect and interact with their target market. This is why it's important:

- *Audience Targeting*

Audiences and demographics are drawn to different marketing channels. Businesses can increase the likelihood of engagement and conversion by targeting their messaging to the appropriate audience groups through a well-defined channel strategy.

- *Resource Allocation*

Resources such as time, budget, and manpower are finite. Businesses can more efficiently use their resources by focusing on channels that provide the best return on investment (ROI) and avoiding wasting time and money on channels that don't connect with their target market by employing a strategic approach to marketing channels.

- *Brand Consistency*

Establishing a solid brand identity requires consistency. Businesses may strengthen brand recognition and audience trust by carefully choosing and managing their marketing channels to maintain consistency in messaging and branding across all touchpoints.

- *Maximizing Reach*

The reach potential of different channels varies. By utilizing a variety of channels that collectively cover a wide range of their target population, a well-thought-out channel strategy enables businesses to maximize their reach and guarantee that no potential consumer is overlooked.

- *Adapting to Consumer Behaviour*

The way that consumers behave is always changing, particularly in the digital age we live in. Businesses may stay relevant and efficiently satisfy the needs of their audience by adjusting to shifting consumer trends and preferences with the help of a flexible channel strategy.

Various Marketing Channels

Marketing channels are the means by which companies engage with their intended market, advertise their goods, and increase sales. The following are some of the main categories of marketing channels that companies frequently use:

1. Social Media

Social media platforms like LinkedIn, X, Instagram, and Facebook give businesses the chance to interact with their audience directly. These platforms facilitate businesses in reaching a wider audience through influencer collaborations, targeted advertising campaigns, and content sharing.

Social media marketing is very dynamic, enabling in-the-moment conversation and cultivating deep connections with customers.

2. Email Marketing

Email marketing is still a dependable and affordable way to reach customers, even in the face of more modern marketing platforms. Email marketing is a useful tool for businesses to maintain client relationships, issue promotions, and notify clients about upcoming events and new offerings.

Email marketing enables segmentation and personalization, guaranteeing that messages are suited to the interests and preferences of the recipient.

3. Content Marketing (Blogs, Articles)

The goal of content marketing is to draw in and keep a target audience by producing insightful and timely information. By means of blog entries, articles, films, and infographics, companies can exhibit their proficiency, instruct their readers, and establish brand legitimacy.

Search engine optimization (SEO) is heavily dependent on content marketing since well-written content raises a website's exposure and ranking.

4. Search Engine Optimization (SEO)

To raise a website's position on search engine result pages, SEO entails improving its meta-tags, content, and structure. Businesses may improve brand awareness, draw in more organic traffic, and make their websites more visible by ranking higher in search results.

SEO is a low-cost marketing tool that helps companies compete successfully in the online market by focusing on high-quality traffic.

5. Pay-Per-Click (PPC) Advertising

Businesses can use pay-per-click (PPC) advertising to display adverts on search engines and other websites, only having to pay when people click on the ads. Platforms like Microsoft Advertising and Google Ads allow companies to target niche markets and obtain rapid exposure.

PPC advertising offers straightforward campaign performance measurement, fast campaign results, and precise targeting possibilities.

6. Direct Mail

Sending physical mail to specific recipients, including letters, post-cards, or catalogs, is known as direct mail. Targeting particular geographic regions or demographics is made effective with this marketing channel since it is extremely personalized and concrete.

Personalized offers, loyalty programs, and event invitations are a few examples of how direct mail marketing may help businesses interact with clients in person.

7. Influencer Marketing

In recent years, influencer marketing has become increasingly popular. Engaging in partnerships with influencers who command a sizable following among your intended audience can increase the visibility and legitimacy of your brand. Influencers may help you sell more products and build your brand by promoting them through reviews, suggestions, and interesting content.

8. TV

One of the most widely used marketing channels for expanding brand awareness and reaching a large audience is television advertising. TV commercials give companies the chance to use the visual storytelling power of television to present their goods and services to a wide range of consumers.

TV advertising is excellent for mass marketing efforts since it has a large impact and a wide audience despite its potential expense.

NOTE: These are but a handful of the numerous marketing avenues businesses can utilize. The secret is to choose the channels that will work best for your target market, business objectives, and overall marketing strategy.

How to Choose the Right Marketing Channel for Your Business

A company's overall success and growth can be greatly impacted by choosing the appropriate marketing channels. The following seven essential actions will help you successfully navigate the process:

1. Define your goals

Make sure your marketing goals are well-defined first. What do you hope to accomplish through your marketing efforts? Your channel selection approach will be guided by clear and measurable goals, whether they be for growing sales, generating leads, driving website traffic, or enhancing brand awareness.

2. Know your audience

Know your target market inside out. Perform comprehensive market research to find out their pain points, interests, preferences, and demographics. Having a deep understanding of your target demographic enables you to select marketing methods that will appeal to them and successfully deliver your message.

3. Evaluate channel relevance

Not every marketing channel is made equal, and what functions well for one company might not be suitable for another. Analyze how each channel relates to your target market and your company's goals. Take into account elements like cost-effectiveness, reach, engagement potential, and compatibility with your brand values.

4. Conduct competitive analysis

Analyze your competitors' marketing tactics and keep a watchful eye on them. Which channels are they using? Are they having success with particular strategies or platforms? Even if you shouldn't directly mimic your rivals' tactics, you may learn a lot from them about what approaches are most effective in your sector and where to concentrate your efforts.

5. Test and iterate

Don't be scared to try out various marketing strategies and channels. To assess the efficacy of each channel, set up small-scale tests and make adjustments in response to the findings. Keep an eye on important indicators like ROI, click-through rates, and conversion rates to find out which marketing channels are working best for your business.

6. Create a multi-channel strategy

Instead of putting all your eggs in one basket, think about implementing a multi-channel marketing strategy. To increase your chances of success, attract a larger audience, and reduce risk, diversify your marketing efforts over a variety of media. But be careful not to overextend yourself; instead, concentrate on platforms that complement your objectives and appeal to your target market.

7. Monitor and optimize performance

The effort doesn't end after your campaigns are started and your marketing channels have been chosen. Keep an eye on each channel's performance at all times, and adjust your tactics in light of current information and insights. If certain channels do poorly or if new chances present themselves, be ready to change course.

Step 6: Developing a Content Strategy

A content strategy involves the planning, creation, dissemination, management, and governance of material. A strong content strategy will draw in and keep the target audience interested while advancing organizational objectives.

Importance of Content Strategy

A content marketing strategy is essential for the success of your digital marketing initiatives, regardless of the type of business or sector you operate in. These are a few of the causes.

1. It aligns the team on goals and objectives

A content marketing strategy makes sure that all members of the marketing team are aware of the general aims and particular targets of the business.

When content creators, social media managers, authors, and other team members are on the same page about goals like brand exposure, lead generation, or customer interaction, they can create material that consistently supports these objectives. This raises the likelihood of obtaining noticeable results.

2. It guides content creation and distribution

A content marketing strategy necessitates planning the types of content to produce, such as blog posts, infographics, videos, and podcasts.

Additionally, you will ascertain which distribution channels—such as the corporate website, email marketing, or social media platforms—are the most successful.

By ensuring that the material is timely, relevant, and suited to the interests and requirements of the audience, this planning promotes advocacy and brand loyalty.

3. It optimizes resources

Planning out a comprehensive content marketing strategy will help you allocate resources—money, time, or personnel—more effectively in order to execute the plan.

You can allocate your time and resources to projects that will yield the highest return on investment (ROI) if you know what kind of content you must create and the channels you plan to use to share it.

4. It improves online visibility

This issue can be resolved with a well-executed content marketing plan, which raises a brand's exposure in search engine results pages (SERPs).

Search engines reward superior, search-engine-optimized content and appear higher in search results, increasing natural traffic.

You can bring in more quality leads to your website by focusing on keywords and subjects that are pertinent to your intended audience.

5. It builds brand authority and trust

You can establish your business as a thought leader in its sector by continuously generating excellent, pertinent, and useful content.

Establishing credibility with your audience is essential for fostering enduring relationships and retaining customers.

A content marketing plan makes sure that your content offers value draws in readers, and entices them to return and engage with the business on a deeper level.

How to Create a Compelling Content for Your Audience

1. Understand your target audience

Knowing your target audience is the cornerstone of creating content that is both strong and engaging. Shooting arrows without knowing where to aim is not possible. There's a chance that you will eventually connect with your target audience. That likelihood is as remote as it gets, though.

What steps can you take then to better understand your target audience? You must first investigate their hobbies, pain spots, and demographics. You may create buyer personas with your data to learn more about the goals, obstacles, and motivations of your target audience. This knowledge will help you create material that speaks directly to their needs and will also help you personalize messaging.

2. Be authentic and relatable

Sometimes, flowery language or shallow content in posts or advertisements confuses readers. When it comes to engaging material in this day and age, relatability and authenticity win out.

Sincere communications are necessary to engage your audience since people long for true connections. Make sure the personality and core values of your brand are reflected in your engaging content. Correlate how your brand becomes essential to meeting a need or a pain point in the audience's life at the same time.

In your communications, strive to be relatable, human, and friendly. To establish trust, you can provide personal narratives, behind-the-scenes photos, and user-generated content. You may build deep connections with your audience in this way.

3. Tell strong and captivating stories

Being human, our natural tendency is to hear, see, or read stories. Because of this, crafting social media content that connects with your audience requires strong storytelling.

Write compelling stories that arouse feelings and grab readers' attention. You may provide relatable anecdotes, customer success stories, or journeys of overcoming obstacles. Whatever the subject, storytelling enables you to establish an emotional connection with your audience.

This is a fantastic approach to demonstrate the influence your business has on users' or customers' lives.

To improve the storytelling experience and make your material more memorable and click-worthy, incorporate visual elements like photographs and videos.

4. Produce informative and educational content

Valuable and insightful content about your brand, goods, and services is another kind of content you may create. Your readers will be drawn in by captivating content that provides insightful knowledge or solutions to difficulties.

Here are some content structures that you can use:

- Craft compelling content that educates, informs, and adds value to their lives. (How to solve a problem? Why is your product or service important?)
- Create tutorials or instructions on things about your product or service.
- Provide tips, guides, and industry insights relevant to your niche or your audience's problems.

You can position your business as an industry authority and develop trust with your audience by creating instructive material. Your audience will be more engaged the more value you offer.

5. Spark interesting conversations and encourage engagement

Social media is all about exchanges and conversations. You have to use this approach to highlight your product or service.

Encourage questions, opinions, and discussions to get your audience involved with your information. Answer messages and comments right away to demonstrate that you sincerely value what people have to say.

Additionally, the majority of today's social networking networks allow you to broadcast live.

In addition, user-generated content campaigns, competitions, and interactive surveys are excellent means of engaging your audience.

6. Optimize your content for each platform

Every social media platform has its distinct features and expectations from its users. As a result, you need to modify your engaging content to match the format and design of each platform.

For instance, you can produce captivating videos for YouTube, Reels, or TikTok, brief and concise tweets, and visually striking images for Instagram. You can increase the impact and reach of your content by making sure it is optimized for each platform.

Depending on the platform, you can also test different things with your material. In order to keep your audience interested, variety is essential. This is an opportunity to go beyond a single format for content. Examine several formats, including interactive quizzes, webinars, live videos, podcasts, and blog postings.

This enables you to accommodate the various tastes and consumption patterns of your target audience. To increase the value of your material and attract a larger audience, repurpose it for several channels. For instance, post brief segments of a lengthy video on Reels or TikTok, then submit it to YouTube.

7. Produce relevant and timely content

The timeliness and relevance of your intriguing content are another element that appeals to your target audience. It is, therefore, crucial to be abreast of the most recent developments, conversations, and trends in your sector. Additionally, you want to think about the best time to post content.

Keep track of current events and social media topics that are relevant to your expertise. Include your viewpoint, insights, or relevant solutions in your content strategy to address these issues or events that are currently trending. Your strategy and captivating content establish your business as a thought leader in your industry and community and show off its significance.

Establishing a Content Calendar and Distribution Plan

Now that you've learned how to create compelling content for your audience, it's time to know the steps to create a content calendar and distribution plan. A content calendar and distribution plan helps you organize and schedule your content creation and distribution efforts. Here's a step-by-step guide to get started:

1. What are your goals?

When organizing any future content, begin by identifying its main goal. Selecting the appropriate channel and format should be based on the response to the question.

Is the content intended to:

- Produce new leads
- Direct readers to a website
- Gain visibility
- Grow the number of your social media followers

The specified goals have a significant impact on who, where, and how frequently you post content. For this reason, everyone on your team must be aware of your objectives both before and during the planning phase.

Therefore, setting goals should come before putting a content calendar into action. Distributing information without a defined goal will not help your business; on the contrary, it will be a waste of resources.

Every individual working on a project or item on the calendar needs to be fully aware of the intended outcomes.

2. Create a template for the calendar

You can find a lot of software applications with calendar functionality; feel free to select the template that works best for you. However, because switching to new software can be time-consuming, your content schedule might be as simple as a spreadsheet.

If you're organizing content with the entire organization, the calendar ought to feature a share button. Using the free Google Sheets tool, for instance, you can make a calendar template that everybody involved in content development can amend on their computer to contribute ideas and comments.

While the exact requirements of your team will determine how your content calendar is put together, it should, at the very least, contain the following:

- The channel in which the content will be published
- The topic
- The type of content
- The date and time for publishing
- The person in charge
- Follow-through: has the content been published according to schedule?

Here is an example of how to create a content calendar and what a simple content calendar template can look like:

Date	Content-Type	Topic/Title	Platform	Responsible	Status
July 15	Blog Post	Summer Marketing Tips	Blog	Jane	Drafting
July 18	Video	Product Demo	YouTube	John	Editing
July 20	Social Post	Customer Testimonial	Instagram	Sarah	Scheduled
July 22	Email	Monthly Newsletter	Email Campaign	Mike	Sent

3. Choose your channels

Determine which channels your present and potential clients use. This will assist you in determining what type of content you should focus on developing. Does your blog need to publish articles? What about pictures on Instagram and Twitter? What about videos on YouTube? How about a Facebook survey? TikTok and Instagram short video content?

Publishing content on several platforms and in multiple formats can help you reach a larger audience. However, ensure that you have enough resources to devote to the platforms on which you intend to appear. Instead of posting on every network you can think of, choose your most critical channels and focus on providing high-quality content. This way, you can stay on track by producing high-quality content rather than partaking in every content production trend that adds little value to your organization.

Social media posts are typically the quickest and least time-consuming sort of content to publish, but it's also important to explore how you can use video content to promote your business — even if planning and creating films requires more time and work. However, ensure that your content calendar includes more in-depth information than just social media.

Press releases, in-depth articles, and guest blogs ought to be a part of your annual communications and marketing strategy since they will probably offer more information and benefits to prospective clients.

Additionally, cross-promoting and sharing your more in-depth information can be efficiently accomplished with social media. You can increase traffic and attract visitors to your website by sharing an article on LinkedIn or Twitter or by posting an infographic from a blog post on Instagram.

4. Begin with the calendar year

When it comes to content planning, start with the calendar year. Make a list of all the major events that you want to base your content on, such as holidays, trade shows, seminars, and training.

HINT: Holiday wishes are a simple approach to creating content and engaging consumers.

This simple step will help you determine the type of seasonal content you will require in the future, as well as estimate the incoming workload, allowing your team to plan accordingly.

5. Add your content

Once you've written down all of the crucial dates, begin filling in the blanks with related content ideas. This content could contain:

- Theme posts: Are you attending a trade fair or seminar? Is there a current discussion about your operations? Follow the broad conversation in your profession and quickly grasp the current topics.
- Serial posts: Do you specialize in a service and want to share it with your customers? Serial posts are an excellent approach to educating and highlighting your expertise.
- Write expert articles and guest blogs about your services and current themes in your field.
- Publish press releases about product launches, research results, and worldwide expansion.
- Seasonal or holiday greetings
- Videos or images from events, promotions, products, and projects
- Testimonials from customers and interviews presented as a case study or video
- Fascinating and funny facts about the business: Who works there, and what happens when there's a coffee break?

Make sure your timetable is filled with enough pertinent ideas. Your content will remain intriguing if you provide variation.

6. Keep evergreen content at hand

Content that isn't limited by time or date will always be beneficial to your clients and business. Even after the first buzz following publishing, this kind of material is likely to continue receiving hits and visitors because contemporary issues are still relevant and are frequently searched online.

By including links to them in your more recent content on related topics, you can also effortlessly reconnect your readers to your classic blog posts and articles from the past.

When your schedule is delayed, timeless content might also come to your rescue. It is beneficial to have ready-made content saved somewhere so that it may be used when your team needs to focus on other duties because it can be developed and released whenever you want. Timeless content ideas that may be used at any moment should have a designated spot on your calendar.

7. Make use of prior content

When making a content calendar, you don't always have to create all of the content from scratch. The majority of businesses have valuable content on hand that hasn't been used, like consumer survey responses and CRM system data.

Previous blog entries can also be updated and repurposed via various platforms, such as making them into quick films. It can be a good idea to give comparable concepts in different formats because your potential clients may search for information on multiple platforms. By addressing various target groups, you will maximize the value of all the valuable information you have produced.

It is imperative to ensure that the content on your website is current since a considerable number of prospective clients may peruse your previous blog entries or articles. Occasionally, checking and updating them to make sure your content is correct will give you a trustworthy and professional appearance.

Mark the articles that have been updated to inform your viewers that your content is current and that you are constantly working to improve its value to them.

8. Decide on the publishing frequency and set time limits

Consider how frequently you can actually provide new content. Since content creation takes time, it's critical to determine a publishing frequency that suits your needs. The effectiveness of the calendar depends on your ability to recognize your boundaries. The content will suffer if it is overstuffed. Nonetheless, there needs to be adequate content to drive visitors to your website and consistently add value for your clients.

You can identify the busiest periods for your business with the aid of a content calendar. By guaranteeing that initiatives are initiated and completed well in advance of the publishing date, planning will assist people as well as the team in getting ready for the busiest months of the firm. Stated differently, time constraints should constantly be applied to the planning process to ensure that deadlines are met. Scheduling social media posts on a different posting platform like SEMrush and blog posts on your CMS platform is another way to make sure that content creation stays on course.

A certain amount of flexibility should be taken into consideration and permitted in the scheduling when designing a content calendar, though. There may be times when your business needs to react fast to outside events or news in your industry. As a result, it may occasionally be a good idea to postpone the material that was initially scheduled and less important in favor of responding to current events.

9. Update and review your plan

The question of how far in advance to plan your content cannot be answered with certainty. A number of variables affect planning, including the degree of volatility in your industry and even some that are unique to your organization.

However, bear in mind that the more in advance you arrange your content, the more seamlessly the content will flow. One easy rule of thumb is to plan the major content for the entire year and then, for the next month, plan the weekly and daily material more thoroughly.

Individuals should be able to voice their opinions and revise their ideas as needed. Reviewing the content calendar with the entire team on a regular basis could be a smart idea. This will assist you in staying on course and adjusting to any changes that may occur.

10. Monitor how your content is received

The fact that practically everything in digital marketing is measurable is one of its best features. However, assessing the true impact of the content is sometimes neglected after a business invests a large amount of effort in producing and disseminating high-quality content.

Take some time to review your data and processes and incorporate them into your future strategies. Which social media posts have generated the most discussion? Which blogs have received the most shares? To what extent have the media outlets covered your press releases?

The following metrics can be followed on your tools:

- Newsletter tool: open rate, click-through rate, subscribers
- Press release tool: open and click rates
- Media monitoring tool: the amount of mentions and what, where, and how it is said.

Since many social media platforms come with built-in analytics tools that let you gauge the effectiveness of your content, you can track a lot of social media data directly from the tools themselves. Knowing what kind of content your readers are interested in can help you to develop and produce even more captivating content in the future.

Step 7: Implementing, Monitoring, and Adjusting Your Strategy

Creating a marketing plan alone is not good enough. A strategy is nothing more than a theoretical exercise that you can put off for weeks, months, or even years. The goal of every marketing strategy is to bring about the intended change by means of events that must occur after it is put into place. An amazing strategy and plan can be created by combining the beautiful elements of vision, inspiration, cranial gymnastics, and the glamour of naval gazing. All of it can be fascinating and even entertaining. All is for naught, though, until superb marketing execution makes it truly happen.

Every aspect of marketing that is required to bring a strategy to life is made possible by execution. To create leads, for instance, tradeshows, advertising, PR, social media participation, and blogging can all work together. To make the strategy work and yield results, each component must have all the specifics covered and contribute correctly.

Important Marketing Execution Tips

1. Ensure it is adaptable

A solid marketing plan lays the groundwork, but the world of marketing is constantly evolving. The implementation phase needs to be flexible in order to accommodate new social media platforms, changes in consumer behavior, and revisions to search engine algorithms. Being inflexible in your approach can result in wasted time and opportunity.

2. Utilize data in fine-tuning the execution

Data analytics are essential to the successful implementation of marketing. Resources such as CRM software, Google Analytics, and specialized marketing platforms can offer up-to-date information on the effectiveness of each component of your approach. You can maximize your results by making quick adjustments with the help of this data. It's important to continuously improve the plan rather than just putting it into action.

3. Don't rely solely on automation

Automation tools can handle monotonous activities like sending emails, updating social media, or even segmenting audiences in today's technologically advanced world. But depending only on automation can deprive your marketing plan of the human element that fosters real connections. Effective marketing execution strikes a balance between automation and human interaction to keep your brand relevant and genuine.

4. Align marketing execution with sales goals

A typical mistake made when executing marketing is to confuse the goals of sales with marketing. The most effective marketing plans target conversions rather than merely brand recognition. The efficiency of the sales pipeline is increased when the marketing and sales teams work closely together to make sure that lead-generation activities are directed toward qualified prospects.

5. Evaluate and adjust your strategy

Your plan is not set in stone, even once execution has started. As a matter of fact, the first round of execution might yield insightful information for future strategic planning. It is important to keep a careful eye on Key Performance Indicators (KPIs) and have flexible plans that can adjust to changing market conditions or performance targets.

NOTE: Effective leadership is essential to the successful implementation of the marketing plan. A capable team leader can swiftly reach important choices, settle disputes, and maintain focus. They serve as the conductor of your marketing orchestra, making sure that each instrument plays its note at the appropriate tempo and tone to produce a tune that appeals to your target audience.

Tracking Key Performance Indicators (KPIs) and Metrics

KPI tracking is the tools and processes used by businesses to keep an eye on performance indicators. The process of measuring key performance indicators (KPIs) entails gathering particular data and transforming it into meaningful metrics that can be evaluated and presented in dashboards and charts that are simple to understand.

Every business produces data from its everyday activities, which may be tracked and evaluated to gauge efficacy. Operational improvements can then be implemented with the use of these metrics.

KPIs can be tailored to meet the demands of different industries, departments, or even just one. They provide insights into many facets of an organization's operations.

However, tracking KPIs entails more than just gathering data. It is possible to ascertain whether these indicators point to a need for improvement or highlight areas within an organization that require optimization by taking a wider view of them.

NOTE: In today's workplace, efforts to constantly modify and correctly orient businesses for success depend heavily on KPI tracking.

Creating a relevant KPI library is the first step in effectively tracking performance metrics for your business. When relevant KPIs are identified and tracked effectively, numerous areas can be addressed right away.

Sales is one of the sectors where KPIs are used the most frequently since it allows for simpler tracking and quantification of overall success and goal progress. This involves monitoring metrics such as monthly revenue, sales growth, and sales as a function of converted leads.

Businesses can gain insights into where their sales funnels can be improved by using KPI tracking to determine how their funnels are doing from lead to conversion.

Making Data-Driven Adjustment for Optimization

The last step in putting a winning marketing strategy into action is optimizing your efforts using data-driven adjustments. Use the knowledge you get from monitoring your KPIs and metrics to hone your strategies and boost output. Finding patterns, trends, and places where your campaigns are falling short is what this method entails. Make any necessary adjustments to your strategy based on this data. You could want to try new marketing techniques, refocus your investment on high-performing channels, or change your messaging.

To boost engagement, experiment with alternate subject lines, sending timings, or personalization strategies if your email marketing campaign, for instance, has a poor open rate. Examine the ad creatives, targeting settings, and bidding techniques to find areas for improvement if your social media advertising is not bringing in the anticipated return on investment.

Chapter 8
Operations and Management

Operations and management are very significant in the daily running of a business. Operations management focuses on all the activities that are involved in converting the inputs to outputs that the customers require. This entails aspects such as ensuring that things are done on time, the costs are within the required budget, and the quality is good. Thus, good operations management ensures that these processes are properly coordinated to minimize time and costs while meeting the customers' needs.

Management means that all the activities within the business are well coordinated. It includes identifying, scheduling, directing, monitoring and assessing the activities of the organization to achieve the company's objectives. Managers come into play to provide important decisions, form groups, and oversee the performance. They also provide for the development of the right culture within the organization and ensure that the business is ready for any changes that may occur in the market. Operations and management are two functions that run the business and make the business grow in the competitive world.

In this chapter, we shall discuss how you can properly operate and manage your business in the right manner.

Setting Up Your Workspace

As a business owner, your workspace is the area where you work, whether it's an office, a shop, or even your own home. It's where you do your job, handle tasks, and organize everything you need to get work done effectively.

It's important to follow certain steps to successfully set up your workspace for effectiveness and efficiency.

1. Choose a suitable location

When choosing a location for your workspace, whether it's at home or in a dedicated office space, consider several important factors. First, think about how noisy the area is—try to find a spot away from loud sounds or distractions that could interrupt your work.

Next, think about how easy it is to access the location. It should be convenient for you to get to, whether that means being close to home or easily reachable by public transport or car.

Lastly, consider the amount of space you'll need. Make sure there's enough room for your desk, chair, computer, and any other equipment or supplies you use regularly. Having a comfortable and organized workspace can help you focus better and be more productive in your business activities.

2. Organize your equipment

Get all the tools and equipment you need for your work. This includes your computer for managing emails and documents, a printer for producing hard copies, and a phone for communicating with clients or suppliers.

Additionally, gather any specialized tools or equipment specific to your business, such as machinery, software, or instruments. Ensure these items are easily accessible within your workspace and are positioned in a way that facilitates efficient workflow.

Keep them in good working condition by performing regular maintenance or updates. This ensures they are reliable when needed. This setup helps to enhance productivity and reduces frustration by having everything you need readily available and functioning properly.

3. Arrange furniture

When arranging your furniture, focus on setting up your desk, chairs, and shelves to make your work easier. Your desk should have plenty of space for your computer, paperwork, and any tools you use frequently. Make sure it's organized so you can find things quickly. Your chair should be comfy enough for long periods of sitting, with good support for your back. Arrange shelves or storage nearby for easy access to files, books, or other materials you need. The goal is to create a setup that helps you stay organized and comfortable throughout your workday. It makes tasks smoother and more efficient.

4. Manage your supplies

Keep a stock of essential items like stationery, paper, pens, and any other materials you use regularly in your work. Make sure you have enough of these supplies so you don't run out unexpectedly. Keep them organized and easily accessible within your workspace. This could mean using drawers, containers, or shelves to store them neatly.

Labeling or categorizing items can also help you find what you need quickly when it's time to use them. Staying stocked up and organized helps you avoid interruptions in your work and maintain productivity throughout your day.

5. Personalize your space

It's important to create a space where you feel comfortable and at ease, as this can positively impact your mood and creativity. Personalize your space by adding personal touches that make it feel comfortable and inspiring for you.

Consider including plants to bring some greenery and freshness into the space. Artwork or photos that inspire you or remind you of your goals can also be great additions. Choose decorations that reflect your personality and motivate you to work productively. The goal is to create a more inviting environment that supports your well-being and enhances your enjoyment of your work.

6. Ensure good lighting

Having proper lighting in your workspace is crucial for reducing eye strain and creating a productive environment. If possible, position your desk near a window to take advantage of natural light, which is not only easier on the eyes but also boosts mood and alertness.

Supplement natural light with task lighting, such as a desk lamp with adjustable brightness, to illuminate specific areas where you work. Ensure that the lighting is adequate and evenly distributed across your workspace to avoid shadows or glare that could cause discomfort.

For example, in an office setting, overhead lighting can provide general illumination, while a desk lamp can be used for focused tasks like reading or writing. Good lighting contributes to a more comfortable and efficient work environment and enhances your overall productivity.

7. Consider ergonomics

Ergonomics focuses on designing your workspace to fit your body and reduce the risk of discomfort or injury. Start by positioning your computer screen directly at eye level to prevent neck strain. Use a chair that offers good back support and allows your feet to rest flat on the floor or a footrest if needed. Adjust the height of your chair so that your elbows are at a comfortable angle when typing, and use armrests if they help you maintain a relaxed posture.

Remember to take regular breaks to stretch and move around, which can alleviate tension and improve circulation. By paying attention to ergonomics, you can prevent repetitive strain injuries and work more comfortably for longer periods. For instance, ergonomic accessories like an adjustable monitor stand or an ergonomic keyboard can further enhance your workspace setup, promote better posture, and reduce physical strain.

8. Set up storage solutions

Establishing effective storage solutions helps keep your workspace organized and your documents easily accessible. Consider using filing cabinets to store important paperwork, categorizing them by project or type for quick retrieval. Shelves can hold reference books, supplies, or decorative items, keeping them off your desk and reducing clutter.

Digital storage systems such as cloud storage or network drives can also be invaluable for storing electronic files securely and accessing them from anywhere. Use labels or color-coding systems to identify different categories of items, making it easier to locate what you need when you need it.

Setting up efficient storage solutions enables you to streamline your workflow and create a more productive environment where everything has its place. A good instance is having a home office with a combination of digital storage for electronic documents and physical storage like shelves or file drawers. This can maintain organization and efficiency.

Procurement and Inventory Management

Procurement and inventory management are crucial parts of how businesses get and keep the goods they need. Procurement involves finding suppliers and making deals to buy goods or services from them. It's important because it ensures that businesses get the best materials at the right prices. Inventory management, on the other hand, tracks how much of those goods a business has at any given time. It's vital to know this in real-time so businesses can always know when to reorder and keep enough stock on hand. Studying supply chain management gives you the skills to handle these kinds of tasks and solve problems that come up in managing a business's supply of goods.

What's the Purpose of Procurement and Inventory Management?

Procurement and inventory management aim to acquire products or services efficiently and economically. This means keeping stock levels low and minimizing extra inventory while ensuring the right amount of goods is always available to meet customer demand.

Inventory is the products a company keeps ready for sale. Effective inventory management aims to reduce costs by only producing goods when customers need them. It also provides reliable information about available stock to guide decision-making for employees.

When planning inventory management and procurement, consider the following:

- What you're buying (like computers or farm products)
- How much demand there will be
- If local suppliers can provide what you need
- How much it costs to make the product

What are the key features to look for in a procurement management system solution?

When choosing features for a purchasing system, focus first on managing how items are bought to meet the company's needs. This ensures that the right products are acquired to support the business operations.

1. Need

To ensure that each purchase of a product is appropriate, it's essential to have clear answers to specific questions. These include understanding how many units should be ordered to meet current demand and future needs. Additionally, knowing the exact details, such as specific colors, sizes, or quality requirements, ensures that the purchased items meet the company's standards and customer expectations. Clarity on these aspects helps streamline the procurement process, ensuring that the right products are acquired in the right quantities and specifications.

2. Analysis

Managing the above questions for every product can be daunting, especially for larger organizations that deal with thousands of different items. To make smarter purchasing decisions, it's helpful to use forecasting and analysis. This involves predicting future needs based on trends, seasonal changes, promotions, and shifts in market conditions. By analyzing these factors, businesses can plan better, ensuring they buy the right products at the right times.

3. Vendor management cost

When managing vendors, it's important to consider more than just the price they quote. A good purchasing management software helps in assessing the total cost of a product, including shipping and other expenses. Tracking spending across the company also reveals opportunities to get discounts when buying in larger quantities from suppliers. This approach helps businesses make the best decisions that maximize cost savings and efficiency in procurement.

4. Vendor effectiveness

Evaluating how well vendors perform helps businesses plan better, make smarter spending decisions, and manage suppliers more effectively. By analyzing supplier performance, companies can gain insights that lead to improved processes and cost savings. Setting clear expectations for new vendors becomes easier, and ongoing evaluations using factors like their quoted prices, previous costs paid, and delivery times ensure they meet the company's needs consistently. This structured approach strengthens supplier relationships and enhances overall operational efficiency.

Hiring and Managing Employees

The hiring and management of employees is one of the biggest concerns facing business owners. This is an extremely difficult issue that all business owners deal with.

People manage companies. People are a business's most valuable asset, not the goods or services they provide. The right—or wrong—people a company hires can have a significant impact on its success or failure. Thus, disregard this section at your peril.

Some businesses favor recruiting people gradually. Before employing a candidate, they take their time to get to know them, evaluate their skills, and conduct interviews. Some people also support firing swiftly. They let someone go as soon as they discover they made a mistake and that the person they recruited is unfit for the job, within the bounds of the law, after trying every reasonable means to make things work.

Finding and hiring the appropriate people for your business is ultimately the aim, followed by trying to hang onto them for as long as possible—which isn't very long these days.

Let's look at some tips to help you navigate this difficult area.

Tips for Hiring the Right Employees

1. Define the Qualities and Abilities You're Looking for

It's astounding how many business owners are unsure of what kind of expertise they require for their enterprises. They declare, "I want this person for this job," but they don't take into account the skills and attributes required for that role to succeed.

It's important to take the time to determine the precise requirements of a position before hiring someone. Armed with that information, you can draft a precise job description and use it as a guide to interview candidates.

In the event that the qualifications and skills a job candidate needs to possess for a specific role are not clearly stated, you will eventually find that the individual you hired is not a suitable fit.

REMEMBER: You won't find what you're looking for if you don't know what it is.

2. Post Attractive and Detailed Job Offers

Once you've decided what you're searching for and written a job description, you can post a job offer. The job posting should have the following details: job title, job summary, location, keywords, "about us" section, compensation details, and qualifications like education, experience, and hard and soft skills. Inadequate job applications from unclear or incomplete job postings prevent you from selecting the best candidate for the position.

3. Use Social Media to Promote Job Openings

Job sites are useful, but social networking is also an option. Since it's so simple to distribute job posts and get the word out to appropriate audiences, you may post jobs on a range of social media channels. Additionally, social networking is less intimidating for job seekers. (Have you seen the problems they have when using employment sites to search and apply for jobs?)

Spread the word, whichever you decide to do it. And keep in mind that it takes time and effort to find and attract the proper people. Therefore, exercise patience and diligence.

4. Be Meticulous About Interviews

Comprehensive interviews are necessary in order to find and hire the best people. They can take place in a coffee shop or a boardroom, professional or informal, but you still need to go over every detail (do you still have the map? ;-) to make sure the individual you end up hiring is a good fit for the position and the organization.

Before becoming too enthused about experience, abilities, and credentials, take into account your business culture. Examine the candidates' energy, attitudes, values, and communication styles carefully. Do they uphold the same company values and work ethic as you? With the rest of your squad, would they get along?

It's your opportunity to pitch the business and discuss your ideas after you've identified the ideal candidate. Ultimately, it's not only about you selecting the appropriate people; it's also about the appropriate people selecting you.

5. Offer Competitive Salaries and Benefits

This brings us to the aspect of recruiting that causes anxiety in everyone. Once you've chosen a candidate, it's time to discuss pay and incentives. A competitive salary, excellent benefits, bonuses, and opportunities for professional advancement are all components of an attractive job offer.

Candidates can see the potential career path of large, established firms if they choose to accept the position. However, because the company is still young and you have no idea when or how these opportunities might come up, it can be challenging to offer professional progression opportunities when you're first starting. Therefore, be extremely patient with your staff and assure them that they will grow along with the company.

People with an entrepreneurial spirit and a desire to help build and grow a business are in high demand by certain employers. Individuals who work for startups have the opportunity to learn and develop far faster than those who work for large, well-established corporations in the style of corporate America.

Remember that although salary and benefits are always significant, the priorities of today's job hopefuls differ from those of past generations when it comes to remuneration. People place high importance on work-life balance, democratic corporate structures where people feel heard and respected, flexibility, a feeling of meaning and purpose at work, and access to coaching and mentorship. They desire to be involved in the business and contribute to the solution. They want to work for organizations and executives that will value their opinions and be willing to have them contested. Put differently, they find it unacceptable to merely perform a task and receive compensation for it.

NOTE: You cannot succeed in running your own business by yourself, so the next time you are deciding what kind of compensation to offer a candidate, go beyond a salary and benefits package. Not everything is about money.

REMEMBER: You have to figure out a way to retain them when you hire them. Good employee management is just as vital as finding the proper candidates because contented workers are more engaged, productive, and efficient and are also less inclined to quit.

How to Effectively Manage Your Employees

Employee retention is advantageous for business. Employee turnover is not. A high turnover rate lowers productivity, causing businesses to miss deadlines and lose clients. It reduces team morale since employees must take up the slack left by departed teammates. It harms the company's reputation since word spreads that it could be a horrible place to work.

Employee turnover is also pricey. Losing an employee can cost a company anywhere from 100% to 150% of their income, depending on their degree of seniority--it costs less for hourly workers and more for technical and executive roles. Turnover costs include recruiting, onboarding, training, ramp time to peak production, loss of employee engagement as a result of high turnover, errors, and negative effects on corporate culture.

What exactly does this mean? This means that efficient personnel management is vital to the survival and success of any firm.

Let's take a look at how to properly manage your personnel like you know what you're doing.

1. Create a good work environment

People leave managers, not jobs. Employees are frequently mistreated by company executives, who disappoint them, make promises they cannot keep, ignore them, refuse to listen to them, fail to include them in the process, and fail to mentor or teach them. That is why most individuals leave—to find someone better to work with.

As a business owner or leader, you should create a pleasant working atmosphere in which employees feel comfortable, safe, and engaged. The work environment encompasses everything from company culture to management methods, equipment and resources available to employees, and clothing codes.

It also entails putting people in situations where they can shine. Remember that today's employees want to contribute to the success of the firm they work for, not merely to earn a paycheck. They want to know that the work they do has a meaningful, positive impact on the business.

REMEMBER: A positive work environment encourages good employees to stay.

2. Establish clear expectations and objectives from the start

At the start of the employer-employee relationship, both parties must be clear about what they can expect from each other. Some firms discuss their do's and don'ts with new workers during their first meeting to let them know what they expect of them. In turn, new employees want to know what they can expect from the organization.

Expectations and goals are more important than ever in the present employment environment, where job hopping is the norm. According to statistics, millennials (those born between 1980 and 1996) have an average job tenure of 2.8 years. They're also continually looking for a better job; nine out of ten say they plan to shift employment every three years. You can expect to have your personnel for a few years, so make the most of it.

NOTE: Expectations work both ways. Define and express your expectations and objectives from the start.

3. Offer career development opportunities

How can your staff learn and improve if you do not teach them? Learning is not a magical process. It is a method of communication and education.

If you want your staff to perform better at work, you must assist, educate, mentor, and coach them. That is your responsibility as a leader: to help your people excel in their tasks.

4. Conduct job performance evaluations

One thing that younger generations value is feedback. They genuinely want to know how they are performing and what they can do to improve. Sure, you can provide informal feedback here and there, but you should also arrange meetings to review their performance.

Like job interviews, job evaluations can be formal or informal. The key thing is to do them. Do not skip them. Evaluations provide the information you and your employees require to excel at your positions.

Genuine insight necessitates honesty. To keep valuable personnel, you must understand how they feel. To find out how they feel, ask them and provide a comfortable environment for them to be honest. You must also be willing to receive honest critiques. It is the only way to know where you stand. Dishonest feedback is ineffective and causes more issues than it solves.

To fully evaluate your personnel, you must measure their performance. Several metrics can be used for this purpose. Some agencies, for example, use systems to measure areas such as effective project management, cost-effectiveness, and profitability (whether or not the services provided by employees generate a profit for the company), as well as the net promoter score (how likely their clients or customers are to recommend the agency).

You can conduct quarterly performance evaluations. Ask your clients to evaluate your personnel, and the company's leadership should do internal reviews. Then, ask your staff to review you. It is preferable to hear the truth that hurts rather than the lie that feels wonderful.

5. Act on the feedback you received

After you've evaluated each other and shared feedback, it's time to act on it. Knowing what to do isn't enough; you also need to know how to do it. Now, it is up to you to be a successful mentor and coach. If you're not sure where to begin, start by reading a few books about the subject.

Make sure your staff understands that comments and evaluations are not intended to be personal. It is business. Encourage them to adopt a growth mentality. They must want to hear the feedback. Only then will they be able to take the necessary steps to advance professionally.

Customer Service Strategy

Great customer experiences do not happen by accident. A well-defined customer service plan provides the foundation for every memorable interaction between a company and its consumers.

As market competition heats up, providing outstanding customer service on a constant basis becomes more important than ever. Connecting the dots across various communication channels—phone, email, chat, social—is an important step toward future-proofing your firm.

However, doing so requires connecting the dots between the people and procedures that manage those touch points. A single support request may be routed through multiple tools and personnel. Your customer service strategy acts as a road map for negotiating that complexity with ease.

Before we go on to look at the various customer service strategies, let's first understand what customer service strategy is.

A customer service strategy is a well-planned approach to dealing with client inquiries. It enables you to provide a consistent customer experience throughout the whole customer journey. Better customer service leads to a more loyal client base. Customers who are loyal to you buy more frequently, spend more money, and refer their friends and family to you.

Why is Customer Service Strategy Important?

1. It drives customer satisfaction and retention

The modern customer has more choices than ever before. Keeping their attention is no longer enough to earn their commitment. It is an issue of earning their trust.

The only way to earn that trust is to constantly satisfy expectations, which requires a dedicated customer service approach. It offers the structure and organization required to help your team achieve (and surpass) goals.

Happy customers are more likely to stay loyal, make repeat purchases, and refer your products or services to others.

2. It connects customer-facing teams

Numerous people drive your customer experience, including those in the customer success, service, and social care teams. A well-documented customer service strategy serves as the glue that holds together complicated team structures and prevents duplication of effort.

This degree of efficiency offers two benefits for your organization. First, consumers benefit from fewer transfers and escalations, resulting in reduced wait times. Second, support teams can do their best job without the stress of internal back and forth, resulting in superior agent experiences.

These elements work together to provide a positive feedback loop that continually improves consumer and service experiences.

3. It builds brand reputation

Research shows that building brand reputation and loyalty is the top goal for marketers across sectors, with 66% of businesses putting it first in today's economic environment.

Businesses looking to enhance their market share in the next years are focusing more on their customer service offerings--and for good reason. An excellent customer service strategy establishes and preserves your brand's reputation throughout both good and bad times.

When things are going well, you may utilize audience sentiment data to determine what your consumers are enjoying. For example, perhaps individuals appreciate that your representatives take the time to customize answers. You may use this information for other elements of your plan that require comparable customization strategies.

If the market falls or a crisis occurs, a strong brand reputation can protect against long-term damage. Customers who have had favorable interactions with your brand are more inclined to extend their goodwill and remain loyal.

Strategies to Improve Your Customer Service

1. Identify a customer journey

To create an effective customer service management plan, first under-stand how a consumer interacts with your business. This entails assessing all touchpoints throughout their journey, beginning with their first visit to your website and ending with recurrent purchases.

Let's imagine a consumer visits your website and inquires about price details. And after speaking with your customer support personnel, they fled rather than check out. Isn't this a bad situation? This is an example of a poor customer experience. By examining it using a customer journey map (Awareness-Interest-Purchase-Retention-Advocacy), you may determine the exact roadblocks that affected the consumer's choice not to purchase a certain product.

Inspecting the difficulties that customers encounter might help you understand how to better answer their concerns and anticipate client demands. By doing so, you'll be one step closer to improving your services and encouraging people to purchase your items. This will help you minimize turnover while increasing client loyalty.

When creating a customer journey map, you need also consider the following:

- How often do your customers contact you?
- Which channels do they use?
- Do customers who most often abandon their cart contact you beforehand, or do they not contact you at all?
- What are some of the questions your customers ask most often?
- Does the speed at which you reply (i.e., in real-time or with delay) to them seem to affect their buying/cart abandonment decision?

By evaluating these questions, you may give more information to your customer support staff and better identify client touchpoints. Finally, you'll be that much closer to developing a successful customer service plan.

2. Focus on building a dedicated team of employees

Let us begin by stating that having great personnel on your team with a customer-centric approach is essential. What exactly does this mean? First and foremost, you must have personnel with important customer service abilities. These include the capacity to prioritize customers' satisfaction and handle their demands with patience and care.

Furthermore, your support staff personnel should be able to see themselves in their client's shoes. Empathy and a thorough knowledge of client complaints, inquiries, and concerns will help you gain their trust and build a long-term connection with them.

Consider the possibility of having a disgruntled or unhappy customer because anything went wrong with their delivery. They contact your customer service, but your support representative lacks the patience and empathy required to deal with such a consumer. So, either they answer their communications in a chilly or unprofessional manner, or they take too long to respond.

The ultimate consequence is that the buyer is utterly unsatisfied and will never buy from your brand again. Isn't this a bad situation?

The reality is that your customers will notice when your customer service representatives care. And they'll respect you and your brand much more for it.

Here are a few of the considerations you must take into account while developing a team of people with a customer-first mindset:

- Ensure that your employees align with your business culture and values. If they do, they are more likely to enjoy their time working for you. As a result, they will be more eager to deal with even the most unsatisfied consumers. Furthermore, they will better comprehend and communicate your company's goal. This might lead to more clients who identify with your brand and what you provide.
- Ensure your team members have empathy. We've previously addressed empathy, and we can't overstate its value. If your customer care agents lack empathy for your client's worries, they will be unable to grasp how they feel. This increases the danger of clients being dissatisfied with your brand since they did not receive adequate assistance.
- Ensure team members have a genuine desire to help others. Employees that are natural people-helpers might be critical

to sustaining client happiness. Customers will feel more respected and appreciated if they truly desire to go the additional mile by supporting and advising persons in need.

3. Install live chat software

To get the most out of your customer support approach, consider adding a live chat button to your website.

However, you might wonder whether implementing live chat on your website is worthwhile.

Suppose you have a product with several price plans. There may be several features and plan options available. As a result, a consumer may require some assistance to sort everything out. Furthermore, people may welcome obtaining extra information when considering which choice is best for them.

This is when having a live chat widget put on your website may come in helpful. Your consumers will be able to swiftly and simply obtain the necessary information by contacting your customer service directly via live chat.

Live chat is one of the most popular forms of customer care software available, as well as the most efficient. According to statistics, 87% of consumers had great experiences with live chat. Additionally, 41% of customers choose live chat help above any other medium.

This demonstrates that using live chat is one of the most effective customer support strategies.

Furthermore, most live chat software solutions available on the market are extremely simple to deploy. Using this sort of software to communicate with customers can benefit both your front-line employees and your consumers. That's because your reps will manage all interactions from a single panel, and your clients will receive assistance faster than any other channel.

For example, some live chat systems include useful features such as a live visitor list. This sort of functionality allows you to keep track of all new and repeat visitors to your website. Then, you may utilize this information to send them personalized messages at the appropriate moment.

4. Use chatbots

When it comes to developing an effective customer care strategy, it only makes sense to include chatbots.

Simply simply, chatbots are algorithms that identify user intent and replicate client discussions. By including a chatbot on your website, you will be able to automatically answer people's inquiries, assist them as they place an order, invite them to join a mailing list, give them discounts, and much more.

Chatbots are fantastic because they may assist in removing a major burden off your agents' shoulders, allowing them to focus on more complicated questions. As a result, you will be able to improve customer happiness, create more leads, decrease cart abandonment, and eventually increase revenue.

5. Ask your customers for feedback

Requesting input from consumers is one of the most effective strate-gies to enhance your customer strategy. By doing so, you will not only gain all of the required information for improving your customer service and overall company practices, but you will also demonstrate to your customers that you respect their feedback. And this is a tried-and-true strategy for increasing their loyalty over time.

There are several benefits to soliciting feedback from your customers on a regular basis.

For example, you may discover that your consumers are puzzled about how your shipping works or that they are having difficulty with the price information. Then, you may focus on refining all of the information you've provided on your dedicated website page or just create a FAQ page that answers their inquiries.

Alternatively, your clients may express a preference for receiving help through another channel, such as a phone call or WhatsApp chat.

But how should you seek feedback to achieve the greatest results? According to Survey Monkey, 85% of customers are eager to provide feedback to firms whose products they purchase. Approximately 75% of consumers are inclined to react to post-purchase surveys, while 58% are eager to provide feedback via chat support systems.

There are several methods for gathering client feedback. However, the optimum time to do this is immediately after giving customer assistance. For example, you can easily automate the process using chatbots, as mentioned earlier.

You can also utilize your live chat software to integrate surveys and feedback forms or just request a rating of your services.

Alternatively, you may send feedback emails or use social media by making a dedicated post where users can vote, comment, and share their thoughts.

Remember, feedback is the cornerstone for improving each aspect of your organization. So, don't forget to include it in your customer support strategy and prepare to make data-driven decisions.

6. Know your key performance indicators (KPIs)

When it comes to data-driven choices, you must understand which data to analyze in order to maximize the effectiveness of your customer service strategy.

But how do you judge which data is important and which isn't? Identifying this relies on the sort of client service you provide. For example, some customer service metrics may differ based on whether your consumers may contact you by phone, social media, or website.

So, to assist you in determining which data is vital for your customer service strategy, we've compiled a list of basic key performance indicators (KPIs) to analyze. Take a look at each one and select ones that are relevant to your field:

- *Customer satisfaction score (CSAT)*

CSAT is excellent for identifying the so-called pain points in your client's journey and assessing overall customer pleasure. Using the survey mentioned earlier or delivering a simple message with a rating option following a client encounter might assist you in collecting this sort of data. We believe that every form of customer service might benefit from this statistic.

- *Net promoter score (NPS)*

You may use NPS to assess client loyalty by asking a simple question: "Would you recommend our product/service to a friend?".

Measuring this measure will help you gain a better understanding of how much your consumers respect your products and brand enough to suggest them through word of mouth.

- *Customer effort score (CES)*

This type of measure can assist you in determining how your clients interact with your products or services. You may simply conduct a poll asking clients how difficult it was to utilize your product or services.

- *First response time*

This measure will allow you to calculate how long your clients are on hold. According to Klipfolio, most consumers expect a response from a ticketing system within 24 hours. Live chat should last less than 1.5 minutes, while phone engagements should be no more than 3 minutes.

- *Average resolution time*

This number is fairly self-explanatory: it indicates the average time required to address a customer complaint. To get the average resolution time, just add up the time required for all resolutions. Then, divide your result by the total number of requests that were resolved.

- *First call/contact resolution rate (FCR)*

FCR allows you to track how many times consumers have to contact you to resolve their issues. It may be computed by dividing the number of cases resolved on initial contact by the total number of instances. Then double that by 100. Customer service criteria for a good FCR are estimated to be about 70%.

In no particular order, here are a few additional relevant KPIs you should consider:

- Active issues
- Resolved issues
- Average abandonment rate
- Customer retention rate

Before you test any of these measurements, you should determine which ones will help you the most. Then, try measuring them monthly or quarterly.

This might lead to the discovery of several interesting insights. For example, you may notice that while your average resolution time is good, your customer satisfaction level is still lower than you would want.

Suppose you continue to actively watch these or any other indicators that appear to be most important to your organization. In that case, you will become more aware of where you may improve.

Then, you'll be much closer to identifying solutions and developing a superior customer service strategy in the long term.

7. Personalize customer experience

Customer service is much more than just assisting consumers in need. This is also a fantastic time to establish and nurture consumer connections.

To actually create an excellent experience that your consumers will value, make it as individualized as possible.

Did you know that more than 54% of consumers demand individualized customer service experiences?

In other words, individuals are more likely to trust a business that employs a customized approach when communicating with customers.

If they are on your list of loyal, returning customers, simply stating their name would be enough. However, you may also provide them with exclusive discounts and limited-time deals, as well as propose goods based on their buying history.

Fortunately, most customer care software systems provide access to the whole client contact history. When dealing with a repeat consumer, you may benefit from this understanding. This may help you adapt their entire experience to be as personal and authentic as possible.

8. Offer top-notch customer service across all online channels

One of the most crucial parts of an effective customer service plan is being accessible to your consumers. Essentially, this means being able to serve clients across all channels relevant to your business.

If your clients want assistance, they will want to contact you as quickly as possible. Your goal should be to make this procedure as simple as possible for them.

First and foremost, make sure your website offers customer assistance using popular customer service technologies such as live chat. Furthermore, you may provide omnichannel customer support across numerous channels, such as social media, phone, and your website, and combine them all.

That being said, if the majority of your consumers appear to prefer interacting via a single channel, you should direct your resources and agents to that channel.

Assume your customers choose to interact with you via a customer phone service. Then, ensure that your call center operators are available to your consumers around the clock. You may also insert a pre-recorded message in case your phone operators are busy or unavailable, informing them that the first available operator will be able to help them.

In summary, you should constantly be freely accessible to customers across all of your platforms. This will undoubtedly help consumers respect your efforts and your brand as a whole.

Time Management and Productivity Tips

When it comes to beginning and operating a business, timing is everything. It makes no difference what stage you are at. Making the best use of your time would be really prudent. The objective should be to work smarter rather than harder. That requires discipline, patience, and foresight.

Good time management leads to more productivity, reduced stress, and more opportunity to do the things that matter. Using the following strategies can help increase your productivity:

1. Ensure your goals are SMART

Set objectives that are attainable and quantifiable. Set goals using the SMART technique. In summary, make sure your goals are Specific, Measurable, Achievable, Relevant, and Timely.

2. Prioritize wisely

Prioritize tasks by priority and urgency. For example, consider your everyday chores and identify which are:

- Important and urgent: Do these tasks right away.
- Important but not urgent: Decide when to do these tasks.
- Urgent but not important: Delegate these tasks if possible.
- Not urgent and not important: Set these aside to do later.

3. Set a time limit to complete a task

Setting time limits for completing chores helps you stay focused and efficient. Making the tiny extra effort to determine how much time you need to devote to each work might also help you identify possible difficulties before they occur. That way, you can devise strategies for coping with them.

For instance, imagine you need to complete five reviews in time for a meeting. However, you realize that you will only be able to complete four of them in the time available before the conference. Suppose you are aware of this information in advance. In that case, you may be able to easily assign the writing of one of the reviews to another person.

Nevertheless, suppose you didn't have to run a time check on your responsibilities beforehand. In that case, you may have discovered your time problem only one hour before the meeting. At that point, it may be much more difficult to locate someone to assign one of the reviews to, as well as to fit the work into their schedule.

4. Take a break between tasks

It is more difficult to stay focused and motivated when you are working on many projects without taking a break. Allow for some pause between jobs to clear your mind and revitalize yourself. Consider taking a little sleep, going for a short stroll, or meditating.

5. Organize yourself

Use your calendar for better long-term time management. Write down the deadlines for projects or activities that are required to complete the overall project. Consider which days might be optimal for completing various activities. For example, you may need to schedule a meeting to discuss cash flow on a day when the company's CFO is accessible.

6. Remove non-essential tasks/activities

It is critical to eliminate unnecessary activities or duties. Determine what is meaningful and worth your attention. Removing non-essential tasks/activities allows you to devote more time to what is truly important.

7. Plan ahead

Ensure that you have a clear understanding of what has to be done on a daily basis before you begin each day. Make it a habit to jot down your "to-do" list for the next workday at the end of each day. This will allow you to get things started the next morning.

Chapter 9
Scaling Your Business

Business scaling is the act of expanding a business in a manner that will enable it to be in a position to handle the increased business productivity. Let me put it this way: your business is like a plant. When you size it, you are providing it with care to make it bigger to produce more flowers or fruits and not drop or die out.

This normally entails identifying strategies through which the production of goods or services that you offer can be enhanced without necessarily affecting the quality or the consumer satisfaction level. It may mean more people, better tools or reaching out to new territories. The aim here is to take your business to the next level and add more value over time to the extent that your business is capable of addressing the needs of more customers without bowing out.

NOTE: When it comes to the concept of scaling, it means growing but doing it as efficiently and sustainably as possible.

Recognizing Growth Opportunities

Growth opportunities are the actual ways by which it is possible to increase the market share, income, or even profit through diversification of services offered to clientele or the geographical area of operation. The search for opportunities is one of the critical elements of a strategy since it enables one to match resources, strengths, and objectives with new/consequent market conditions and client needs. However, how can one distinguish and evaluate the most potential development areas for the business?

But first, it is necessary to discuss why growth opportunities should be sought for your business.

Why Do You Need to Identify Business Growth Opportunities?

- *Sustainable Expansion*

The recognition of opportunities helps businesses expand in a systemized manner and in the proper scalable direction. By this, they can gain more market share, cover new geographical areas or add new services and products to their portfolio as a way of making their businesses sustainable and profitable in the long run.

- *Competitive Advantage*

This way, businesses do not get caught unaware; that is why aggressiveness has to be maintained in the business world. This may entail creating new services or products, redoing business processes, or moving into new areas before competitors.

- *Maximizing Resources*

Opportunities can be considered as the strengths of the business since they indicate the areas that can generate growth once utilized optimally. From updating technologies and building the skills of the employees to improving the marketing strategy, enterprises can apply resources wisely with the intention of meeting business development goals.

- *Meeting Customer Needs*

Organizations that have discovered growth prospects are in a good position to address changing customers' needs. Because of this, they are able to introduce products and services that accommodate the shift in trends, customer needs, or emerging issues in the market.

- *Financial Health*

The concept of growth opportunities can have a very strong influence on the value of an organization's objectives. It can result in additional sources of income, higher margins and better investors' trust, which lubricate the process of financing and business living.

Strategies for Identifying Business Growth Opportunities

1. Conduct comprehensive market research

When one decides to undertake market research, it is akin to deciding to become a detective in one's industry. It entails researching the trends, analyzing people's consumption patterns, and looking into what rivals have been doing. In this way, you will be able to identify the sectors that actually have limited options for consumers or the issues that many people face but for which there is no satisfactory solution.

For instance, if you observe that many people in your locality are involved in outdoor activities, but most of them find it difficult to access environmentally friendly equipment for camping, then that is a niche that could be filled. What you will get to know are the weak areas, or I should say the unfilled zones where the customer is not fully satisfied and where you can offer a product or a service, bringing out the specific need better than anyone else. Obviously, this can draw more customers whose requirements can be met with those solutions in order to grow your business.

NOTE: Market research is not restricted to figures but instead people so that you provide solutions that people want.

2. Gather feedback from your customers

Conducting Customer feedback helps you pay attention to the Customer's feedback about the goods and services they purchase or experience from your business. To achieve this strategy, it enables you to identify their passions, needs as well, and pain when dealing with other organizations. For instance, problem reports, where a number of customers complain about a certain aspect of your products or services or where they demand a particular service that your firm is yet to offer, are green lights to growth.

Besides, such feedback from the customer acts as a guide to the next line of development and innovation. What makes your work extraordinary, apart from improving the level of customer satisfaction, is that you also gain more loyal customers, and others go looking for similar solutions. This strategy enables the business to respond effectively to the ever-increasing customer demands and the ever-changing market needs.

3. Industry networking

Industry networking can be defined as the social relations development process with peers, suppliers as well as other experts who belong to the same business sector/ industry. It is the concept of reaching out to people or firms that have useful information, skills, and materials for achieving your business objectives. These are usually established in the course of attending fairs, trade unions and professional bodies, news-groups, discussion lists and partnerships on development projects.

It is worth noting that industry networking plays several critical roles where the objective is to identify growth opportunities for businesses. First, it holds information from inside the industry and trends that may affect the industry in the future that you can obtain. You would find out there is an introduction of new technologies, modification of consumer tastes, or a change in the regulatory practices that may present an opportunity within your business niche.

Secondly, networking involves the sharing of ideas and experiences among employees or managers from different organizations. One may also learn from the competitors' new market areas that have not been explored, unique opportunities, or customers' needs that your business can satisfy.

Furthermore, networking results in the creation of partnerships or alliances often culminating in the formation of joint ventures, additional product lines, improving the organization's service delivery, or breaking into new markets.

4. Stay updated on technological advancement

Being updated with technological developments can be well likened to the act of sharpening the utensils and tools of your business. It is a process of enhancing one's knowledge of what is new in the market that can benefit your business in terms of expansion or efficiency. Innovation, at its core, implies that you are actively seeking better methods of practicing your trade or creating your goods.

For instance, suppose you are operating a bakery business, and you come across an oven that can bake cakes faster and to perfection. This particular innovation in your baking business would be instrumental in enhancing the production ability, better quality cakes that would attract more customers and thus enhance sales. Likewise, expansion in new software that can help run inventory more effectively might be an effort-saving technique that eliminates the incidence of mistakes. This is due to the fact that more of your concentration will be specific on providing your customers services and growing your business.

REMEMBER: conveying the notion that technology is not only an array of appliances, but it is the proper utilization of technologies that can make your business successful and progressing. Whether this is using new machines to increase efficiency, optimizing your business solutions with top-of-the-line software and hardware, or even incorporating smart systems into the organization, keeping up with technology creates possibilities that can take your business to the next level.

5. Stay informed about economic and regulatory trends

Monitoring the changes in economic conditions and regulations is similar to observing the conditions before going on a journey. It is all about being alert to how the rules and the economic systems might work or impact your business. For instance, if there is a new law, it means that it might be easier to deal with some aspects in some regions, thus cutting the expenses. Thus, you may possibly think of marketing in that area. On the other hand, it may be revenue decrease because of the change of taxes that may add costs to your company; hence, prepare for the changes early enough by either charging higher prices or looking for ways to cut costs.

Similarly, being aware of certain economic indicators means that you are ready for changes in a notion, such as customers' behavior or demand in the market. If many people are spending more on, say, household products, you could try to tap into that market and try to sell them some more products.

NOTE: By keeping abreast of these trends and regulations, one is in a better position to make better decisions that will allow the business to expand or brand itself while at the same time being unable to identify pitfalls that are likely to affect the business in the future.

6. Foster a culture of innovation within your organization

This can be done within the organization by coming up with new ideas. Internal brainstorming is the process of establishing conditions that help the organizational members generate ideas freely. It begins by creating an environment that supports the generation of ideas with top management encouraging ideas from any employee, no matter the business unit. For instance, establishing weekly meetings for mind sharing or introducing boxes where people can type in what they would like to see changed about products or services made within the organizations can go a long way in engaging the employees.

When employees are encouraged to participate in coming up with recommendations, it not only motivates the workers but also brings in upfront various considerations that the employees may possess. A frontline employee may come up with a way of handling the numerous questions that customers present to the company in a shorter period than usual, which will make the customers more satisfied. Similarly, a person in operations might suggest a new way of manufacturing that saves materials as well as money.

However, generally internal brainstorming is not merely a way of creating ideas but also a way of creating an environment where these ideas could be developed and later put into practice. By establishing ways of open communication and valuing the drivers of innovations, you will be able to create a progressive environment for your business to respond actively to the changes in the market and actively search for new opportunities for its development.

7. Form strategic partnerships or alliances

Entering into a strategic partnership or strategic alliance with other businesses is one of the most efficient ways of expanding your business by leveraging on available resources and capacities. By partnering with such companies, you find a way to expand your markets and capacities because the companies complement or offer products or services to similar markets.

For instance, a telecom provider and customer relationship management (CRM) software firm can work together to create solutions that enhance organizational communication. Thus, via this type of partnership, each business may better leverage its strengths in order to offer the other more valuable and comprehensive solutions.

The partnerships and agreements can offer opportunities to obtain entry to fresh modes of distribution. For instance, a small local producer may increase product visibility and, at the same time, gain access to large numbers of customers through an established retail chain. In a similar manner, alliances can aid in the coordination by coming up with noble resources, an amount that none alone is capable of manufacturing advanced products in the market.

Another benefit is cooperation in marketing support when partners can effectively promote packaged services or create demand for a large audience. The formation of relationships and connections is a planned mode of expansion that offers mutual returns to the businesses from their associations and enables them to tap the benefits of cooperation, use synergy, and speed up their growth process in the new fields.

Strategies for Expansion

At some point, virtually every commercial organization or start-up has to consider the issue of growth. Several incentives might be related to business growth to the owners of the businesses. Benefits that the business owners may enjoy due to business growth include the following. It is for these reasons that expansion has such advantages as increased market share and clients, reduced costs and enhanced operations.

However, it also opens up a lot of risks, and if not well addressed, the expansion, more often than not, exhibits a sign of doom for a struggling corporate. It may be a massive process, particularly where you have no idea of the instruments that can be utilized to enhance the achievement of the firm goals. Consequently, in the pursuit of success, the business owner has to comprehend the definition of business development and strategy.

There is normally a process of expansion in business, especially when a business reaches a certain growth stagnation, and the business looks for opportunities to increase its profits. There are several ways through which it is done; let us look at some of the ways business expansion is done comprehensively. It includes obtaining extra facilities, opening more outlets, recruiting more salesmen, launching more and more advertising campaigns, expanding outlets in the shape of franchises, venturing into new areas, introducing new products or services, etc.

This can be attributed to the following several causes why small businesses do not grow. The most profound reason devoted by experts is the issue of resources. Another factor that may act as a deterrent for expansion attempts is the fact that in some businesses, there might be a few personnel, and as a result, one might spend a lot of time training the new staff, most of who may not possess the kind of experience and knowledge that the older personnel possess.

Another risk that many company owners, especially the new ones, pointed out is a slowdown of sales attributed to economic factors. There are different market-driven business events that every entrepreneur must be acquainted with. Indeed, the majority of start-ups of new small firms are owned by people who have not even a clue about what is in demand and what is out of demand.

Some of these employers have to conduct research in markets to find out which products are hot bestsellers in order for them to expand their business. This study may be particularly relevant if a company heavily uses direct mail or television advertising as its promotional tools.

Before the start of any expansion program, the entrepreneur must draw up a well-coordinated business development plan. Unfortunately, the dream of most business owners reaches a dead end because they do not have a clear company expansion strategy. Suppose a business owner lacks a deliberate business development strategy. In that case, they may likely work more harm than good for the business.

The process of expansion of a firm is a deliberate effort that requires thorough planning, objective assessment of business conditions, and an investment decision. To make the expansion of business more contusive, it is very necessary to have a vision, goal and business strategy properly defined. Organizations, hence, have to choose the type of growth they want for their business. After this, they may go to formulate the right business expansion plan depending on the factors mentioned above.

Following the formation of a business expansion strategy, an entrepreneur is faced with the question of how they will implement new ideas. For instance, they might employ specialist personnel like financial consultants and operational strategists. These experts can provide them with the exact business ideas and figures of their expected revenues. Otherwise, they may turn to business coaches regarding commercial and operational planning challenges.

Nonetheless, it is high time that we briefly discuss, in general, some of the possible tactics that businesses can employ in their bid to expand.

1. Market penetration strategy

Market penetration is one of the business strategies applied to expanding the market share of a particular company's products or services in a given market. It is the objective of achieving a higher client base of customers who draw on the products or frequently visit the company for services, which in turn increases the general earnings and profit of the firm. This strategy usually involves the identification of a particular targeted market segment and increasing the marketing communication activities in an attempt to reach the customer who has not previously dealt with the company's products.

Market penetration entails offering special price offers, increasing on advertising budget, increasing outlets, improving product quality, and offering additional services to existing customers. Thus, the employment of these techniques will help the business organizations increase their exposure and attraction among the consumers in the market domain and, thus, increase the market share and income.

The major benefit of using this technique is that it assists business organizations in increasing sales without necessarily going for product development. Besides, market penetration might well lead to increases in one's own market share coupled with a relative reduction of share by competitors.

This form of expansion is especially suitable for new firms that aim at entering a specific industry of production or existing firms with a large number of regular customers as it is a cheap method of expanding the number of clients and sales growth.

2. Marketing and promotion

Another method of developing your business is to have a good marketing and promotional campaign that can help you exploit the market. Marketing success does not have a specific recipe, and often, what is effective for the first business may not be effective for the second business. To be specific, though, one possibility is to reinforce your firm by finding and utilizing methods of marketing and promotion that will create dedicated clients.

Customer loyalty may be cultivated in different ways. Promoting a business through having special offers and seasonal deals, using the so-called client reward program, and actively using social networks for advertising are some of the ways to maintain client loyalty.

Since marketing and promotional activities are directly proportional to business advancement, you will be in a better place to create a powerful brand within the shortest time possible, making it easier for customers to recognize your business as the market leader in your specific sector.

3. Expansion into a new market

When a market becomes oversaturated with a particular kind of product or service, it can potentially become stagnant. You see a typical business cycle where companies expand to previously unprofitable areas due to the saturation of markets. This is termed as 'Market penetration'. Market penetration is a marketing concept that involves finding new markets to invest in or expanding the current markets in which a firm is active. Thus, on occasion, it might involve expanding a firm's line of products or services in a bid to spur growth.

Market expansion is suitable for firms that have stagnated in their current markets and require an upgrade on the right markets to venture into. Organizations that have established a solid presence in the current markets and have the customer base and brand recall are often in a good stead to expand, into several segments.

4. Expand your business abroad with EOR solutions

Companies, at some point, come to a time in their operations when they have captured almost all the local market share, and the only remaining option is to export. It is this stage that many businesses have a lot of fear about because of the problems it poses, but at the same time it is a source of many opportunities since it opens up the avenue for reaching out to a lot of consumers.

International expansion can alter your business model or enable you to acquire new skills that were previously unobtainable. For instance, global market expansion may compel you to decide on outsourcing and the advantages that constitute it, as well as understanding how to lead a teleworker workforce.

In addition, international expansion translates to being involved in issues to do with HR and payroll in those new countries, coming to terms with the labor laws of those countries, and figuring out how to operate legally. Here, your business may require the services of an EOR or Employer of Record as this enables your business to offshore its Human Resources and Payroll tasks with the risk of non-compliance with various country laws, especially when employing personnel in other countries.

Managing Increased Workload and Responsibilities

If there's one thing project manager education has taught them, it's that work management results in decreased efficiency. Still, there are other issues concerning practice.

The common effects that employees in organizations complain of due to unsuitable scheduling of workloads are stress, unhappiness, and inefficiency. As seen from the above list, while it can be regarded as far from complete, it still gives us some prior facts for the discussion on enhanced task management. Hence, the definition of workload management, its significance, and ways of its application to increase team performance.

Workload management means the distribution of workload in a team or with a group to monitor their productivity and, next use of identifying key performance indicators of personnel and sharing the work with those who have the capabilities. Workload management is also referred to as the ability to allocate work equitably; each person gets what is due to them and no more. You should not push someone to the extent of overworking them in a normal working environment unless there is some reason that requires it. Regardless of your good motives, these may one day turn out to be counterproductive and have a devastating effect on team performance.

Importance of Workload Management

Proper distribution of the workload among the team members proves to be decisive for the efficiency of the whole project and company results. Depending on what your company offers, think about how significant that shift is to your employees' satisfaction at work, efficiency, work-related injuries, turnover, stress indicators, and burnout. Actually, a Gallup poll revealed that up to 66% of full-time employees are affected by burnout at work. Taking that into consideration, the idea of developing a concrete and efficient approach to organizing the tasks might be beneficial to everyone.

It will ensure that the respective teams do not deviate from the set plans and ensure that the required tasks are accomplished as soon as possible. Following are some of the things to look at when coming up with a good and full-proof plan for the accomplishment of tasks:

Strategies to Manage Increased Workload and Responsibilities

1. Understand business priorities

It is important to know what your business's priorities are before distributing the labor. This pertains to the short-term as well as the long-term agenda of the organization.

There are constraints in business where resources are limited, and when using them, another resource has to be given up, which leads to trades. In deciding what work needs to be done, the relevance of the business has to be taken into account. That will help you to identify which activities are profitable in achieving the company's most significant objectives.

Cashiers are indispensable for controlling transactions in a retail business, but they also take on the responsibility of restocking shelves with products. Thus, in the business-to-business context, customer service within the segment of clients with major purchasing power may be more appropriate than within the segments of those who purchase a lesser amount of goods.

This is the reason why most companies classify their customers and give different levels of value and service depending on the amount that the consumer spends.

Clarity of business goals allows you to be precise in your decision-making process, especially in relation to your task management approach. Perhaps these priorities determine the tools that one uses and the procedures that are followed.

TIP: Here is how you should incorporate business priorities into task management:

- *Use business acumen*

As much as any person may be sure about their company's goals, the realities of doing business mean that the workload is managed in such a way that the organization has to make tradeoffs on a daily basis. For instance, if an employee fails to report to work due to illness, business acumen enables one to make sound decisions given that there are many aspects which have been affected, such as elements, stakeholders and all possible outcomes in business.

- *Collaborate on daily priorities*

Business objectives may remain unaltered from one day to another, while the tasks may differ. Hence, when tasks are transferred without communication, there is likely to be confusion to the teams especially the cross-functional teams. It may be required to change work to adapt it to everyday problems, but the task managers should know why such changes are being done.

2. Evaluate tasks

Choosing which tasks to take on at any given moment requires considering a variety of aspects, including the following:

- What are the objectives and goals of the work? This involves aspects such as whether the task requires specific skills or specialism to complete; for instance, the ability to code software and the extent to which 'many hands' are involved.
- How long will it take to complete the task compared to another?
- What is the timeframe given to each task?

- What level of priority does each work have? Are there any specific jobs that need to be done first before others can start?
- Who are the stakeholders that could be affected by the tasks? Were some of these duties requested by the customers or business partners?

When creating your work list, you should try to address the following features in relation to the priorities of the company. This is a general description of the tasks that the team, which is to implement the proposed solutions, is to accomplish.

TIP: These tools will help you to evaluate tasks easier.

- *Employ WBS*

The work breakdown structure (WBS) should be used to illustrate all of the tasks involved in the project. The work breakdown structure (WBS) is one of the ways of outlining all that needs to be done within the context of the project and the time estimated to complete each task. The WBS proves most helpful on big complex projects such as the construction of a building or the design of a system.

- *Create a prioritized list*

Organize your tasks in a sequence with the most urgent (or essential) tasks on top. When identifying the order in which activities should be completed, consider the level of difficulty of the task. If a work is challenging and requires more time to complete or is critical and needs to be delivered as soon as possible, consult with the stakeholders about the possibility of increasing the resources needed or changing the deadlines.

3. Align tasks to people

Assigning work involves two essential components: your to do list and persons who are depending on you to do it. However, workload management does not only concern the aforementioned two concepts.

While seeking talent, then, one also needs to consider whether the person selected can finish the job before the due date. Otherwise, it is possible that the employee will be overloaded and, therefore, behind schedule regarding the project.

That is why it is essential to take into account work rhythm and other factors which can influence efficiency: from attitude to the appointed work to the personal disposition of a worker. For instance, when a particular task requires the operations of different groups, do not assign it to a person who has a strict NO to teamwork.

TIP: One of the challenging tasks that many people face with regards to workload management is how to allocate tasks to the various workers. The following tips may help.

- *Determine team capacity*

When giving new tasks to the team, look at other tasks that each member was assigned and see if there is anything that should be done or if such a task should be given to someone else. It let me test the weighed staffing on the WBS to determine if the resource has too much or too little work and rebalance the workload assignments of workers.

- *Explain the work*

When apportioning sub-tasks to various team members, describe what the different roles are, the duties they will be performing, deadline, and why the work is important. It is necessary to select the strategy for communicating in such situations. Proper communication may ensure that works are done through the set time and quality standards and may motivate the groups.

4. Apply a process framework

Procedures assist management in ensuring that tasks are completed in a standard manner, hence making them reliable, credible, and fast. Any time an employee takes long to finish an assignment that is provided, there could be a deferment of project schedules, but this is not the case with a procedural structure.

Select a process structure that will make it easier for you to plan and allocate tasks particularly based on the aspect that practices well in your firm. Using an employee self-organizing method, such as kanban, which provides employees with the autonomy to choose their tasks, is only one of many approaches that may be applied to the management of tasks for your employees' delegation. Another way is to provide assignments on a daily basis in the morning when the employees are coming to work.

TIP: How you manage the work largely depends on choosing the correct method for the sort of work you are engaging in. Consider the following recommendations.

- ### Opt for an automated system

Ensure that there is an implementation of a process structure that makes the process more of an automated one most of the time while only occasionally requiring the intervention of people. Implement work order systems that select items for you or a system like Kanban and as tasks are completed new work is easily distinguishable without having to wait for job assignments.

- *Keep evolving the process*

Be open to reorganizing the way of how the tasks are distributed in the team. Keep on looking for ways of rationalizing and enhancing the rate of the processes while at the same time promoting fairness in the distribution of the tasks. Trial different methods to find out which is most appropriate for the team.

5. Adapt to workflow changes

Workload management is not easy due to the variability of work; that is, work is not always steady at all times. One day things go perfectly, and you are way ahead of the schedule. Then there is the time that the boss assigns you more work than the crew can carry out. Your approach to task management should enable you to cope with such phases where there is low productivity.

NOTE: Provide your team with help as to how this difficulty could be mitigated. Of the referred approaches, those that are highlighted below are of the same advantage.

- *Reassess*

When new work comes in, then treat priorities and deadlines, especially for employees, with a pinch of salt so that one is not working hard to beat a mirage.

- *Be proactive*

Flexibly adjust the workers' workloads in anticipation of their vacation and holidays.

- *Discourage multi-tasking*

Inform the team that it is necessary to emphasize on the given job and work efficiently in order to improve the quality of the product.

TIP: Also, use the following to ensure that you are ready to handle fluctuations in demand:

- *Perform cross-training*

Whenever possible, cross-train your team members. The broader the exchange of training where team members are familiar with other members' tasks then, the more responsive the particular team is likely to be in terms of workflow. In case one of the team members begins to feel overloaded with work, a team member who has been cross-trained can help out.

- *Confirm task priorities*

The inability to find much work to do may make some of the team members appear to look for other means to spend time. However, do such responsibilities allow you to meet your business goals? Be sure to communicate task sequences to team members about what they should do next after they are done with a task. Also, record the tasks being done to be sure that the team is on the right track and working on the right tasks.

6. Adopt workload management tools

Employing the principles of project management may substantially enhance the processes of task accomplishment. Depending on the specifics of the team and tasks, a whiteboard with task postings, specialized software, a spreadsheet, scribble, or other tools will be useful for simplifying assignments and tracking the team's workload.

It is useful to note that project management software simplifies several elements of task organization and proves to monitor your progress in relation to the general project objectives.

It can assign work orders and offer other reports that give an outlook into every project's status, the team's available capacity, and other useful details pertaining to workloads. The bigger the number of the staff, the more necessary it is to delegate the tasks with the help of the corresponding software.

TIP: The following are some guidelines to consider as one uses the workload management tools:

- *Give visibility to the team*

Choose a system that provides visibility of the work to your staff members. This is, in that way, assisting group participants to implement what they need to do next within the shortest time possible and without necessarily having to look for a boss and be told what the next task is.

- *Use the Eisenhower matrix*

Among the tools used in managing incoming work, there's one called the Eisenhower matrix, which is a form of the prioritization matrix. It categorizes jobs into four quadrants based on their priority: These can be described as urgent and important, important but not urgent, urgent but unimportant, and unimportant and not urgent. The Eisenhower matrix can be considered being one of the most effective tools for consistently prioritizing tasks.

7. Leverage feedback loops

Use the feedback give and take in a team to enhance the flow of communication and cooperation. It may be simply checking on the employee's success or may be a daily or weekly check with the organizational team to discuss the status of the work, and ideas about the anticipated problems.

More specifically, in the scrum process, there is, for instance, a sprint retrospective, which is a meeting that the team performs on a regular basis to define what must be kept and what should be removed.

Feedback loops can offer data regarding the applicability of the current workload management strategy in distributing responsibilities fairly across the team. Let us now assume that in the same team, some employees are always complaining that they are under pressure for time and work more than others, while some employees complete their work much earlier than others. In that case, it implies that the present procedure has to be reconsidered.

TIP: The following are effective methods that can be adopted and implemented in the improvement of the workload and feedback processes:

- *Employ milestones*

In large-scale projects that may span several months or years, it is helpful to set markers to check the pace and progress toward set dates. One can use milestones as checkpoints and ensure the project delivers what is expected by the team in line with the set goals at predetermined intervals.

- *Combine different feedback*

Feedback mechanisms can be made up of any indication. It could be employed with applications for tracking the status of the team's work and the capacity for further work or with the framework of checklists or status reports. Employing various techniques offers more information for making alterations to the workload during its operation.

Scaling Your Operations Effectively

Scaling up a business means "to increase in size or quantity in a similar and usually successful and controlled way." The concept of scaling is different from the concept of growing. When a company increases, its expenses also follow the path of income Books of accounts suggest that. When the size of a business increases, the sales increase and the costs for operations decrease. Organizations that have learned how to grow to acquire customers quickly, and indeed, there is never any need for a firm to seek additional resources to enhance its growth as it will continue to chase the market and negotiate better margins with each passing year.

NOTE: As a business owner, you constantly find yourself in a position where you have to look for solutions and be ready to embrace the most unconventional ideas. To experience business success, you have to be willing to run well-organized projections and plans. Of course, the concept of increasing your activities entails some risk. But the right one may save you from obvious mistakes, and will help you create proper development of your business for the further success.

Strategies to Scale Your Business

1. Have a plan in place

When leaving your comfort zone, planning is not the problem. On the contrary, it is crucial. If there is a need to pivot from certain plans, it means that other new or alternate plans have to be made. That is true with smart business scaling. With a plan of action in place, it will be easier to sustain high standards when delivering quality performances and introducing other procedures as the operation size increases and, at the same time, minimize the level of risks and losses. An initial step could be to write down all the factors that may slow you down or even stop you from getting to your goal.

2. Know your customers

It is your consumers who generally make or mar your business. When expanding your business, it is important not to forget about the quality of the services being offered to customers. In decision management, it is useful to step into the consumer's shoes and assess how various actions in the business development plan would affect you as a customer. Consumers do not have to be given a new set of tricks while scaling because if their demands are considered during each level of scaling, they can essentially become your best brand ambassadors and take your profits to the roof.

3. Spend time wisely

When it comes to developing your business (and keeping that expansion under control), time is money. For all the actions for scaling and growing do make sure that they are all time-bound.

Sometimes critical activities come as a surprise and may show up in the wrong time like during scaling or expansion. Thus, it is necessary to coordinate time management techniques to maintain your team's productivity while undergoing the growth process and accept possible variations in plans and actions.

Teach your staff members on how to adhere to time. There are a number of tools and software packages available, ranging from Microsoft Project to ClickUp and TaskQue, through which your firm can make the best use of time. Staffing up and means bringing in a project manager may also alleviate the situation.

4. Consider big data

Big data means the processing of a large and complex amount of data in detail to find specific details like trends, customer preferences, patterns and unexpected correlations. It assists you in arriving at prudent decisions on the extent of expansion that you want for your business.

Knowledge about big data and its use might enable you avoid some losses and make correct decisions for your business development and expansion. It can also used in cases of identifying and eradicating the root causes of inefficiencies in your processes for better internal productivity.

5. Anticipate the adjustment pace

When it comes to implementing changes, it is always a good idea to think about how each change will impact the rest of the organization's team, though in any case, there will always be some reaction time needed. Let them understand there is a need for change and there is no need to fear the challenges that this opportunity brings. Most importantly, they need some time to grasp their roles in the overall strategy of your company's growth plans as well as to evaluate how they can benefit from the new objective of your business and how they can add value to a new direction of the company. Think about the methods of adjustment and dedicate a sufficient amount of time to such changes in the scaling plans and processes.

More often, large organizations have change leaders who work at creating effective and realistic blueprints and helping to impose order on the implementation process. Forecasting the degree of your organization's preparedness for change will require an understanding of your people. In certain cases, it is useful to discuss and negotiate with your personnel about the specifics of scaling that you have in mind. Adapt customers as vital sources of feedback, which is crucial to take anything – criticism and concerns – and improve the means of interacting with them. It will help you estimate the rate of their adjustment to your change and get their backing to expand.

6. Know your team

Sustaining operations give an opportunity to identify the vulnerabilities of your business. Thus, the focus is on incorporating your team's opinions regarding when and how to scale as well as assessing their performance during scaling. The idea of scaling up organizations with a team of employees who are quite rigid or incompetent will not give better results, but rather it can be worse.

Thus, knowing your team better can help you and your company in making business decisions in the future and help to develop the potential of the growing corporation on the basis of understanding the capabilities, talents, and personalities of the team. If one comprehends their people, organizational values, as well as client expectations, they will be in a better position to determine when and how to grow. This can be done by collecting other people's input in a faceless and, therefore, bias-free manner.

7. Hire reliable managers

There is no doubt that a team's performance is always proportional to the performance of its leader. Every enhancement in the operations and production shall demand that you employ more people at one point or another. When this occurs, you must count on administrators who abide by the same long-term development strategy and will defend it.

Ensure you get the right human resources who are worthy to protect the brand and capable of meeting the obligations. It is useful to offer incentives to workers from all tiers of the organization and affirm their capability for being held accountable for concepts and responsibilities and for making employees feel wanted. Any company, in the course of corporate upheavals, counts on people who do not just do things but who appreciate the vision and would strive to make it operational.

8. Decentralize and automate

This is especially true if the structure is a work that was created from the ground up, and now a capable professional is taking it over from you. Nevertheless, to achieve business growth quite often, it is necessary to decentralize and automate the process to a certain extent. Though it is likely to pose difficulty for the new generation of entrepreneurs, it fuels the business and provides an opportunity for the top echelons to channel their attention towards strategic management. Therefore, by showing that you are indeed receptive to your team's ideas and decisions, you encourage the concept of your company being the rightful place for your employees to grow and stay for the rest of their careers.

Likewise, by employing the measures in relation to the workflow automation technologies, you will be able to devote more amount of time and money to other better and significant operations rather than bothering about petty repetitious tasks. They want to integrate the system to perform repetitive work ranging from social marketing to email marketing, customer relationship management, and lead management.

Various Mistakes You Must Avoid When Scaling Your Business

As mentioned above, some acts, similar to the techniques outlined above, may help you in the right direction as you move forward with the growth of your business, whereas other acts can deter progress. The following are the risks to be averted.

1. Hiring the wrong people

Employment of the right personnel, especially managers, should be a vital quest for business organizations. Are their goals in life right for your business, or do they have the right attitude? The groups must therefore include their individual goals in the new undertaking and whether those goals are in line with the mission of the organization. Recruit employees for the fact that you have many years of dedication that they're willing to bring to the table so that they do not become a hindrance to the growth process.

2. Prioritizing short-term growth over long-term sustainability

You could consider it logical that if your business were to grow as fast as possible, it would bring even more benefits and positive recognition to the brand. However, this attitude is profitable in the sense that it disregards substantial product quality as well as customer service experience. The greater part will recommend your product and your brand if their shopping experience is good. This is opposite to what would be termed as a fad as it would help in the long run rather than just the current fad.

3. Having messy accounting

If you own a small business, you can be economically responsible by paying close attention to your money. Nevertheless, one does not want to relax once the enterprise has evolved because one needs to monitor the results, including the margins, conversion rates, predictions, and taxes. Using CPA services either on a full-time or on a part-time basis can also help in easing some of this pressure and you spend your time doing the other work. It is also advisable for you to use good quality accounting software that will help in managing your information.

4. Relying on projections

It can be enticing to base your expansion of the firm on sales estimates. However, planned revenues do not accrue in a planned manner or at a rate that downscales the personnel number while boosting the cash inflow. Play it safe and increase your firm's operations only if you have the relevant data and not projections.

5. *Exhibiting poor leadership*

With sound leadership in place, performance will be boosted among the employees, and the maximum returns will be achieved for the organization, not just in the usual runs of the business but also during the process of growth/development. Organic growth implies using a new set of managers who will have the suitable competence that match the direction in which your firm is growing. While a leader possessing all the essential skills and possessing a vision may build great accomplishments, unsuitable leadership may give the opposite.

6. *Ignoring issues that arise*

When beginning a business, it could be easier than when you decide to scale up. This may sometimes make you feel uneasy when you encounter new threats. This may, of course, encompass problems concerning employees, processes, or merchandise. Difficulties have to be dealt with as soon as they arise and not to be set aside – and thereby lie low to gather fungus and make situation worse in the future.

REMEMBER: Every efficient organization may have to expand someday, and risky policies need to be adopted to survive and grow. However, to mitigate such risks and guarantee that your expansion efforts are beneficial, you need to observe the following measures: Understanding when to use which strategy and how to avoid these pitfalls will assist in reducing problems and increase the likelihood of successfully managing the expansion of your firm.

Maintaining Quality and Customer Satisfaction

There are several advantages to growing your business; it will create additional revenue, capture more market share, and increase brand recognition. However, it might pose some challenges, like the ability to maintain high-quality standards as well as customers satisfaction across multiple sites, people, and products. Expanding the business can pose a threat to the set standards or even the overall reputation of the business as it is expanded to other areas; how do you avoid this? The following is a guide to help you in the management of quality control and client satisfaction as you embark on an expansion of your business.

1. Define your quality criteria

Before trying to expand the operations and the processes, you should establish what is meant by quality in the eyes of that particular company. What does your consumer, partners, and regulators want and/or require out of your companies system? Tell me about critical performance indicators and their measures that you apply to assess the quality? In what manner do you communicate and record the quality standards and procedures to be followed? An organization should strive to have a clear and consistent definition of quality so that it may align its growth plan with the quality objectives and principles.

2. Implement quality management systems

Quality management systems (QMS) are the processes and practices for directing and controlling an organization's quality management activities for its goods, products, and services. Thus, QMS may help you define your processes, point out the weaknesses and mistakes, control and evaluate the results, as well as recognize the corrective and preventive actions needed. QMS can also assist you in attaining regulatory and industrial requirements such as ISO 9001, Six Sigma, and Lean. Based on the requirements that you have and your goals, you may choose from the different QMS models and frameworks that are out there in the market, or perhaps you might develop your QMS models and frameworks that seem good for your company's CP.

3. Train and empower your staff

It is your staff that directly interacts with the consumers through their delivery of the product and service; therefore, the quality and happiness aspect is very vital. The communication model also implies that you must educate and enable your employees on the acceptable organizational quality standards and controls, clients' feedback and complaints. The employees should also be encouraged and rewarded if they perform exceptionally well with promotion opportunities availed to them. Taking better care of your inside insures management of quality and excellent services within the organization.

4. Collect and use customer feedback

Customer feedback on products is a valuable source when it comes to getting data on improving the quality of a product and customer satisfaction levels. The information from customers should be gathered and applied on a continuous and planned approach using methods such as questionnaires, feedback, references in approach, and social media, among others. You need to analyze and respond to customer feedback by ascertaining the key advantages and limitations of your goods and services, your customer's needs and wants and the opportunities and risks in the market. You should also accept the consumer feedback, show them your appreciation and indicate to them what action has been taken.

5. Review and improve your processes

Quality control and customer satisfaction are moving and growing concepts. They have to be continuously pressure-checked and optimized, like in the case of monitoring and interpreting quality, in the search for the best practices, and in creativity involving coming up with a few innovations and piloting them. You also have to ensure dynamics and qualify them to suit to new clients' tastes, business environment shifts and new technologies. Thus, through process analysis and improvement, one may enlarge the performance, efficiency, and competitiveness.

6. Collaborate and communicate with stakeholders

Quality assurance and customers' satisfaction are you and your suppliers, distributors, contractors, or partners' responsibility. You have to work and talk with your stakeholders by building and developing the stakeholder relations, initiating both sides' expectations and necessary conditions, sharing and exchanging necessary information and experience, as well as handling and preventing potential issues. Engagements with your stakeholders will ensure that the quality standards, as well as the added values, accord with the set expectations across your value chain.

Chapter 10
Legal and Regulatory Compliance

Regulatory compliance can be defined as the process of adhering to laws and or rules and regulations. The regulatory agency, which could be the government or an industry body, usually imposes the regulations in order to assist firms to carry on business and prevent adverse actions by the regulator.

Regulatory compliance has existed for a long time, but its importance has grown with the advancement of technology. As more firms use technology to generate products and services, there is a greater risk that they may violate rules or fail to comply with all of them. This is where regulatory compliance comes in: it outlines how these businesses may remain compliant while still utilizing technology as an asset.

Many companies underestimate the significance of regulatory compliance. As a result, they face fines and punishments from authorities for failing to comply with their rules.

Understanding Business Laws and Regulations

Business law, which is also referred to as commercial or mercantile law, can be defined as the body of laws which govern business and commerce, including companies.

Business law is the branch of law which sets out the legal framework for the formation and conduct of a business. Business law encompasses all of the laws and norms that regulate how a business can be established, how to start and manage it, how to operate it legally, and how to sell or close it.

Business law also encompasses rules governing corporations, contracts, commercial papers, intellectual property, secure transactions, income tax, and other business-related interactions.

Importance of Business Laws

company law is primarily concerned with preserving order, establishing a set of widely recognized norms, settling disputes, and defending freedoms and rights in the context of a company, including its relationships with customers, government agencies, and other businesses.

1. A comprehensive set of standards established universally

Before, there was no sufficient law that could protect consumers or their money invested or their interest, and hence, many consumers lost a lot of money. Since there were no rules and regulations for the management of companies and the protection of customers' rights, the majority of company owners defined their own rules to get as much profit as possible, which led to the suffering of customers. With the advent of business law, firms all over the world are now required to follow international norms that protect both customers and companies.

2. Reduced possibilities of fraud

Business law benefits business owners by raising their awareness of the many laws and regulations governing persons and enterprises. Furthermore, it benefits customers by making them aware of their rights against business owners, preventing them from falling victim to the firm's suffering and deceit.

3. Business laws help maintain an equilibrium

Customers feel more satisfied and secure when there is business legislation in place. In the absence of business law, each business had distinct rules governing commercial transactions, making it impossible for sellers and customers to reach an agreement. However, all countries now adhere to the same rules, making it much easier to reach an agreement between seller and buyer. This has eased and made international commercial transactions much more efficient.

4. Ethical conduct

The formulation of business laws helps business people to make the right decisions. They now know when to report to a lawyer. Ethical principles have to be complied with by every business. Nonetheless, this is not the case since many organizations neglect such measures with the aim of generating more revenue. Business law states that all businesses should adhere to ethical practices in order to make the consumers content and portray a good image of the business.

What You Need to Know About Business Laws as a Small-Business Owner

It is common for small business owners to face numerous legal questions and concerns, and thus, they need to know the specifics of business law.

It can be said that commercial law covers a broad area of small business development and its functioning, like retail contracts, taxation laws, employment laws, contract laws, civil laws, commercial transactions, and laws related to the universal commercial code.

Business lawyers are central in handling and providing solutions to business-related legal matters and the law on employment and corporations, among others. An attorney may assist a small business with its legal problems, negotiate with other companies regarding a business' affairs, and draft certain documents such as purchase agreements or nondisclosure agreements.

It is highly recommended to have a business lawyer or a law firm on your payroll as one of the best protection strategies for your small business against litigation and ensuring that all the applicable laws are followed. This means that with a good business lawyer, the firm is protected and well-represented thus taking away any fears that may be there. Business owners should also gain knowledge on the steps they need to take in order to protect their ideas and concepts. This entails the registration of trademarks and copyrights and the protection of company assets, which are secrets.

Compliance Requirements for Small Businesses

As a small business, the compliance requirements that you may need to meet might depend on your location and the type of business that you are running. The laws may vary with the cities, states, or even countries, meaning that there are legal frameworks that businesses must follow. For instance, the permits and licenses you need to have when opening a shop in one city may not be the same as that of another city. Similarly, industries have certain laws that are provided to govern the operations of the particular industry. For instance, a healthcare organization will have guidelines that govern issues to do with patients' confidentiality whereas a manufacturing firm will have guidelines to do with safety and the environment.

These compliance issues necessitate the identification of the laws that govern your business in relation to the geographical location and activity undertaken. It is, therefore, important for small business owners to understand these laws and seek counsel from lawyers or business associations in order to meet all the legal requirements.

But, the following are the general compliance requirements for small businesses.

1. Ensure your business is officially recognized

The first thing that one has to do is to get the business registered and recognized by the government which is the first step to meeting the business Laws and regulations. This entails the process of filing your business name and the type of legal entity that you are, for instance, LLC or corporation, to the local, state, and federal government, depending on the area of your business operations. It is important because it legitimizes your business as a legal entity and enables it to transact its business within the legal framework. The specificities of the registration process may differ depending on the country or state, but usually, one has to read and complete some forms, provide certain documents and pay some money to the relevant government agencies. When you register your business, you will get a certificate of registration that will show the legal existence of your business; this is important, especially when opening a bank account, recruiting employees and any other business transactions that require one to be legally recognized.

2. Obtain necessary licenses and permits

Licensing and permits are a way of getting legal permission from the government to be allowed to run your business in your region and field. Some of these licenses and permits may include;

For instance, a restaurant may require health permits, food handling licenses, and zoning permits, and on the other hand, a contractor may require construction permits and trade permits. These permissions guarantee that your business complies with some set measures, for instance, health and safety measures or environmental measures.

The licenses and permits that your business needs, how to obtain them, and when to renew them are crucial, and your business must meet those requirements to avoid legal consequences.

3. Understand and fulfill your tax obligations

This is well understood as the aspect of understanding and fulfilling the legal mandates of the government when it comes to taxes pertaining to your business. These are filing income tax for the money you make in your business, filing and remitting sales tax on the goods or services you sell and filing payroll taxes if you hire employees.

Income tax is paid on the basis of the profits of your business, while sales tax is collected from the buyers and remitted to the government. Payroll taxes refer to the process of withholding taxes from the employees' salaries and remitting the amounts to the government on behalf of the employees.

REMEMBER: The following are some of the responsibilities which, if well observed by your business, will make sure that it meets all the tax requirements and does not have to face any problems with the tax laws:

4. Comply with employment laws

This includes adherence to the principles spelled out in the employ-ment laws that govern employee relationships and remuneration. Some of the issues that are regulated by these laws include wages that are required to be paid, the cost of overtime, policies against discrimina-tion in the workplace, and measures and practices to be applied regarding workplace safety.

For instance, one needs to remunerate the employees fairly, ensure that they work in a healthy environment, and follow set laws on the number of hours they can work and the number of rest periods they are required to have.

Also, in the legal systems of businesses, there are mandated benefits such as health insurance and family leave, among others. Thus, obeying these laws not only helps to exclude legal problems and possible fines but also guarantees the effectiveness of organizational and personnel functions as a result of ensuring workers' health and wellness.

5. Protect your intellectual property

You've to protect your ideas, inventions and creations from being used, copied or reproduced by a third party. They include trademarks for brand names and logos, copyrights for writings or art and patents for inventions and special processes.

By providing your work to the relevant authorities of the right govern-ment, you are provided with legal jurisdiction over your Inputs, and, thus the right to stop other people from appropriating your work or benefiting from it in any way. Being strategic assets, the businesses are obliged to search for theirs, protect them where it is possible through application for protection in accordance with the laws of the specific country and even enforce them to retain their competitive advantage in the market. It assists in avoiding such incidences of infringement and allows people to protect the legal rights of inventions and hard work.

NOTE: We will discuss more on how to safeguard your intellectual property in the subsequent segment of this chapter.

6. Ensure privacy laws

Privacy laws are policies that provide guidelines on the proper way through which the information of persons should be collected, processed, stored and protected. It is pertinent that the business infor-mation of customers and employees needs to be protected according to the privacy regulation. This entails the safeguarding of data acquired by your business establishment.

For instance, you have to give information to customers and workers about what data you are gathering and for what purpose, acquire permission where required, and uphold measures that can prevent unauthorized exposure of the data or hacking. Businesses that operate in the EU region need to abide by the GDPR regulation, while Californian firms have to adhere to the CCPA regulation, for managing personal information responsibly, processing requests for data access, and reporting the breach to the authorities.

REMEMBER: When your business complies with these laws, you create customer confidence and employee trust, and you also get to steer clear of any legal troubles that come with the mishandling of such information.

7. Adhere to environmental laws and regulations

Paying attention to environmental compliance essentially entails having to follow specific legal requirements aimed at safeguarding the environment. These regulations may encompass many areas based on the type of the organization, including environmental standards for air and water, methods of waste disposal and dealing with hazardous substances. For instance, regular plant manufacturing organizations may require permits to release wastewater or emissions up to specified quantities, while construction firms may be required to regulate the effect of their activities on the environment. Compliance entails keeping records and making regular reports that would guarantee a company's compliance with the laws in its business, hence avoiding the negative impact on the environment.

Policies related to sustainable development practices and energy management also influence a firm's impact on the external environment. This may refer to the utilization of renewable energy, establishing a recycling system within the firm or the utilization of environmentally-friendly technologies. If the organization does not meet environmental standards, it can be subjected to fines or face a lawsuit, making it necessary to institutionalize environmental management principles.

8. Contractual obligations

In respect of contracts, make sure that all the terms are legal, and can be readily enforced. This indicates that the contracts with customers, suppliers, and partners have to be well drafted, negotiated, and implemented to minimize the incidences of entering into unprofitable and unlawful agreements. It entails agreement on areas such as the rights and duties of the parties, the agreed price and payment method, the delivery time and date and any conditions and warranties pertaining to the business.

Contracts also need to show possible risks and their management through a shoulder action to mitigation by including clauses on the measures that will be taken in case of such a disagreement, like arbitration or mediation.

Furthermore, business people need to make sure that their contracts do not offend the law on the formation of contracts and their performance. This includes realizing the essentials of contractual admissibility, which are offer acceptance, consideration, and mutual and bilateral intention to be bound. It is advisable for contracts to be drafted in simple language to reduce cases of misunderstandings and to make sure that each of the parties knows their responsibilities well.

The contracts held by the business may also require frequent review and amendments to help cater for changes in business relations or legal provisions to protect the business's interests.

9. Comply with health and safety regulations

The protection of health and safety at work is crucial in fostering an environment that minimizes threats to the health of persons in the workplace with the aim of reducing accidents. This entails following a number of standard operating procedures and state and federal requirements that pertain to risks such as physical, chemical, ergonomic, and so on.

Managing risks is crucial, and organizations must conduct risk analyses to determine possible risks and take appropriate actions to avoid them. Some of the general requirements include offering relevant safety training for the workers, offering the relevant PPEs and also having correct measures in place in cases of accidents and emergencies.

While compliance promotes the safety of workers and employees and reduces work injuries and illnesses, compliance with health and safety regulations helps to improve the work culture and increase organizational effectiveness in the delivery of work. Employers, organizations, and companies that value the health and safety of employees, customers, and the public will experience low turnover rates of experienced personnel, fewer employee absences resulting from work-related diseases or accidents, and compliance with legal requirements on health standards and associated legal actions.

10. Financial reporting

Ensure that you have a proper record of all the business financial activities that your business is undertaking. This process ensures that financial statements, which include the balance sheet, income statement, and the cash flow statement, among others, are a true reflection of the financial situation of the business for a particular period.

The concept of reporting requirements entails following the principles set by accounting standards and other regulatory authorities like the GAAP or IFRS as per the jurisdiction and industry, respectively.

Financial reporting is crucial in giving clear and correct information to the various stakeholders, such as investors, lenders and government agencies, on the financial status and performance of the business. It promotes good governance by ensuring proper decision-making and availability of funds through loans or investments and proves legal and compliance with the laws and regulations.

In business, accounting software is applied to keep financial records, while qualified professionals like certified public accountants (CPAs) are employed to ensure compliance with standards and legal requirements.

Intellectual Property Protection

During this time of global information accessibility and globalization, protecting your ideas and inventions from piracy and counterfeiting is a major predicament.

Irrespective of the nature of the business you are running, be it a new-born start-up, or a global conglomerate, protecting your intellectual capital should be sacrosanct. It is important to emphasize that while beginning to work on patents, trademarks, copyrights, and trade secrets, you also have a vested interest in protecting your efforts and unique selling proposition in the public domain.

Overall, the protection of IPR enables companies to avoid legal pitfalls concerning infringing on other people's work, providing the necessary control over generated ideas and products, as well as answering market challenges in the contexts of furthering technological advancements and global competition.

To discuss further details about how to protect it, it is crucial to learn what it encompasses first.

Intellectual property or IP means all those articles which are produced in the human mind or by the genius of an individual or a company. Intellectual property in business deals with inventions, trademarks, copyrights, patents and industrial designs which offer exclusive privileges to the inventors or holders of the property.

These assets can be very important for the business since they create the company's specific brands, work on new products or services and thus become competitive in the specific market. Policies like patenting, trademarking, and copyrighting are crucial within the business world since they guard work results from imitation or implementation by undesired violators and personnel.

Steps to Protecting Your Intellectual Property

1. Identify your intellectual property

First, it is crucial to categorize all possible or existing types of the business's IP. This consists of Inventions and products, protectable code and software, symbols and trademarks, writings and artistic works, and all proprietary methods and recipes. Take stock of the following in order to be able to appraise its worth and its dependability:

2. Understand legal protections

Identify legal protections for different types of intellectual properties. In regard to inventions or new processes, patents can be sought, which provide the holder with the production, using, and selling rights of the invention for a predefined time. Trade marks or brand names and types, logos and slogans are common in a market of products and services in commerce. Copyrights cover literary pieces like novels, music, software programmers, and even artwork; this is because they give one person or company sole rights to reproduce the creative piece and putting it on the market. The concept of trade secrets focuses on preserving the business information that provides a competitive advantage, for instance, the lists of clients, manufacturing methods, or recipes.

3. Secure intellectual property rights

After identifying one's intellectual property and being aware of the available protections, ensure that one protects the rights of their invention, trade secret or logo. For patents, this may include submission of patent applications to the relevant patent examining authority. For trademarks, this may include registering trademarks with the trademark registry in the respective territory and for copyrights, submission of the copyrighted work to the copyright agencies in the relevant jurisdiction. Regarding trade secrets, use Non-Disclosure Agreements (NDAs) for the employees, contractors, and business partners gaining access to such information.

4. Monitor and enforce

Constantly be on the lookout for unauthorized use or infringement of your intellectual property right. Online sources, industry magazines and newspapers, and legal databases should be used to identify the possible violations. As soon as one finds that their rights are being infringed, one should act fast in an effort to try to reclaim the violated rights. This may involve writing letters to stop infringement and contact infringers as well as negotiating the use of the invention in legal forms such as licensing and taking legal action through the help of intellectual property lawyers to stop people from using the invention without permission and also to claim for compensation.

5. Educate employees and partners

Brief your employees, business associates and counterparts about intellectual property rights and the IP assets possessed by your organization. Adopt strategies that clarify that everyone has an equal obligation to protect the organization's IP rights, confidentiality, and data security. Develop a workshop for the employees in order to raise awareness about how to recognize possible IP infringement and how to report it to avoid an accidental infringement or leakage.

6. Update and maintain

Protection of intellectual property is not just a onetime process that needs to be done, but it requires continuous checks and updates. Be aware of emerging changes in the laws and policies relating to IPs to be on the right side of the law. Re-register and register to renew and keep a record of ownership of the license agreement and usage permissions. Copyright Check your IP strategy from time to time so that it can be revised depending on the current goals and conditions in the market so that your valuable assets will go on protecting your business and contributing to its success.

Contracts and Agreements

A business contract entails the legal relationship between two parties where each of the partners has specific expectations based on the contract. A business contract most often refers to a document that provides the terms of business relations and the legal regulation of business operations.

Business entities use contracts and agreements as modalities in running their enterprises, irrespective of the size of the company. The relations between the companies are based on legal agreements making corporate relations substantial.

It is legally binding in civil courts and can be used to control expectations and the flow of relations more efficiently in a company. Contracts are especially useful in the provision of revenues and control of risks among the companies.

The existence and complexity of business increase the knowledge of other types of contracts that incorporate legal undertones and written words that a business owner is most likely to subscribe to.

Difference Between Contracts and Agreements

Generally, contracts and agreements are two different legal terms, although they are often employed to refer to similar concepts.

A written agreement is a type of ordinary consensual bargain where two or more parties decide on some course. These contracts can be expressed or implied or entered orally or in writing, and some of these agreements are at arm's length. It means it is usually not required that one has to observe or document them.

On the other hand, a contract is a legitimate and legal business understanding between two or more individuals which is written and executed. A contract can be oral, but a formal and written one is more appropriate and can hardly be challenged.

An enforceable contract is sometimes referred to as a legal contract. One of the situations is when you need to use it in the court in order to make a decision on which of the parties is right when solving a disputed issue according to the Contract Law.

When using business contract templates, you should consult with a lawyer as to whether it is viable to do so or if the legal proceedings should draft a formal company agreement with all the legal documents. Only a lawyer can give you competent legal advice since this is his line of profession.

What's the Importance of Business Contracts and Agreements?

Business contracts and agreements are important tools for sustaining, controlling, and developing the affairs of an enterprise. They are employed to set payment conditions and reciprocal small company contracts.

Accordingly, small business owners are encouraged to sign contracts on all forms of business with third parties due to the legal framework provided by contracts that are vital in the operation of any business.

It minimizes risk and is effective in the resolution of conflict when at the same time maintaining private communication with the other party.

Types of Business Contracts and Agreements

1. Sales and Purchase Agreements

These contracts are used when entering into a transaction, whether it is the purchase or the sale of goods or services. There are basic characteristics, including the number of pieces, the price for one piece, the delivery conditions (for example, who pays for the delivery), and the warranties/ guarantees. For instance, if a firm sells computers to another firm, the sales contract will indicate how many computers, the agreed price per each, the delivery date, and any warranties regarding the computers' quality and usability.

2. Service Agreements

The service agreements legalize relations where one party is involved in rendering services to the other. These contracts describe tasks to be completed, the length of service, torts fee, and both the rights and duties of the client and the professional. For example, the service agreement of a marketing agency and its client would define what kind of marketing services are going to be rendered, the remunerations for the services and the timeframe within which the work is supposed to be done.

3. Employment Contracts

An employment contract provides the legal framework under which an employee is hired in a particular company. They are the position held, tasks assigned, and role expected to be performed, the remuneration earned in cash or kind, provisions for medical care and retirement, among other provisions, and lastly, the provisions for withdrawals or dismissal or resignation. An example is an employment contract that spells out the position of the employee, the amount they will be paid, working hours and the termination clause of either the employer or the employee.

4. Partnership Agreements

These are contracts entered into when individuals collaborate in the management of a business concern but do not own equal stakes or capital. In a partnership agreement, every partner defines their role and duties, the division of profits or its distribution, management powers, and the guidelines for resolving the conflict. For example, suppose two friends want to open a restaurant. In that case, the business organization structure will determine who does what, how many of the profits each friend will have and how personnel such as employees will be hired.

5. Non-Disclosure Agreements (NDAs)

NDAs commonly apply to situations when parties organize a business relationship and share sensitive data that should not be disclosed to third parties, including business secrets, marketing strategies, or customer lists. These contracts restrict the use of the information, and the recipient cannot divulge or expound its use in other activities. For instance, if a potential investor invests in a firm, a company's technology will be revealed to the investor, and therefore, this will mean that the company may call for an NDA to avoid the investor passing the technology to other firms.

6. Lease Agreements

Lease agreements are used in the renting of property or equipment. They state provisions like the length of the lease, the amount of rent to be paid per month, who will be paying for the bills and when, and any clauses pertaining to the renewal or the evasion of the lease. For example, a lease of office space would show the length of time the tenant would be allowed to occupy the premises, the amount of rent chargeable on the premises, and who is legally responsible for any repairs in case of plumbing or electrical faults.

7. *Joint Venture Agreements*

These contracts are used when two or more businesses work together on a particular project or undertaking. JV agreements cover the scope of each participant's work, how profit or loss is to be shared, who gets to make decisions, and how disagreement is to be handled. For instance, in the case where two construction firms collaborate to develop a new shopping mall, the JV agreement will indicate how the expenses will be split, who will control the project, and the manner in which the returns from the constructed mall will be split.

8. *Franchise Agreements*

Franchise agreements are legally binding contracts that define the legal relationship between a franchisor, who controls a certain concept and offers it for licensing, and the franchisee, who is an independent person or company. The following are the most essential contracts that describe the manner in which the franchisee may conduct the franchisor's business in terms of fees for use, the operational regulations and guidelines, marketing specifications, and the franchise agreement and its terms. For instance, the franchisee Formula, for example, under the fast-food restaurant franchise agreement must pay what percent of his gross sales in royalties, what numbers of products are to be sold in the restaurant and how the restaurant has to be decorated in order to match the franchisor's brand.

9. *Licensing Agreements*

A licensing agreement is a legal contract in which one party in a legal agreement is authorized to utilize a work invention or symbol owned by another party under certain terms and conditions laid down in the contract. These contracts include issues like the royalty or the license fee, the term of the license, any restraints as to the use of the IP, and the duties and liabilities of the participants. For instance, a software developer can sell their application to a firm or company by an agreement that they will get a certain percentage of the product's revenue and another with the conditions of how the product will be marketed.

10. Insurance Contracts

This is an agreement between an insurance provider and an insured whereby the rights and responsibilities of each party are outlined. These contracts also specify which risks are to be covered and their limits (property damage or liability, amounts of coverage, premiums (payments made by the policyholder), and deductibles, which refer to the amounts that the policyholder has to contribute before the insurance organization's contribution begins, and how claims are to be submitted and processed. For instance, it can involve insurance where a business has a contract with an insurer for coverage of fire risk and the coverage amount, and what the business must do to seek compensation if the business experiences fire at its place of business.

11. Payment Contracts

Payment contracts define how and when a payment will be made, conditions of payment, and who will make the payment. These shall detail the payment terms, including means of payment like bank transfers or checks, due dates, interest for late payment and other conditions such as award of the payment on the achievement of certain conditions. For instance, engaging in a payment contract means the sharing between a client and a contractor how and when the parties shall make payments in regard to the specific phases of the project.

12. Security Agreement

A security agreement is applied in financing deals whereby one individual (the creditor) offers security (tangible and intangible assets, property, inventory, equipment, etc.) to a second individual (the debtor) for a credit grant. Commendable stipulations in these contracts include the type of security to be pledged, the purpose which the security is to serve (for instance, repayment of a loan), circumstances that would warrant the sale or release of the security pledged, as well as the measures to be taken in case of default. For example, a security undertaking between a borrower and the bank states the business properties surrendered to back the business advance.

13. Influencer Agreement

Influencer agreements outline the legal relationship between a business and an influencer or content creator. Such contracts include the expectation of the influencer side and include duties like generating content, showcasing products/ services, refraining from violating brand directions, payment methods (one-time or per sales made), and usage rights of content developed by the influencer. For example, an example of collaboration with an influencer between a brand of cosmetics and an Instagram influencer would contain the kind of content that the influencer will post, the frequency of the posts, and how the influencer will mention the brands in the posts.

14. Independent Contractor Agreement

This type of contract defines business relations between an entrepreneur, on one side, and an independent contractor, or a freelancer, on the other side, to whom certain services or works are to be assigned. They explicitly state that the contractor will not be an employee and cover aspects such as work to be performed, work timeline, rate of pay (if hourly or project-based), ownership rights, confidentiality, and limitations of legal responsibility. For instance, an agreement between a graphic designer who is an independent freelancer and a marketing company would state the specific graphic design projects to be offered, the amount of money to be charged per project, and ownership of fundamental graphic designs produced.

15. Inbound Agreement

Inbound agreements are well-known in digital marketing and sales and are commonly applied in inbound marketing. These contracts outline the agreement between a business (in most cases, SaaS or services provider) and an affiliate or a reseller through which the latter brings leads or customers to the former. Inbound agreements define the parameters of the relationship, including the terms of the referral arrangement and, if there is such a thing, commission, the roles of each party in relation to the leads and sales, and when and how the relationship can be discontinued. For instance, an agreement that is inbound in nature between a software firm and a marketing agency details the manner in which the agency will direct traffic to the software firm's site and the compensation to be offered for every sale made to clients referred by the agency.

NOTE: In deciding the right type of business contracts and agreements, various factors come into consideration as discussed below:

- Type of business
- Industry
- Location of operation
- Nature of the transaction
- Other relevant business contexts.

Every businessman should hire a small business lawyer to help in developing good contracts that will protect the company. A professional lawyer will explain the various types of company contracts and agreements and things to avoid.

Elements of Business Contracts and Agreements

There are several elements of a business contract that are usually included in most contracts. These are the transaction characteristics and the rights and obligations of the parties that the agreement has set.

In addition to such provisions, the terms of a contract often include the following information:

- Details of limitations, for example, what actions are prohibited for both parties while the contract is in place
- When and how to terminate the contract
- Whether the parties have a right to renew the contract
- What happens when a party breaches the contract
- Definitions of terms used
- Privacy policy terms

Chapter 11
Troubleshooting and Problem-Solving

Starting a small business or launching a startup always brings challenges. No matter how well you plan or test things, problems will come. That's why, as an entrepreneur, it's important to be good at solving business problems.

Problem-solving in business means creating ways to deal with difficult issues that are hindering you from reaching your business goals. These problems can be tricky and might be affecting just one part of your team, a process you use, or your whole company. They're not usually things you can fix right away.

To solve these problems effectively, you need to set up consistent ways to handle them. This involves looking carefully at the situation, brainstorming different ideas to fix it, deciding which ideas to try first, and then checking if those solutions actually work. It's a bit like doing a monthly check-up on your business, where you dig deep to find out what's going wrong and figure out the best ways to make things better. Without this approach, it's hard to solve problems quickly or make sure your business runs smoothly.

Identifying Common Challenges for Startups

1. Fierce Competition

Starting a new business is tough because big companies are always competing fiercely. This competition is even harder if you're doing business online. Startups must be perfect because any mistake can be costly. Both businesses that sell to other businesses (B2B) and those that sell directly to customers (B2C) feel this pressure.

To succeed, startups need to be bold and find ways to stand out. They have to work harder than bigger companies to get noticed and build a place for themselves in the market.

2. Unrealistic Expectations

Success often brings along high expectations. These expectations might seem reasonable at first, but in reality, they can be too much to achieve. This is especially true for young startups.

After a big success, startups sometimes set goals that are too ambitious. They forget that success doesn't last forever and that expectations keep growing. Startups need to figure out what they can realistically achieve. Sustainability becomes crucial here. It means putting in consistent effort over time.

To thrive in a competitive business world, startups should aim high but be realistic about what they can accomplish. They need to consider their available resources, how much they can grow, and what the market conditions are like. This balanced approach helps them stay on track and build a lasting business.

3. Hiring Suitable Candidates

One of the most important things that shapes how a startup works is how well its team members work together. A team is made up of people who have similar skills and focus on the same goals. To build a really successful team culture, startups—and companies in general—have to choose the right people.

There are lots of people out there who want to work for startups. Picking the right person for the job can be really tricky. It's one of the biggest challenges that startups face nowadays. When a startup hires someone, they should remember this important idea: people who have similar goals and qualities that fit with the business tend to get along better and work well together.

4. Partnership Decision Making

Partnership is important for success, especially for startups in our current digital world. As businesses fight hard to survive and thrive, startups face a big challenge in finding reliable partners they can trust. This challenge is even greater for tech startups.

Collaborating with the right partner can bring huge rewards for startups. However, before deciding to work together with another company in the same industry, startups must carefully consider several factors. They should look for partners who have a strong reputation in the market and are respected by industry leaders.

Choosing the right partner can help you achieve your goals more effectively. It's about finding someone who not only shares similar goals but also brings valuable expertise and resources to the table. This strategic approach to partnerships can be a game-changer for startups aiming to succeed in a competitive business environment.

5. Financial Management

Money attracts more money. When a startup earns more, its expenses also tend to increase—it's just how things work. Managing finances is one of the biggest challenges startups face today.

Small startups often rely heavily on financial support from investors. Sometimes, when they receive a lot of money, they struggle to manage it well and feel overwhelmed.

To handle this, startups should be cautious with their finances, keeping a close eye on everything. Getting advice from a trusted financial consultancy firm can really help them manage the financial pressures they face today.

6. Cyber Security

In today's digital age, small startups, especially those operating online, must be extremely quick and adaptable to tackle the growing threats of cyber attacks. Hackers are always on the lookout for vulnerabilities in startup systems, making cybersecurity a critical challenge.

Cybercrimes have risen sharply in recent years and are expected to continue increasing. Startups that operate online are particularly vulnerable to these threats. Hackers target sensitive information like employee records, financial data, and other crucial details that are vital for a tech startup's survival.

To protect their valuable online data, startups need strong and highly secure systems. One effective measure is using a virtual private network (VPN) connection. This technology encrypts communication channels, ensuring that sensitive information remains safe from unauthorized access. By implementing robust cybersecurity measures like VPNs, startups can significantly reduce the risk of cyber threats and safeguard their business operations.

REMEMBER: Ensuring cybersecurity is not just about protecting data; it's also about safeguarding the trust of customers and stakeholders. Startups that prioritize cybersecurity build a reputation for reliability and secure business practices, which is crucial for long-term success in today's competitive digital landscape.

7. *Winning Trust of Customers*

The customer is incredibly important, and that's absolutely true. Gaining a customer's trust is one of the biggest challenges facing all businesses today, especially startups. With a satisfied and loyal customer base, startups can grow and move closer to achieving excellence.

Customers play a pivotal role in a startup's success. Their recommendations and social media presence can give tech startups an advantage over traditional businesses.

To earn and maintain customers' trust and loyalty, startups must adopt a customer-focused approach. This means prioritizing the needs and satisfaction of customers in every aspect of their operations. By doing so, startups can succeed in achieving sustainable growth and progress in today's competitive and tech-driven business environment.

Strategies for Overcoming Obstacles

All businesses encounter obstacles. What distinguishes one firm from another is how it solves business challenges. While some people allow difficulties to derail them, others have learned to anticipate them and see them as a chance to learn and develop.

Certain obstacles can be avoided. They might be the result of mismanaged emotions, established behaviors, or repetitive blunders. Unattended, these impediments become emotional robbers, stealing concentration, draining mental energy, and occasionally derailing the most critical projects.

What can you do to overcome these business challenges and capitalize on possibilities for success? Here are some ways to assist you in overcoming typical business challenges.

1. Establish frugality as a fundamental value within the company

It is not unusual to see a startup receive investment and proceed to spend like a Fortune 500 company. Euphoria and the joy of victory can override common reason. Uncontrolled expenditure is a corporate impediment that can be readily overcome. In the early days of Microsoft, they sent out a "Shrimp and Weenies" message to all workers, instructing them to be thrifty with corporate money—to order weenies, not shrimp, when the firm paid the bill. It advised staff to think of Microsoft as "the biggest small company in the world." Maintaining a thrifty mindset while your business expands is sound long-term advice.

2. Understand your worth and steer clear of pricing decisions driven by emotions

One of the most common business issues that small business owners encounter is developing effective pricing strategies for their products and services. Sometimes, emotions decide the price charged. For example, fear of losing the business leads to pricing too little, which gradually reduces the profit margin. This can lead to insurmountable business issues on the road.

Emotional pricing can also stem from a sense of pride—what one consultant referred to as "the joy of the hunt," which involves obtaining the contract at any cost and feeling good about beating the competition. On closer examination, this is a hollow victory—price with your mind, not your emotions. Know your expenses, be informed about your competitors, and assess your rates on a regular basis.

If you consistently receive negative responses to your offers, solicit input from clients about your pricing strategy. Many people are eager to share their experiences, and this feedback might provide valuable information in the future.

3. Be ready to let go of what isn't effective or working for you

Some products or services offered by a business may no longer be functional. We tend to fall in love with our own products and services and find it difficult to let them go. It's almost as if we create blinders that prevent us from seeing what is obvious to others but not ourselves. To maintain success, you must be ready to discard things that are no longer effective.

Evaluate what doesn't work and be willing to walk away from it before it becomes a business concern. The energy you unleash by letting go will boost your concentration on what works, allowing you to apply the intensity of a laser focus to the proper target.

4. Replace outdated strategies with innovative ones

Some business issues stem from our established habits, such as adhering to obsolete modes and methods of doing business since they are what we are most familiar with. For example, depending on outward marketing approaches while overlooking the benefits of inbound marketing initiatives. Inbound marketing entails recruiting customers through a variety of channels, including blogs, podcasts, videos, social media marketing, and many other types of content marketing. It is the precursor to outbound marketing, which includes tactics like cold phoning and direct email marketing.

Being open to trying new marketing methods that you may not have used before might help you develop your business and stay competitive. Embrace social media, develop quality material to freely share on your website, and think about hiring an expert to help you improve your website or even outsource your small company marketing campaign.

5. Understand the primary challenge your business is up against

What would you do if you could remove one major impediment to your business's exponential growth?

Finding and educating the proper individuals to help develop the organization, as well as gaining easier access to money, have been common approaches. What would your response be? Gaining clarity is the first step toward taking action to keep barriers from impeding your path to success.

For example:

- Do you have inadequate IT that slows things down?
- Are there inefficiencies in using the technology and software?
- Are you understaffed?
- Are people confused about roles and responsibilities?
- Is the decision-making process slow because all decisions must go through you?
- Is a growing workload slowing down progress?

6. Stay engaged with the sales function

During the startup phase, entrepreneurs typically serve as sales leaders. They are the experts on their product or service since they produced it. Some entrepreneurs may step away from sales as their businesses expand and hire more people. They gradually separate themselves as they concentrate on finance, personnel management, and other operational concerns. That becomes a significant business challenge since sales may make or ruin a company.

The standard advice offered to entrepreneurs is to avoid wearing too many hats and not micromanage the firm. While this is true, when it comes to sales, it's best to keep sales in your peripheral vision so you're not taken off guard and can change before major business difficulties and issues arise.

Furthermore, don't let a hectic schedule keep you from training and improving your sales team. Sales teams are essential for every company seeking to develop and thrive. Investing time in providing continuing training for your sales force is critical.

Handling Financial Difficulties

When your business faces financial difficulties, it primarily struggles to generate sufficient revenue to cover expenses or meet financial obligations. These difficulties can manifest as cash flow problems, where there's a shortage of available funds to pay suppliers, employees, or creditors on time. They may also include declining sales, increased operating costs, or excessive debt burdens that strain the company's financial health. Such challenges can impact profitability, hinder growth opportunities, and jeopardize the overall sustainability of the business if not effectively managed and addressed.

Below are effective strategies to handle financial difficulties and ensure your business gets back on track.

1. Assess your business' financial situation

Assessing your business's financial situation is crucial when facing difficulties. Start by gathering all your financial records—like bank statements, sales reports, and expense receipts. Look closely at where your money is coming from and where it's going. Are there patterns showing declining sales or increasing expenses? Understanding these trends helps pinpoint the root causes of your financial challenges. It could be that your market has shifted, or perhaps there are inefficiencies in your operations that are costing you money.

Once you've identified the problems, prioritize them based on urgency and impact. For instance, if cash flow is tight because customers aren't paying on time, focus on improving your invoicing and collection processes. If expenses are too high, look for areas where you can cut costs without harming your core business operations. By assessing your financial situation thoroughly, you'll have a clearer picture of what needs to change and where to focus your efforts to stabilize your business.

2. Prioritize and cut costs

In times of financial difficulty, prioritizing and cutting costs can make a significant difference in your business's financial health. Start by categorizing your expenses into essential and non-essential items. Essential costs are those necessary for your business to operate smoothly, like rent, utilities, and salaries. Non-essential costs, on the other hand, may include things like subscriptions, luxury expenses, or excessive marketing spending that can be reduced or eliminated temporarily.

Once you've identified non-essential expenses, explore ways to reduce or eliminate them. This could involve renegotiating contracts with suppliers for better terms or finding alternative vendors offering lower prices. Consider implementing cost-saving measures such as energy-efficient practices to reduce utility bills or consolidating orders to benefit from bulk discounts. Every dollar saved can contribute to improving your cash flow and financial stability.

3. Improve cash flow

Cash flow is important for any business, especially during challenging times. To improve cash flow, begin by closely monitoring your accounts receivable. Send out invoices promptly and follow up diligently on overdue payments. Consider offering discounts for early payments to incentivize customers to settle their bills sooner. On the accounts payable side, negotiate extended payment terms with suppliers without straining your relationship. This approach can help free up cash that can be reinvested into your business operations.

Another strategy to improve cash flow is to optimize your inventory management. Avoid overstocking on items that aren't selling quickly and focus on products with higher turnover rates. This minimizes holding costs and maximizes the availability of cash for other business needs. Additionally, consider leasing equipment instead of buying it outright to conserve cash reserves.

4. Increase revenue

Generating additional revenue is key to overcoming financial difficulties in business. Begin to evaluate your current product or service offerings and identify areas where you can expand or innovate. Consider launching new products or services that cater to existing customer needs or tap into new market segments. Market research and customer feedback can provide valuable insights into potential opportunities for revenue growth.

Marketing and promotional activities are also crucial for increasing revenue. Develop targeted marketing campaigns to reach your target audience effectively. Utilize digital marketing channels, social media platforms, and email marketing to promote your offerings and attract new customers. Offering special promotions, discounts, or bundled packages can incentivize purchases and stimulate sales. Also, consider forming strategic partnerships or collaborations with complementary businesses to expand your customer base and enhance revenue streams.

5. Renegotiate debts

To explain this more practically, imagine your business finances as a puzzle where each debt is a piece. To solve this puzzle during tough times, think of renegotiating debts as rearranging those pieces to fit better together. Start by examining each debt piece—like loans or credit lines—and understanding its terms and conditions. Reach out to your creditors not just to ask for changes but to propose a new arrangement that benefits both sides. It's like finding a new way to assemble the puzzle pieces so they fit snugly and support your business's financial stability.

Consider suggesting longer repayment periods or reduced interest rates that align better with your current cash flow. This negotiation process is akin to finding the right pieces to complete a challenging puzzle— one that, when solved, provides relief and a clearer path forward for your business.

6. Explore financial options

Exploring financial options means looking at different ways to get money for your business when you're facing financial challenges. It's like checking out various sources where you can borrow money or get funding to help your business keep running smoothly or grow. One way is through traditional bank loans, which give you a lump sum of money that you pay back over time with interest. Another option is a business line of credit, which is like having money available whenever you need it, up to a certain limit, and you only pay interest on what you use.

You can also explore alternative options like crowdfunding, where people donate money to support your business idea or find investors who are willing to invest money in exchange for a share of your business. Each option has its own benefits and considerations, so it's important to research and choose the one that best fits your business's needs and goals.

7. Seek professional advice

Consult with financial advisors, accountants, or business consultants who specialize in turnaround strategies for guidance and support.

This is important because professionals, such as financial advisors or consultants, bring expertise and experience that can provide you with a clear understanding of your financial situation. They can analyze your cash flow, expenses, and revenue to pinpoint areas where you can cut costs or increase income. This analysis helps in creating a realistic plan to manage debts or improve profitability.

Also, professionals offer unbiased guidance. They can offer solutions that you might not have considered and provide an objective view of your financial health. This perspective is valuable because it helps you make the best decisions for your business rather than relying solely on emotions or guesses.

8. Engage employees

Try to engage your employees and keep them informed during financial difficulties. This helps foster a sense of teamwork and shared responsibility. When employees understand the financial challenges facing the business, they are more likely to actively participate in finding solutions. This can lead to innovative ideas for cost-saving measures or new revenue streams that may not have been considered otherwise.

Also, involving employees boosts morale and motivation. When employees feel included and valued, they are more committed to the success of the business. This can translate into increased productivity and efficiency, which are critical during financially challenging times. Moreover, employees often have insights into day-to-day operations that can uncover areas where efficiencies can be improved or costs reduced.

9. Review and adjust business plan

Update your business plan with realistic financial projections and strategies to navigate the challenges ahead. This can help you gain a clearer understanding of where your business stands financially and where it's heading.

To carry out this process, start by conducting a thorough assessment of your current financial standing reviewing income statements, balance sheets, and cash flow statements to understand your cash position, revenue trends, and cost structures. Based on this assessment, set realistic financial projections for the upcoming months or year, considering factors like market conditions and customer demand.

Next, review and adjust your business goals to align with these projections. This might involve revising sales targets, adjusting expense management strategies, or prioritizing initiatives that can generate quicker cash flow. Develop specific action plans and strategies to achieve these revised goals, such as launching targeted marketing campaigns, renegotiating contracts with suppliers for better terms, or exploring new revenue streams.

Communicate these updates transparently with your team to ensure everyone understands their role in achieving the new objectives and remains motivated towards collective success.

Dealing With Legal Issues

Ideally, legal issues should be avoided via deliberate, proactive action. However, even the most vigilant business owners or leaders may encounter a significant legal challenge. Contract conflicts, intellectual property concerns, employment law compliance, and regulatory challenges are among the most typical legal issues affecting small and medium-sized firms.

If your business is embroiled in a legal dispute, you must move quickly and decisively to safeguard your interests. The following are important procedures to take if your business is involved in a legal issue or problem:

1. Prioritize documentation

When facing a legal issue, timely and thorough documentation collection is crucial. This process begins with identifying and preserving all relevant documents that could potentially influence the outcome of the case. This typically includes gathering emails, contracts, invoices, financial records, and any other written communications that pertain to the matter at hand. Each piece of documentation should be dated and organized chronologically or thematically to facilitate easy reference and retrieval.

Preservation of evidence is equally important to prevent any accidental alteration, loss, or destruction of critical information. This involves ensuring that electronic documents are backed up securely and that physical copies are stored safely. Moreover, maintaining a detailed log of when and how each piece of evidence was obtained can provide a clear chain of custody, which is essential in legal proceedings.

2. Use open-ended questions to gather information

When speaking with witnesses or other parties involved in a case, using open-ended questions can help gather comprehensive information. Instead of asking questions that can be answered with a simple "yes" or "no," open-ended questions encourage people to provide detailed explanations and share their perspectives fully. For example, you might ask, "Can you describe what happened leading up to the incident?" or "What was your understanding of the agreement between the parties?"

These types of questions allow individuals to elaborate on their experiences, feelings, and observations, providing a clearer picture of the situation. They help uncover nuances and details that might not emerge from more restrictive questioning.

3. Understand the applicable laws

Taking the time to research the laws relevant to your situation is important. It helps you understand what rights you have, what you need to do, and what choices you can make. For instance, if you're dealing with a contract issue, researching contract law can clarify what the terms mean and how they apply to your case. If it's about a personal injury, knowing the laws around that can help you figure out what compensation you might be entitled to.

By understanding the laws, you're better prepared to make decisions and take actions that protect your interests. It's like knowing the rules of a game before you play—you can plan your moves wisely and know what to expect. Whether you're dealing with a legal dispute or just want to know your rights in a specific situation, researching the applicable laws gives you the knowledge to navigate confidently and make the choices.

4. Be impartial and fact-based

Businesses that maintain a track record of consistent, predictable, and lawful conduct generally fare better when faced with legal challenges. Despite this, unforeseen issues can arise. If your company becomes embroiled in a legal dispute, it's crucial to approach the situation with impartiality and objectivity. In legal proceedings, factual accuracy holds utmost importance, so it's essential to thoroughly grasp the details and circumstances of your case before proceeding further.

Being impartial means avoiding biases and emotions that could cloud judgment. It involves focusing on gathering and presenting facts objectively, which strengthens your position in any legal battle. By prioritizing a clear understanding of the facts, businesses can better navigate the complexities of litigation and make informed decisions guided by the realities of their circumstances.

5. Maintain confidentiality

Keeping information about your legal case confidential is crucial to protect your interests and maintain control over how information is used. It's important to limit discussions about your case strictly to those who have a legitimate need to know, such as your legal counsel or trusted advisors directly involved in handling the matter. This includes refraining from sharing details with friends, family members, or business associates who are not directly relevant to the case.

By keeping a tight circle of those informed, you minimize the risk of inadvertently disclosing sensitive information or opinions that could potentially harm your case. This approach helps maintain confidentiality, preserves strategic advantage, and prevents unauthorized individuals from influencing the proceedings. When in doubt, consulting with your legal team before discussing details with anyone outside of the necessary circle can help ensure that you're protecting your legal position effectively.

6. Work with qualified legal counsel

Seeking qualified legal counsel is indeed crucial when dealing with legal issues. A skilled business lawyer can provide invaluable guidance in navigating the complexities of the legal system. They help you understand your rights and responsibilities, analyze the specifics of your case, and devise a strategic plan tailored to safeguard your interests.

An experienced attorney brings expertise and insight that can significantly impact the outcome of your legal situation. They offer clarity on legal complexities, negotiate on your behalf, and represent your interests effectively in negotiations or court proceedings.

Chapter 12
Exiting Your Business: Knowing When and How

Starting a business is exciting and is a wonderful way to invest time, energy, and passion towards working hard. Nevertheless, one has to consider the possibility of stepping out of their business at some point in their life.

It is crucial to understand when and how to cut one's losses and get out of a business, this could be because of personal factors, changes in market dynamics, or in a bid to pursue other ventures.

Understanding Exit Strategies

An exit strategy is a plan that a businessman or investor wants to follow when he intends to withdraw from a business he has started or invested in. It is a strategic plan that may include the process of business sale, transferring the business to heirs, the process of acquiring another company, or even shutting down the business. It is vital to have exit strategies because they help in planning for the transition process in the best manner possible, optimizing the return on investment, and avoiding disturbing the business and its stakeholders. These are usually done and proposed in the early stages of the formation of the business and its strategies and are in sync with the long-term objectives of the business and the market trends.

Here are the different exit strategies:

Types of Exit Strategies

1. Initial Public Offering (IPO)

An Initial Public Offering (IPO) is a significant milestone where a privately held company transitions to becoming a publicly traded entity by offering its shares to the public through a stock exchange. This process involves extensive preparation, including financial audits, regulatory compliance, and market assessments to determine the offering price and size of the offering. IPOs are often pursued by companies seeking substantial capital infusion to fund expansion, repay debts, or facilitate shareholder liquidity.

For business owners and early investors, an IPO provides a robust exit strategy by enabling them to monetize their ownership stakes through the sale of shares to public investors. It also enhances the company's visibility and credibility in the market, potentially increasing its valuation and access to future capital.

However, IPOs entail significant costs, including underwriting fees, legal expenses, and ongoing compliance with regulatory requirements such as Securities and Exchange Commission (SEC) filings and shareholder disclosures. Moreover, the process can be time-consuming and complex, requiring careful coordination between company executives, investment banks, legal advisors, and regulatory bodies.

Despite these challenges, successful IPOs can offer substantial rewards, including enhanced liquidity for shareholders, increased market capitalization, and the ability to use publicly traded shares as currency for future acquisitions or strategic initiatives.

2. Merger or Acquisition

A merger or acquisition (M&A) involves selling a business to another company (acquisition) or combining two companies to form a new entity (merger). M&A transactions are popular exit strategies because they offer owners the opportunity to realize the value of their investments by selling to a strategic buyer or a private equity firm.

For sellers, M&A transactions can provide liquidity, mitigate business risks, and unlock synergies that enhance operational efficiency or market competitiveness. Strategic buyers often seek acquisitions to expand market reach, acquire technology or intellectual property, or integrate complementary products and services into their existing operations.

From a financial perspective, M&A transactions can be structured in various ways, including cash purchases, stock-for-stock exchanges, or a combination of both. The valuation of the business, negotiation of terms, due diligence processes, and regulatory approvals are critical aspects of M&A transactions that require careful consideration and professional guidance from legal, financial, and M&A advisors.

Additionally, cultural compatibility between the acquiring and target companies, as well as retention of key talent post-transaction, are crucial factors that can influence the success and integration of the deal.

3. Management Buyout (MBO)

A Management Buyout (MBO) occurs when the existing management team or employees of a company purchase the business from its current owners, often with the support of external financing from private equity investors, banks, or other financial institutions.

MBOs are commonly pursued when business owners seek succession planning, desire to retire, or aim to divest their ownership while preserving continuity in operations and management. For management teams, MBOs offer the opportunity to gain ownership and control of the business, aligning their interests with company performance and future growth prospects.

Key advantages of MBOs include insider knowledge of the business, a smoother transition of ownership and leadership, and potential operational improvements driven by management's familiarity with company operations and strategic vision.

However, MBOs require careful negotiation of purchase terms, valuation assessments, financing arrangements, and legal agreements to ensure fairness and transparency for all parties involved. Also, securing adequate financing and managing post-acquisition integration challenges are critical considerations that can impact the success and sustainability of the MBO transaction.

4. Strategic Alliance or Partnership

Forming a strategic alliance or partnership involves collaborating with another company to achieve mutual business objectives, such as accessing new markets, leveraging complementary strengths, or developing innovative products or services. Strategic alliances can serve as precursor strategies that lead to a potential acquisition of the business or a strategic division by the partner company. These alliances are often formed through joint ventures, licensing agreements, distribution partnerships, or co-development initiatives, depending on the nature of the collaboration and shared goals of the participating companies.

For businesses considering strategic alliances as an exit strategy, key benefits include sharing resources and risks, expanding market reach, accessing new technologies or intellectual property, and enhancing competitive advantages through combined capabilities. Unlike traditional M&A transactions, strategic alliances offer flexibility in terms of structure and duration, allowing companies to test collaboration opportunities before committing to more permanent arrangements.

However, successful strategic alliances require clear objectives, mutual trust, effective communication, and alignment of strategic priorities between the partnering companies to maximize synergies and achieve sustainable competitive advantages in the marketplace.

5. Liquidation

Liquidation is a business exit strategy that involves selling off all assets of the company, including inventory, equipment, real estate, and intellectual property, to convert them into cash. This process typically occurs when a business is unable to sustain operations, faces insurmountable financial challenges, or when owners decide to close the business for personal or strategic reasons. Liquidation allows owners to maximize the value of their assets and distribute proceeds to creditors, shareholders, and other stakeholders in accordance with legal obligations and priority claims.

While liquidation provides a straightforward method to wind down operations and settle financial obligations, it is generally considered a last resort due to its implications for employees, customers, suppliers, and the broader community. Business owners contemplating liquidation must adhere to legal requirements, such as notifying creditors, filing necessary tax returns, and complying with state and federal regulations governing asset sales and distribution of proceeds.

Moreover, the decision to liquidate should be guided by professional advice from legal, financial, and tax advisors to mitigate potential liabilities and ensure an orderly dissolution process that minimizes adverse impacts on stakeholders.

NOTE: Each of these exit strategies presents distinct opportunities, challenges, and considerations that should be carefully evaluated based on the unique circumstances, goals, and objectives of the business owners and stakeholders involved. The choice of an exit strategy often depends on factors such as market conditions, business valuation, shareholder objectives, and long-term strategic priorities to achieve optimal outcomes and maximize value creation for all parties involved.

Factors Influencing the Decision to Exit

Being a business owner is an exciting adventure full of unique difficulties, wins, lessons, and progress. It's a route that fosters resilience, adaptability, and a strong personal connection to the company you've fostered and created. However, there comes a point in every business owner's journey when they consider exiting their firm. But why? What motivates someone to walk away from something they've invested many hours, resources, and passion into?

The choice to leave is rarely spontaneous. It's a watershed moment, sometimes caused by a complicated network of variables that progressively tip the scales in favor of leaving the company.

These variables may be roughly classified into two major categories:

1. Push factors
2. Pull factors

Push Factors

Push factors are events that, over time, make the idea of staying in the business less enticing or practical. These are frequently problems or issues that compel the owner to stand aside.

Pull Factors

Pull factors are the appealing alternatives or chances that entice business owners into a new chapter by offering new experiences, personal growth, or financial gains.

Let's look at these push and pull elements to better understand the complex dynamics that influence the choice to exit a business.

PUSH FACTORS

Push factors are frequently the underlying forces that cause a business owner to consider exiting their business. They may not want to abandon their firm, but circumstances may make it increasingly impossible or unsustainable for them to continue. Some frequent push factors are:

1. Burnout

Running a business requires attention, work, and time. Over time, the constant stress and responsibilities of running a business can lead to burnout. Emotional, mental, and physical tiredness can impair a business owner's capacity to lead and make informed judgments successfully. If the burnout becomes too severe, individuals may consider exiting their business as the sole possible choice for recovery and recharging. This permits individuals to pursue other hobbies that they may have had to put on hold owing to the obligations of operating a business.

2. Health complications

Unexpected health difficulties can have a substantial influence on a business owner's capacity to continue efficiently operating their firm. Chronic illness, severe illnesses, or unexpected health emergencies might make it physically or emotionally difficult to sustain the necessary degree of commitment. In such instances, a business owner may have to sell their business and prioritize their health.

3. Family obligations

Personal life might sometimes need an adjustment in priorities. A company owner may be forced to depart their firm due to family responsibilities, such as caring for ill parents, raising small children, or supporting a spouse's work. This choice may be based on factors other than the business's performance, such as the owner's prioritization of family duties.

4. Financial difficulties

If a business is not financially sustainable, it can put a burden on the owner's finances and add to their stress. The firm may be going through a hard patch, trying to produce profits, or dealing with financial issues such as debt accumulation, inability to pay staff, or trouble maintaining operations. Such circumstances lead the business owner to contemplate selling their business in order to avoid financial loss and, in some cases, personal bankruptcy.

PULL FACTORS

Pull factors are the more hopeful, forward-thinking motives that might entice a business owner to exit their business. They are the alluring features that make leaving their organization appealing and personally rewarding. Some frequent pull factors are:

1. Retirement

Many business owners look forward to retirement after years, if not decades, of hard work and management. They worked hard, overcame obstacles, and got the benefits of their efforts. They now desire a less stressful lifestyle in which they can devote time to personal hobbies, family, travel, and leisure activities. The prospect of a well-deserved relaxation might be a strong motivator for them to exit.

2. A desire for new challenges

Entrepreneurs are generally motivated by the excitement of new challenges and prospects. Over time, a business owner may acquire a new love or rediscover an old one. This might include charity endeavors, starting a new business, traveling the world, or professionalizing a pastime. The urge to pursue these new interests might become a strong motivator, leading individuals to leave their current jobs to start on a new adventure.

3. Opportunity to sell

Knowing when to capitalize on the success of your business is an important component of running a successful business. When market circumstances are favorable, the business is prospering, and a profitable offer arrives, a business owner may decide to sell. The promise of making a significant financial profit from the sale might be an appealing incentive. Not only does this bring immediate cash advantage, but it also enables reinvestment, increased financial stability, and funding of new business ventures.

Planning Your Exit Strategy

Planning an exit strategy involves several key steps and considerations to ensure a smooth transition and maximize value for business owners and stakeholders. Let's look at a structured approach to planning your exit strategy.

1. Exit strategy objectives/goals

When starting a new business, it's important to think about your personal goals right from the beginning. These goals could be as clear-cut as wanting a certain amount of profit when you eventually sell the business or as deep-rooted as creating a lasting legacy in your industry. Knowing what you want to achieve helps you stay focused and make decisions that steer the business toward those goals.

For instance, if your objective is to sell the business for a significant profit, you'll likely prioritize strategies that boost profitability, enhance market value, and attract potential buyers or investors who align with your financial aspirations. Having these objectives not only guides your business decisions but also gives you a sense of direction and purpose, ensuring that every step you take brings you closer to achieving your ultimate goals.

2. Timeline consideration

A well-defined timeline ensures that you're ready when the time comes to make a successful exit from your business. It is like having a roadmap for your journey. It gives you a clear direction and helps you prepare effectively. For example, suppose you decide you want to sell your business within five years. In that case, you can start taking steps today to increase its value and make it more attractive to potential buyers. This might include improving operations, building a strong management team, or expanding your customer base. Having a time-line also allows you to set milestones along the way so you can track your progress and make adjustments as needed.

3. Intentions for the business

In planning an exit strategy, it's important to define what you envision happening to your business once you're ready to move on. Whether you intend to liquidate the assets, merge with another company to leverage synergies or pass the business down to a family member, outlining these intentions clarifies your vision and guides your strategic decisions.

For instance, if your goal is to pass the business to a family member, you might start grooming them early, ensuring they're ready to take over when the time comes. Alternatively, if you plan to merge with another company, you would focus on identifying potential partners and aligning your operations to maximize compatibility and value.

4. Market conditions

Considering market conditions is pivotal when planning to sell your business, as they can greatly influence the timing and success of your exit strategy. For instance, if your industry is experiencing a surge in demand or interest from buyers, it may be an opportune moment to execute your sales strategy and aim for a premium price. On the other hand, during economic downturns or when industry trends are unfavorable, you might choose to hold off until conditions improve, allowing you to fetch a better valuation. Understanding these dynamics enables you to strategically time your exit, optimizing financial returns and ensuring a smooth transaction process.

Preparing Your Business for Sale

Preparing your business for sale involves two critical aspects: maximizing its value and addressing potential obstacles and liabilities. Maximizing its value and addressing potential obstacles and liabilities is crucial because it ensures you attract serious buyers and negotiate the best deal possible. Let's look at these two important aspects in detail.

Maximizing Your Business Value

Maximizing the value of your business helps you to attract potential buyers and achieve a favorable sale outcome. Here's a breakdown of how you can do this.

1. Financial performance

Start by maintaining accurate and up-to-date financial records to lay a solid foundation for preparing your business for sale. This involves keeping clear and organized records of income, expenses, and cash flow to provide transparency and reliability to potential buyers, showcasing the true financial health of your business.

Improve profitability through optimizing costs—such as reducing unnecessary expenses and negotiating better deals with suppliers—and increasing revenue streams by expanding customer bases or introducing new products/services.

This can also be achieved by demonstrating strong cash flow management. It ensures efficient handling of incoming and outgoing cash, emphasizing financial stability and sustainability. These steps help enhance the overall value of your business and build confidence among potential buyers during the sale process.

2. Operational efficiency

To prepare your business for sale, streamline operations to enhance efficiency and trim unnecessary expenses. Implement best practices, such as identifying and eliminating bottlenecks or redundancies in workflows.

Also, upgrade technology infrastructure. This can optimize processes and improve productivity, demonstrating scalability and sustainability to potential buyers. NOTE: these measures help you increase operational efficiency and also enhance the attractiveness of your business by showcasing its ability to adapt and thrive in changing market conditions.

3. Market positioning

Market positioning is about making your business stand out in the marketplace by emphasizing what makes it unique and appealing to customers and potential buyers. This involves highlighting your unique selling propositions (USPs), which are the special qualities or features that set your products or services apart from competitors. For example, if you offer personalized customer service or innovative technology that solves a specific problem better than anyone else, these can be strong USPs. Competitive advantages, such as lower costs, higher quality, or faster delivery times, also play a crucial role in differentiating your business. Building a strong brand reputation through positive customer reviews, testimonials, or industry recognition further enhances your market position. Showcase metrics like customer loyalty, repeat business rates, and market share to demonstrate your business's strength and potential for growth.

4. Customer relationships

Your business must reflect a strong customer relationship. A strong customer relationship strategy not only enhances business value but also fosters customer loyalty and advocacy, which can lead to increased referrals and sustainable revenue growth over time.

To strengthen customer relationships and enhance business value, focus on delivering exceptional service, maintaining consistent communication, and responding promptly to customer feedback. Providing exceptional service means going above and beyond customer expectations, whether through personalized interactions, resolving issues quickly, or anticipating their needs. Consistent communication involves staying in touch with customers through regular updates, newsletters, or personalized offers that demonstrate your commitment to their satisfaction. Addressing customer feedback promptly shows that you value their input and are dedicated to improving their experience.

5. Intellectual property and assets

Protect and leverage intellectual property assets such as patents, trademarks, and proprietary technologies. Ensure all intellectual property rights are documented and legally protected to enhance the attractiveness of your business.

6. Management team and talent

Ensure you have a competent and motivated management team in place. This shows your readiness for sale. All you have to do is to evaluate the strengths and capabilities of your current management team. Identify key leaders who possess strategic vision and operational expertise. Also, invest in leadership development programs and ongoing training to nurture talent within the organization, preparing future leaders for potential roles under new ownership.

Implement succession planning strategies to ensure a smooth transition of leadership and maintain business continuity during the sale process.

Addressing Potential Obstacles and Liabilities

This is important in the sale preparation to mitigate risks and build buyer confidence during the sale process. Below is a breakdown of what to keep in mind.

1. Legal and regulatory compliance

Addressing legal and regulatory compliance is fundamental to mitigating risks during a business sale. Conducting a thorough review of all contracts, agreements, leases, and regulatory obligations ensures that potential liabilities are identified and addressed upfront. This includes reviewing the status of any pending litigation or regulatory investigations that could impact the business's legal standing or financial health.

During due diligence, providing clear documentation and explanations regarding compliance efforts demonstrates transparency to potential buyers. Any historical legal issues or compliance challenges should be disclosed along with actions taken to rectify them. Engaging legal counsel experienced in mergers and acquisitions (M&A) can help navigate complex legal landscapes to ensure that all legal risks are properly managed and disclosed.

2. Financial transparency

Financial transparency helps build buyer confidence. It's important to provide accurate and comprehensive financial statements, including balance sheets, income statements, cash flow statements, and any relevant financial forecasts. Also, disclose any past financial losses, irregularities, or significant one-time expenses with clear explanations and corrective actions taken to reassure buyers of the business's financial stability and future prospects.

Engaging with a reputable accounting firm to conduct a financial audit or review can further validate the accuracy of financial reporting. It also helps in identifying areas where financial performance can be improved or where cost-saving measures have been implemented. Clear communication about financial metrics and key performance indicators (KPIs) helps align buyer expectations with the business's financial realities.

3. Operational risks

Identify and mitigate operational risks that could impact business continuity or profitability. Develop contingency plans for key operational functions and address any pending operational challenges or dependencies by thoroughly assessing potential disruptions, such as supply chain interruptions, technological failures, or regulatory changes that may affect operations.

Proactively developing comprehensive contingency plans for critical functions ensures readiness to handle unexpected challenges. This helps maintain smooth operations and profitability, which is crucial for reassuring potential buyers during the sale process.

4. Employee and workforce issues

Identify and address employee concerns while ensuring compliance with labor laws and regulations. Openly communicate with employees about the sale process, providing reassurance regarding job security and offering transparency regarding the company's future direction.

Additionally, proactively tackle potential challenges related to integrating the workforce by outlining strategies for retaining key talent and facilitating a smooth transition for new team members. This clear communication and demonstration of a commitment to fair treatment and stability help maintain high morale and productivity during the transition and enhance their appeal to potential buyers.

5. Environmental and safety compliance

Ensure compliance with environmental regulations and safety standards. Address any potential environmental liabilities, such as contamination issues or improper waste disposal practices, that could harm the business's reputation or lead to legal consequences. For instance, if a manufacturing business discovers a historical site contamination issue during due diligence, it should promptly initiate cleanup efforts and notify relevant authorities to mitigate legal and reputational risks.

6. Intellectual property and data security

Protect intellectual property rights and address data security measures to safeguard confidential information. It's important to implement robust cybersecurity protocols in order to prevent unauthorized access or data breaches that could compromise sensitive information such as patents, trademarks, and proprietary business processes.

For example, a software company should encrypt customer data and regularly update security measures to comply with data privacy regulations like GDPR or CCPA. The prioritization of these measures enables businesses to safeguard their intellectual property and also enhance trust with stakeholders to ensure operational integrity and minimize risks associated with cyber threats during the sale process.

Legal and Financial Considerations

A successful exit does not happen by accident! There are various crucial components to consider along the road, including legal and financial aspects of selling your business. Knowing what to expect from a legal and financial aspect is critical for a successful exit.

As a business owner, you may be thinking, "What are the legal implications of selling my business?" When arranging your leave, there are certain legal considerations to keep in mind. One of the first stages is to comprehend the legal due diligence procedure. Furthermore, it is beneficial to be aware of numerous key legal documents.

Legal Considerations

1. Legal due diligence

When a business is acquired and sold, both parties are interested in ensuring that the transaction is safe and secure. To do this, the acquisition process includes a step called due diligence. During this phase, the buyer and their team go through the business to evaluate all elements of its performance.

Legal due diligence is one step in this process. It provides a chance for the prospective acquirer to evaluate the business's legal processes. Generally, they'll want to examine:

- Employment contracts and contractor agreements
- Supplier agreements
- Warranties
- Intellectual property protection
- Intellectual property infringements
- Distribution agreements
- Compensation practices
- Accounting practices and financial statements
- Pending lawsuits

Furthermore, regardless of whether your company is a S corporation, C corporation, LLC, or sole proprietorship, the buyer will review your articles of incorporation or other formation paperwork to ensure they are in order.

While the buyer and their team commence and carry out legal due diligence, you, as the seller, must also take the necessary steps. Conducting thorough legal due diligence helps to lessen the possibility of future problems.

As the seller, it is your job to assist the buyer with the legal due diligence procedure. This involves promptly addressing any of their queries and giving them the information they have requested.

To make the due diligence process go more smoothly, gather all important information ahead of time. This assures that you'll be ready to depart when the time comes.

2. Letter of intent

The letter of intent is written when a potential buyer learns about your company. It also happens before the due diligence procedure starts. While the LOI is not legally binding, it does specify the parameters of a prospective future transaction.

Essentially, it declares that the buyer and seller agree to proceed with the deal provided that specific criteria are satisfied. The letter of intent would most likely include the final purchase price, anticipated closing date, and essential terms of the final deal. It may also contain an exclusivity period during which the seller cannot accept any other proposals.

3. Asset purchase agreement

The asset purchase agreement is the final and legally binding agreement between you and the buyer. It clearly states the sale's terms. As such, it is the most significant legal document engaged in the transaction process.

While the letter of intent establishes the broad parameters of the agreement, these terms may vary as a consequence of information revealed during due diligence. As a result, the asset acquisition agreement is often created and executed during due diligence.

However, the buyer and seller may agree to draft an interim asset acquisition agreement prior to due investigation and then make any required revisions once due diligence is completed.

4. Promissory note

A promissory note is used when the seller is financing the transaction. The promissory note establishes the terms and conditions of the financing system. This covers the amount to be paid, payment schedule, interest rate, and default consequences of the transaction. Promissory notes are utilized with seller financing; therefore, not all transactions require them.

5. Asset allocation agreement

When you sell your business, all of the assets are classed as capital or noncapital. In addition, each asset is given a value. The asset allocation agreement specifies the value and categorization.

As we shall see in the next section, the value and classification of assets included in the sale have a substantial influence on your post-sale tax liabilities. For this reason, it is critical to collaborate with an accountant while developing the asset allocation agreement. This will assist to ensure that the agreement is properly drafted. It will also assist you in understanding what you might expect in terms of your tax liability as a consequence of the sale.

6. Non-compete agreement

Many corporate deals include a non-compete clause. This agreement merely states that you, as the seller, are not permitted to establish a business or engage in any activity that would directly compete with the new owner.

The specific actions that you may and cannot do in order to compete with the new owner will be determined by the conclusion of talks with the buyer.

7. Bill of Sale

After the final agreement has been prepared and all funds and assets have been transferred, you and the buyer will prepare and sign a bill of sale. The bill of sale confirms that all funds and assets have been transferred and received by both parties. It is intended to prevent future accusations that one party did not completely deliver or transfer the agreed-upon assets or funds.

Financial Considerations

There are several financial factors, including personal finances and post-sale taxes. These are crucial factors to consider while selecting the best selection.

1. Income taxes versus capital gains taxes

When you sell your business, you will be required to pay income taxes, capital gains taxes, or both. The breakdown of your company sales income will determine the specific allocation of income taxes vs. capital gains taxes.

As previously stated, the assets you include in the transaction will be classed as capital or noncapital assets. Any income, or capital gain, derived from the sale of capital assets is subject to capital gains tax. Income earned from the sale of noncapital assets is taxed as ordinary income.

This is relevant since the capital gains tax brackets range dramatically from the income tax brackets. The capital gains tax rate is now significantly lower than the standard income tax rate. Income tax rates currently vary from 10% on the low end to 37% on the high end. The capital gains tax rate ranges from 0 to 20 percent.

As a result, as the seller, it is in your best interests to have as many of your assets as possible classed and sold as capital assets. However, while forming an asset allocation agreement, you must always follow IRS guidelines.

2. Exit timing and taxes

The timing at which you sell your firm can potentially affect your tax liability. Suppose you sell during a year when your company incurs considerable expenditures or losses. In that case, the profits from the sale may be reduced. This can help to minimize your overall taxable income, resulting in a reduced tax rate and amount.

However, this method has several downsides. Selling during a difficult year might have a detrimental influence on your business's worth. As a result, you must determine if the possible tax savings outweigh the potential reduction in business value and sale price.

3. Personal finances

Aside from taxes, you also need to evaluate how your personal financial condition would change if you sell your business. If you were earning a monthly or yearly income from your business, consider how you will manage your budget without it.

Depending on the worth of your firm at the time of sale, you may get a large sum of money. Knowing what you intend to do with this ahead of time will help you transition smoothly into your post-sale life.

Considerations When Hiring Legal Assistance to Sell Your Business

Many business owners worry if they need to seek legal guidance when selling their company and if so, what type of aid they should get.

Hiring a business broker or advisor to help with the leaving process is frequently a good idea. Your advisor, like a real estate agent when selling a home, will assist you in navigating each stage of the selling process. This involves getting your firm ready for the market, locating appropriate buyers, negotiating terms, and finalizing the purchase. They can also guide you through the different legal and financial aspects associated with the procedure.

A competent advisor is also a valuation expert. They may assist you in developing an accurate and detailed assessment of your firm prior to listing. They may also assist you in learning how to maximize your business so that you can obtain top dollar.

If you decide to engage the services of a business advisor, you must compensate them. This is frequently structured as a tiny portion of the profits from the sale of the business. While this adds expense to the transaction, a skilled Advisor should more than cover their fee by assisting you in achieving a better sale price and more advantageous contract conditions.

Your advisor can also advise you on whether or not you need to employ additional legal counsel during the process. If you do, they will be able to determine if a particular candidate is qualified for the position and whether the accompanying legal fees are affordable.

The Emotional Side of Exiting

When it comes to selling your business, it's tempting to get caught up in the numbers, but keep in mind that they only tell one side of the story. Both purchasing and selling a business have major psychological and emotional consequences.

Dealing With Mixed Emotions

Sellers who are not emotionally prepared may unintentionally disrupt the sales process. Typically, sellers have put a lot of time and effort into their firm, and as a result, they may not be completely ready to sell. Before you put your business up for sale, take a moment to consider whether you are really committed.

Let's look at some questions you should ask yourself to determine whether you're actually ready to sell. These questions can also help you deal with the emotions that may arrive after the sale.

Do You Have Future Plans?

Your long-term ambitions are at the top of the list of emotional issues to consider while selling. If you don't know what you want to do with your business once you sell it, you may face issues.

Far too frequently, business owners find themselves at a loss for what to do after a sale. All of the mental and emotional energy invested into running a business must be redirected after it is sold. Before exiting your business, be sure you have something fresh and fascinating to focus on in the future.

Do you have a strong support network?

A second emotional consideration before selling your firm is whether it would result in social isolation and stress. It is typical for company owners to build long-term connections and ties with their staff.

Business owners frequently develop feelings of extended family toward their personnel. Suddenly, not working with that extended family might result in a surprising amount of social isolation.

It is not unusual for business owners to meet many of their social demands while working. When such connections fail, many company owners may feel lonely, which can lead to stress and regret. It is advisable to ensure that your social network is strong enough so that selling your business does not cause unforeseen mental and emotional hardship.

Selling a business is a major choice for most business owners. It is a sensible idea to ensure that you truly want to sell. Once your firm has been sold, there is no going back.

The last thing any business owner wants is to sell their company only to later regret the choice. Don't just think about the money you'll make when you sell your firm; think about how it will affect your life and future happiness as well.

Transitioning to the Next Chapter

Starting the process of selling your business may be an emotional rollercoaster. Whether you spent years nurturing it or it was a recent project, letting go of something you created from the ground up can elicit feelings of exhilaration, anxiety, and even sorrow. Retirement adds a whole new level of complication. In fact, one-third of retirees in the United States have symptoms of sadness at this age, which emphasizes the need to plan for your next stage of life.

As one chapter closes, another begins, full of limitless potential for personal and professional development. Let's look at the actions you may take to carefully negotiate this change and set off on a new road full of purpose and fulfillment.

1. Be open to change

When you sell your business, it's a big change in your life. You might feel different emotions like relief, excitement, or even some sadness. It's normal to feel this way because your business is a big part of your daily life. Embracing change means accepting that your life is going to be different now and being open to new experiences and opportunities that come your way.

One way to embrace change is to stay positive. This means looking at the good things that can come from selling your business. For example, you might have more free time to spend with your family or pursue hobbies you didn't have time for before. Keeping a positive attitude can help you see the possibilities instead of focusing on what you might miss from your old business.

Another way to embrace change is to stay flexible. This means being willing to try new things and adapt to different situations. For instance, if you used to work long hours running your business, you might now have to adjust to a different daily routine. Being flexible allows you to find new routines that work for you in this new phase of your life.

2. Define what you want to achieve post-sale

When you think about setting goals post-sale, start by envisioning what you want your life to look like. Consider both short-term and long-term aspirations. Short-term goals could include taking a few months off to travel or spend time with family, while long-term goals might involve starting a new business, pursuing further education, or retiring comfortably.

For example, imagine you've sold your successful bakery business. Your short-term goal might be to take a six-month break to recharge and explore new hobbies like gardening or photography. Meanwhile, your long-term goal could be to invest in a small coffee shop franchise or to start a consulting business to help other aspiring entrepreneurs.

To break down these goals into actionable steps, start by listing specific tasks or milestones you need to achieve. Suppose you're considering investing in a coffee shop franchise. In that case, your tasks might include researching franchise opportunities, attending franchise expos, and meeting with financial advisors to assess your investment options.

It's also essential to make your goals measurable and realistic. For instance, if your goal is to start a consulting business, set specific targets like acquiring your first three clients within the first six months. This makes it easier to track your progress and adjust your plans accordingly.

Lastly, revisit and revise your goals periodically as your priorities and circumstances change. Life after selling your business can bring unexpected opportunities and challenges, so staying flexible with your goals allows you to adapt and make the most of new experiences.

3. Assess your financial situation post-sale

After you sell your business, you'll receive a significant sum of money from the sale. The first step in financial planning is to understand exactly how much money you have received after any taxes or fees are deducted. This amount will be your starting point for planning your future finances.

Next, it's important to think about what you want to do with this money. You might want to use some of it to live comfortably and cover your expenses for the rest of your life. You might also want to invest some of it to make even more money over time.

To help you figure out how to use your money wisely, you might want to talk to a financial advisor. A financial advisor is a person who is an expert at helping people manage their money. They can help you create a plan for your money that matches your goals and makes the most of your financial situation.

One thing a financial advisor might help you with is creating a budget. A budget is a plan for how you will spend your money each month. It helps you make sure you have enough money for the things you need, like housing and food, as well as the things you want, like travel or hobbies.

Another thing a financial advisor might help you with is investing your money. Investing means putting your money into things that have the potential to make more money over time. This could include stocks, bonds, real estate, or starting a new business. A financial advisor can help you choose investments that match your goals and help you understand the risks and rewards of each option.

Also, a financial advisor can help you plan for the future. This might include things like saving for your children's education, planning for retirement so you can stop working when you want to or making sure you have enough money set aside for unexpected expenses.

4. Stay engaged and prioritize active involvement

This is important for a smooth transition to the next chapter of your life. First, staying engaged means spending less time alone and connecting with people or activities you love. It helps you maintain a sense of purpose and fulfillment. When you have activities that you enjoy and look forward to, whether it's volunteering, pursuing hobbies, or learning new skills, it keeps your mind active and focused on the present and future rather than dwelling on the past. This sense of purpose can also boost your self-esteem and overall well-being, reducing the risk of feeling lost or without direction after leaving your business.

Also, staying engaged helps you avoid falling into a cycle of over-thinking or dwelling on what could have been with your sold business. It provides a healthy distraction and channels your energy into positive endeavors. By staying active in your community, pursuing personal interests, or even exploring new career opportunities, you open your-self up to new experiences and possibilities. This proactive approach helps you adapt to the changes brought by selling your business and also allows you to build a new identity beyond your former role as a business owner.

5. Ensure to network and find support

You must understand that no one knows it all. Even with the wealth of experience you've or the plans you must have put in place to execute after selling your business, ideas from others who've gone through the stage can still be pivotal and beneficial.

Networking means connecting with people who can help you in your new phase of life. These people might include other entrepreneurs, professionals in your industry, or even friends and acquaintances who can offer advice or opportunities. Networking can open doors to new ventures, collaborations, or even job opportunities if you're considering working in a different field.

Consider attending industry events, joining online forums, or participating in local business groups. This can help you meet new people and expand your network. These connections can provide valuable insights, mentorship, or partnerships that may not only enrich your personal life but also open up new professional opportunities.

Another thing is to seek support. You can consider joining support groups or online communities of fellow entrepreneurs who have sold their businesses. It provides a sense of trust, friendship, and understanding during this unique phase of life.

6. Prioritize your health and well-being

Once you exit your business, you might get to have more time on your hands. It's important to use this time wisely to take care of physical and mental health. This includes getting regular exercise, eating a balanced diet, and getting enough sleep. Physical activity like walking, swimming, or yoga keeps your body healthy and also boosts your mood and energy levels.

Also, take time for relaxation and stress management techniques such as meditation or deep breathing. It will help you unwind and cope with any stress that may come with the transition.

REMEMBER: Your mental well-being is just as important as your physical health, so finding activities that bring you joy and peace of mind is crucial.

Why Exiting Can Be Beneficial

Exiting a business marks a pivotal moment in an entrepreneur's journey. It represents the culmination of years of dedication, strategic planning, and hard work. It's a decision that goes beyond financial gain, signaling a transition to new possibilities and opportunities. For many business owners, this step reflects a thoughtful consideration of their professional legacy and personal aspirations. It offers a chance to explore new ventures or simply enjoy the rewards of their achievements.

Let's look at the reward associated with the successful exit of your business.

1. Financial gain

Exiting a business can be a major financial milestone, offering significant benefits to the owner. When you sell your business, you typically receive a lump sum of money based on its value. This sum reflects not just the physical assets like equipment and inventory but also the goodwill and reputation you've built over time. For many entrepreneurs, this influx of capital is a result of years of hard work, dedication, and strategic decision-making. It can serve as a financial safety net, providing funds for retirement planning, investments in other ventures, or personal goals like buying a home or traveling.

2. Relief from stress and responsibility

Running a business is demanding, both physically and mentally. It often involves long hours, constant decision-making, and managing various challenges. Exiting your business can provide relief from these stresses and responsibilities. It allows you to regain control over your time and reduce the mental burden associated with business ownership. This can lead to improved overall well-being and a better work-life balance.

3. Opportunity for personal growth

Exiting a business opens up opportunities for personal growth and exploration. It gives you the chance to pursue other interests, hobbies, or personal goals that may have been neglected while you were focused on your business. Whether it's traveling, spending more time with family, or engaging in philanthropic activities, exiting your business can enrich your life in ways that extend beyond financial gain.

4. Time to pursue new ventures

For many entrepreneurs, exiting one business marks the beginning of another entrepreneurial journey. It provides the time, resources, and mental space to explore new business ideas or ventures that may have greater potential or align more closely with evolving personal or professional interests. This renewed sense of creativity and opportunity can be invigorating and lead to new successes in the future.

5. Legacy planning and succession

Exiting your business allows you to plan for its long-term legacy and succession. Whether passing it on to family members, selling to employees through an Employee Stock Ownership Plan (ESOP), or ensuring a smooth transition to new ownership, careful planning can preserve the business's values and impact even after you've moved on. It ensures that your hard work continues to benefit others and contributes to your legacy in the business community.

6. Adapting to market changes

Markets are constantly evolving, and what may have been a successful business model in the past could face challenges in the future. Exiting your business allows you to adapt to changing market conditions proactively. It gives you the opportunity to exit on your terms, potentially maximizing the business's value before market conditions deteriorate or competition intensifies.

7. Health and well-being

The stress of managing a business can take a toll on your physical and mental health. Exiting your business can lead to improved health and well-being by reducing stress levels, improving sleep patterns, and allowing you to focus on activities that promote overall wellness. Taking care of your health is essential for enjoying the fruits of your labor and maintaining a fulfilling life post-business.

Chapter 13
Conclusion

Now that you are at the end of this book, you can take some time to celebrate just how far you have come. Business creation and management is a milestone that is characterized by many opportunities and challenges. This guidebook has thus led us through each significant stage of your business from the conception of the business idea right up to the challenges of growth and possible exit.

In Chapter 1, you're introduced to the entrepreneurial process, identifying business opportunities, and the attitude that one has to have in order to succeed. You learned about the concept of opportunity and how to distinguish between good and bad ones, as well as how to validate market risks and rewards. We also discussed the mindset of an entrepreneur, innovation, and the ability to overcome failure.

Chapter 2 presented us with the guidebook itself, which describes in detail the general structure and how to use it. You understood how to converge and align your goals with an entrepreneurial mindset; this is besides understanding your priorities and how to manage your reading to enhance learning. The chapter also stressed the importance of interactive exercises, actionable tips, and real-world case studies to help you enhance your understanding.

In Chapter 3, we looked at the legal procedures of forming a business. You got to know about the types of business structures ranging from sole proprietorships to corporations and how to form an LLC. This chapter gave important information on how to get permits and licenses to make sure that the business being put up is legal.

The first three chapters of this book provide the legal and management framework for your business; chapter 4 provides the financial framework. You understood what business finance means, what budgeting entails, and what financial planning is. The chapter explained the relevance of the concept of cash flow and the necessity of proper management of small business accounting. This chapter also explained the basic concepts and principles of bookkeeping and financial statements that are vital in managing the financial aspect of a business.

Strategizing a business plan was the main focus of Chapter 5. You learned about the ten steps for creating the executive summary, company description, market analysis, competitive analysis, and organization structure. We also talked about the products or services to be provided, marketing and sales plans, the financial aspect of the business, the amount of capital needed, and the appendix for other necessary details.

In Chapter 6, we looked at marketing psychology. You understood what consumer behaviour is, the psychology of buying and the factors affecting the consumers' decision process. We looked at the various heuristics that are present in marketing and how one can use these to his advantage. The chapter also focused on building brand loyalty by establishing a strong brand identity and adding value to the customers' experiences to build an emotional bond.

Chapter 7 explains the seven steps you need to take in order to create a marketing strategy. You also learned what your target audience is, how to create marketing goals, how to conduct a competitive analysis, and how to craft your unique value proposition. We also reviewed choosing marketing channels, creating a content strategy, and executing, measuring, and optimizing your plan based on key performance indicators (KPIs).

In Chapter 8, we discussed operations and management. You learnt how to organize the workspace, control the procurement and storage of materials, staff management and customer service. We also talked about some tips on time management and productivity to assist you in managing your business.

Chapter 9 was devoted to scaling your business. We discussed the steps to identify growth prospects, strategies for expansion, and ways to handle more work and higher responsibility levels. This chapter also brought into view the aspects of scaling operations bearing in mind the quality of service provided as well as the satisfaction of the customers.

Chapter 10 was on legal and regulatory compliance. You learned the basics of business laws and regulations, the compliance requirements for small businesses, and the ways of protecting the company's intellectual property. We also highlighted the aspect of contracts and agreements in protecting your business.

In Chapter 11, we were introduced to troubleshooting and problem-solving. You understood such things as typical problems of startups, how to avoid them or at least minimize their impact, and how to deal with financial and legal issues that may arise during your entrepreneurial journey.

Chapter 12 focused on exiting your business, which covered areas such as the concept of exit strategies, planning for the exit and preparing your business for sale. This chapter covered the legal and financial aspects of exiting a business and the emotional aspect of the transition.

Celebrating Achievements and Learnings

Your journey as a business owner is full of accomplishments whether it is a minor or major accomplishment. It is always good to remember such milestones you have covered since they are tangible things that you would have achieved by dint of hard work, dedication and perseverance. Every win, every victory in business from the start of your business, the attainment of the first client or the achievement of the first dollar, demonstrates your competency and your effort.

In addition, there are lessons learned throughout the journey. No one wants to fail, but this is something that happens a lot when one is an entrepreneur, and that is why it is said that successful entrepreneurship is made of as many failures as it is made of success. Every difficulty provides lessons on how to adapt, innovate, and grow. Whether it's a financial downturn, having to be more organized with time or legal hurdles, the experience provides lessons on how to handle future challenges.

Looking Ahead: Lessons for Future Endeavors

Looking into the future, you should not leave this entrepreneurial experience and knowledge and skills learned behind. Here are some key takeaways to keep in mind for your ongoing and future endeavors:

1. Continuous learning and adaptation. The dynamics of business are such that they are constantly in a state of evolution. At all times, remain interested in learning and always be prepared to make changes in the way you conduct your strategies.
2. Resilience and perseverance. Failure and difficulties are inevitable. Cultivate resilience to endure adversities and not to be stopped by them.
3. Innovation and creativity. Generate an innovative culture. Endeavour to identify better ways of doing things even after the business becomes well-established.
4. Customer focus. The customers are the backbone of your business. Always look out for customers, establish good relations with them, and make sure to go the extra mile and meet all their requirements.

5. Effective management. Good management is vital for sustaining the business and for expanding it from one level to another. Focus on efficient operations, timely and quality financial management, and effective team leadership.

6. Networking and mentorship. Build a supportive network of people, including those persons who are experienced in business, those who have business advice to offer and those who are themselves involved in the business, as it will help you to overcome day-to-day challenges. Be it effective suggestions that can enhance the project or the help which may be required for the successful completion of the project, they can provide all.

7. Strategic planning. Whether the scenario is planning for growth, managing adversity, strategizing today or thinking about the future exit strategy, it is recommended to have a strategic goal or plan.

8. Work-Life balance. Create equilibrium between working and having other responsibilities for the long-term sustainability both at the workplace and in terms of personal health. Have time to rest and for the mind to be at ease.

Thank you for taking the time to read my book on creating a small business! Now here is my ask to you.

If you found it helpful or inspiring, **I would greatly appreciate it if you could leave a review.**

Your feedback not only helps other readers discover the book but also supports my work in providing valuable content.

If you are looking for a great, scalable business to start, I highly recommend checking out my book on **how you can quickly build a vending machine business from the ground up.**

Once again, thank you for reading!

- David Whitehead

Appendices

Sample Exit Strategy Template

Section	Details
1. Executive Summary	
Business Name	XYZ Tech Solutions
Owner(s)	Jane Doe and John Smith
Established	2014
Industry	Technology Services
Location	San Francisco, CA
Overview	XYZ Tech Solutions has been a leading provider of innovative tech solutions, specializing in custom software development, IT consulting, and cybersecurity services. The company has experienced significant growth over the past decade and is now looking to explore exit strategies to maximize value for its shareholders.

Section	Details
2. Exit Objectives	
Personal Objectives	Jane Doe: Transition to consulting and mentorship.
	John Smith: Retire and focus on personal interests and philanthropy.
Business Objectives	1. Ensure a smooth ownership transition 2. Maximize the financial return for shareholders. 3. Preserve the company's culture and legacy 4. Secure the future of employees and maintain client relationships.

3. Valuation of the Business

Methods Used	1. Discounted Cash Flow (DCF) Analysis 2. Comparable Company Analysis 3. Precedent Transactions
Current Valuation	1. DCF Valuation: $25 million 2. Comparable Company Analysis: $22 million 3. Precedent Transactions: $24 million

4. Exit Options

Option 1: Sell to a Strategic Buyer	• **Target Buyers:** Larger tech firms seeking to expand their service offerings. • **Pros:** Potentially higher purchase price, resources for growth. • **Cons:** Possible cultural changes and integration challenges.
Option 2: Sell to a Financial Buyer (Private Equity)	• **Pros:** Expertise in scaling businesses, potential for future growth. • **Cons:** May prioritize financial returns over company culture.
Option 3: Management Buyout (MBO)	• **Pros:** Continuity of management, smoother transition. • **Cons:** Financing challenges, potential for internal conflict.
Option 4: Initial Public Offering (IPO)	• Pros: Access to capital increased visibility. • Cons: High costs, regulatory requirements, market volatility.

5. Preparing for Exit

Financial Preparation	• Audited financial statements for the past three years. • Detailed financial projections for the next five years. • Assessment of current liabilities and potential future obligations.
Operational Preparation	• Streamline operations to increase efficiency. • Document key processes and systems. • Secure key client contracts and long-term agreements.
Legal Preparation	• Review and update all legal documents, including contracts, leases, and intellectual property. • Ensure compliance with all regulatory requirements. • Resolve any pending legal issues.

6. Communication Plan

Internal Communication	<ul><li>Inform key management and employees about the exit strategy.</li><li>Provide regular updates and address concerns.</li><li>Offer retention bonuses or incentives to retain key staff during the transition.</li></ul>
External Communication	<ul><li>Notify key clients and partners.</li><li>Develop a press release and media strategy.</li><li>Address customer concerns and ensure service continuity.</li></ul>

7. Implementation Timeline

Year 1	<ul><li>Q1: Finalize valuation and choose the preferred exit option.</li><li>Q2: Prepare financial, operational, and legal documents.</li><li>Q3: Begin confidential discussions with potential buyers or investors.</li><li>Q4: Negotiate terms and finalize agreements.</li></ul>
Year 2	<ul><li>Q1: Announce the transaction and begin the transition process.</li><li>Q2: Complete the transfer of ownership.</li><li>Q3-Q4: Support new owners and ensure a smooth transition.</li></ul>

8. Post-Exit Plan

For Owners	<ul><li>Jane Doe: Start a consulting business and engage in speaking opportunities.</li><li>John Smith: Retire and establish a charitable foundation.</li></ul>
For the Business	<ul><li>Continue monitoring business performance.</li><li>Provide ongoing support to new owners as needed.</li><li>Maintain relationships with key clients and stakeholders.</li></ul>

Additional Resources and References

"5 Steps to Start Your Own Business." U.S. Small Business Administration, 2023, www.sba.gov/business-guide/10-steps-start-your-business

"A Beginner's Guide to Starting a Business." Entrepreneur, 2023, www.entrepreneur.com/article/297899.

"How to Start a Business in 10 Easy Steps." NerdWallet, 2023, www.nerdwallet.com/article/small-business/how-to-start-a-business.

Aaron, M. (2016). Business Startup Guide: How to Write a Business Plan. Aaron Mullins.

Aaron, M. (2016). The Ultimate Business Plan Template. Aaron Mullins.

Abrams, R. (2015). Six-Week Start-Up: A Step-by-Step Program for Starting Your Business. Planning Shop.

Alvin, A. (2019). Mastering Digital Marketing for Starters: The Best Methods, Tricks And Steps for Successful Digital Marketing. Partridge Publishing Singapore.

Ann, C. (2013). Writing Winning Business Plans. Aauvi House Publishing Group.

Arthur, L. (2020). Business Plan Handbook: Practical guide to create a business plan. BoD - Books on Demand.

Aulet, B. (2013). Disciplined Entrepreneurship: 24 Steps to a Successful Startup. John Wiley & Sons.

Barker, Eric. "How to Start a Business in 2023: The Ultimate Guide." Shopify, 2023, www.shopify.com/blog/how-to-start-a-business.

Barrow, C. (2016). Starting a Business for Dummies. John Wiley & Sons.

Blank, S., & Dorf, B. (2012). The Startup Owner's Manual: The Step-By-Step Guide for Building a Great Company. K&S Ranch.

Brian, H. (2013). The Pocket Small Business Owner's Guide to Business Plans. Allworth.

Brian, T. (2019). Entrepreneurship: How to Start and Grow Your Own Business. G&D Media.

Cherry, Kendra. "How Emotions Influence What We Buy." Verywell Mind, 2023, www.verywellmind.com/how-emotions-influence-what-we-buy-2795170.

Craig, A. (2011). First Small Business Cash Flow Workbook. Craig Alexander Orr, MBA, MSc, HND.

Craig, A. (2011). Improving Corporate Cash Flow. Craig Alexander Orr, MBA, MSc, HND.

Darlington, G. (2022). How To Start A Business. Dgatsi Derek, G. (2020). Entrepreneur Dreams: Start Your Own Business. DGone Publishing.

Eric, T. (2019). Small Business Taxes For Dummies. Wiley.

Erickson, K. (2018). Corporate Finance: A Simple Introduction. K.H. Erickson.

Additional Resources and References

Eva, R. (2020). Small Business Taxes Made Easy, Fourth Edition. McGraw-Hill Education.

Gary, S. (2018). The Forty Plus Entrepreneur: How to Start a Successful Business in Your 40's, 50's, and Beyond: How to Start a Successful Business in Your 40's, 50's, and Beyond. G&D Media.

Georgia, M. (2023). HOW TO START A BUSINESS: How to Turn Your Ideas into a Successful Venture (2023 Guide for Beginners). Georgia Miles.

Gerardus, B. (2020). Cash Flow A Complete Guide - 2020 Edition. 5STARCooks.

Gerber, M. (1995). The E-Myth Revisited: Why Most Small Businesses Don't Work and What to Do About It. HarperCollins.

Guillebeau, C. (2012). The $100 Startup: Reinvent the Way You Make a Living, Do What You Love, and Create a New Future. Crown Business.

Hugh, C. (2020). How to Start a Business: Starting a Business, Learn Entrepreneurship Skills and Understand What It Means to Start and Develop a Business. Hugh Covey.

James, B. (2021). Starting a Small Business. Anne Bradshaw.

Janet, A. (2018). Business Plan: The Basics. Personal Growth.

Jim, P. (2012). How to Develop a Business Plan. Dr Jim Porter.

John, A. (2011). Cash Flow For Dummies. Wiley.

John, D. (2015). How to Start a Business: Developing Products and Selling Them Online. Mendon Cottage Books.

John, M. (2013). The One-Hour Business Plan: The Simple and Practical Way to Start Anything New. Wiley.

John, N. (2015). Starting A Small Business. Shaharm Publications.

John, S. (2021). Business Plan Basics. John Shenton.

Ken, C. (2019). Starting a Business QuickStart Guide: The Simplified Beginner's Guide to Launching a Successful Small Business, Turning Your Vision into Reality, and Achieving Your Entrepreneurial Dream. ClydeBank Media LLC.

Lee, Nathan. "Setting SMART Goals for Marketing." HubSpot, 2023, blog.hubspot.com/marketing/smart-goals.

Lee, Nathan. "Starting a Business: The Ultimate Checklist." HubSpot, 2023, blog.hubspot.com/marketing/how-to-start-a-business.

Linda, P. (2013). Anatomy of a Business Plan: The Step-by-Step Guide to Building a Business and Securing Your Company's Future. Out Of Your Mind And Into The Mark.

McCarthy, John. "How to Start a Business with No Money." The Motley Fool, 2023, www.fool.com/the-blueprint/start-a-business/.

Mads, F. (2018). Entrepreneur: Building Your Business From Start to Success. Wiley.

Manuel, T. (2015). How to Write a Business Plan: Step by Step guide. Mendon Cottage Books.

Mark, S. (2018). Taxes for Small Business: Step-by-Step Guide to Small Business Taxes Tips Including Tax Laws, LLC Taxes, Sole Proprietorship and Payroll Taxes. Mark Williams.

McKeever, M. (2018). How to Write a Business Plan. Nolo.

Additional Resources and References

Mullins, J. (2013). The New Business Road Test: What Entrepreneurs and Executives Should Do Before Writing a Business Plan. FT Press.

Martin, M. (2016). Self-Discipline for Entrepreneurs: How to Develop and Maintain Self-Discipline as an Entrepreneur. Meadows Publishing.

Mary, E. (2013). Guide to Starting a Business. AuthorHouse.

Matthew, C. (2020). Personal Finance for Beginners - A Simple Guide to Take Control of Your Financial Situation. Matthew Collins.

Matthew, N. (2012). How to Start Your Own Business in 10 Days. Matthew Needham.

Michael, B. (2013). Be the Boss: How to Start a New Business, How to Buy an Existing Business, How to Purchase a Franchise! AuthorHouse.

Michael, K. (2017). How to Start a Business for Beginners: A Complete Guide to Building a Successful & Profitable Business. justhappyforever.com.

Michael, T. (2012). Corporate Finance For Dummies. Wiley.

Nicholas, R. (2022). How to Start a Business 2023: Step-by-Step Beginners Blueprint to Plan and Launch your first successful LLC, Sole Proprietorship, and Startup, including Groundbreaking Strategies for Lowering Taxes. Nicholas Regan.

Nicholas, R. (2022). Taxes for Small Businesses 2023: Beginners Guide to Understanding LLC, Sole Proprietorship, and Startup Taxes. Cutting Edge Strategies Explained to Lower Your Taxes Legally for Business, Investing. Nicholas Regan.

Nkem, M. (2015). The Entrepreneur: A Lean Startup Culture for Smart Entrepreneurs to Build a Sustainable Business. Nkem Mpamah.

Oral, B. (2015). How to prepare a business plan: Entrepreneurship and Small Business. Shefflorn.

Osterwalder, A., & Pigneur, Y. (2010). Business Model Generation: A Handbook for Visionaries, Game Changers, and Challengers. John Wiley & Sons.

Patel, Neil. "Creating Buyer Personas: The Complete Guide." Neil Patel Blog, 2023, neilpatel.com/blog/creating-buyer-personas.

Patel, Neil. "How Cognitive Biases Impact Your Marketing." Neil Patel Blog, 2023, neilpatel.com/blog/cognitive-biases-marketing.

Peter, A. (2020). The Ultimate Guide To Cash Flow Management. Peter Adams.

Ries, E. (2011). The Lean Startup: How Today's Entrepreneurs Use Continuous Innovation to Create Radically Successful Businesses. Crown Business.

Robert, W. (2016). Business Law. Barrons Educational Services.

Robin, B. (2010). Start-up Smart: How to start and build a successful business on a budget. Harriman House.

Rose, H. Business for Beginners. Usborne Publishing Ltd.

Stuart, W. (2010). Finance Basics. HarperCollins UK.

Sutton, G. (2012). Start Your Own Corporation: Why the Rich Own Their Own Companies and Everyone Else Works for Them. RDA Press.

Timmons, J., & Spinelli, S. (2008). New Venture Creation: Entrepreneurship for the 21st Century. McGraw-Hill Education.

Vaynerchuk, G. (2018). Crushing It!: How Great Entrepreneurs Build Their Business and Influence—and How You Can, Too. Harper Business.

Veechi, C. (2014). Creating a Business Plan For Dummies. Wiley.

Additional Resources and References

Vindimear, D. (2015). 101 Entrepreneur Mindset. Vindimear D Heart.

Wade, A. (2023). How To Start A Business - Step By Step Guide To Turn Your Idea Into A Thriving Startup. Royce Publishing.

Weinberg, G., & Mares, J. (2015). Traction: How Any Startup Can Achieve Explosive Customer Growth. Portfolio.

Zook, C., & Allen, J. (2016). The Founder's Mentality: How to Overcome the Predictable Crises of Growth. Harvard Business Review Press.

Glossary of Business Terms

Someone new to the business world may find it challenging to understand the many phrases and terminology used in the field. The purpose of this extensive glossary is to provide definitions and explanations of terms and expressions used often in business contexts. It will help you feel more capable of handling the challenges that come with being a business owner.

A

Asset

Anything owned by a company that has value and can be used to generate future economic benefits.

Accounts Payable

Amount due to a firm to supplier or vendor for products and services acquired through credit.

Accounts Receivable

The amount of credit that consumers and businesses have accepted to pay to another firm for products rendered or goods purchased in the course of business.

Amortization

The act of writing off the expensing of an intangible asset over its useful life as defined by the company.

Annual Report

An official statement containing accounts of a company's achievement of its business objectives in the financial year ends.

Acquisition

When one company purchases another company's assets or shares to gain control over its operations.

Angel Investor

An individual who provides financial backing to startups or small businesses in exchange for ownership equity or convertible debt.

A/B Testing

A method of comparing two versions of a webpage, email, or other marketing asset to determine which one performs better.

Audit

A systematic review or examination of a company's financial statements, processes, or compliance with regulations.

Assets Under Management (AUM)

The total market value of assets that a financial institution manages on behalf of its clients.

Annual General Meeting (AGM)

A mandatory yearly meeting of shareholders and directors where company performance is reviewed, and important decisions are made.

Accounts

The financial records of a company's transactions, including revenues, expenses, assets, and liabilities.

Accrual Basis

A method of accounting where revenues and expenses are recorded when they are earned or incurred, regardless of when cash transactions occur.

Anti-Dilution Clause

A provision in an investment agreement that protects investors from dilution of their ownership stake if new shares are issued at a lower valuation.

Agent

A person or an organization is given permission to act on behalf of another person, most often in business transactions.

Asset Allocation

Investing money in a range of securities such as equities, fixed-income securities, and cash instruments so as to get an optimal risk return.

Absenteeism

The act of workers not showing up for work eventually costs the company money because they aren't working.

Absorption Costing

A way to figure out how much something costs that takes into account all of its costs, both direct and indirect.

Automated Clearing House (ACH)

It is an electronic network used for banking in the US, like for direct transfers and paying bills.

After-Tax Profit

The amount of money a business has left over after all taxes are taken out.

B

Backward Integration

When a company expands its operations to include activities that are upstream in its supply chain.

Balance Sheet

A financial statement that summarizes a company's assets, liabilities, and shareholders' equity at a specific point in time.

Banker's Draft

A check drawn by a bank on its own funds in exchange for cash, typically used for large transactions where security is important.

Bankruptcy

A formal state in which a person or business can't pay its bills, which leads to the process of reorganization or liquidation.

Base Rate

The lowest rate of interest that a central bank sets and that other banks use to set their own rates.

Bear Market

This is a kind of financial market with declining price trends and a pessimistic outlook among the buyers.

Benefit-Cost Analysis

A technique applied to determine whether the values of undertaking a given project or undertaking an activity are worth the cost of disadvantages.

Benchmarking

Benchmarking involves the evaluation of your firm's practices and accomplishments in relation to the most effective players in your industry or competitors.

Bid-offer Spread

The difference between how much someone wants to buy an asset (bid) and how much they want to sell it (offer).

Black Swan

A negative event can happen at any time and has bad effects that are hard to guess using normal predicting methods.

Blue Chip

A well-known, financially stable company with a good name for quality and dependability. This term is often used to refer to large-cap stocks.

Bootstrapping

Building or growing a company with little or no external capital or funding.

Brand Ambassador

A person hired by a company to represent its brand positively and increase brand awareness.

Brand Equity

The perceived value or strength of a brand, including customer loyalty and brand awareness.

Brand Extension

Putting out new goods or entering new areas with a well-known brand name.

Broker

A third party that helps buyers and sellers make deals, usually in the financial markets.

Budget

A statement that indicates the amount of money an individual or business expects to earn and the amount expected to be spent in a given period of time. It is used to plot and monitor items.

Buildings Insurance

People who own properties can take insurance for their houses that are threatened by fire, theft, natural disasters, and many more.

Bull Market

A type of financial market where prices are going up, and buyers are feeling good about the future.

Business Continuity Plan (BCP)

A plan that spells out the steps and rules that must be followed to keep a business running during and after problems like natural disasters or cyberattacks.

Business Cycle

Some of the repetitive cycles of activity are characterized by the process of growth and diminution, for instance, growth and decline.

Business Intelligence (BI)

Techniques for collecting, storing, processing, and visualizing business information with the help of various tools, software, and approaches.

Business Model

A strategic approach in which a business venture operates in order to turn dollars and provide value to people.

Business Plan

A text document that details the aim or goals of a venture, strategies and the anticipated revenues or earnings it will generate.

Business Process Outsourcing (BPO)

The act of contracting another party for the performance of some business tasks or activities that are within the internal capabilities of the organization.

Burn Rate

The speed with which a business uses up its cash or capital within a specified period of time; this term is mainly applied in businesses that are new.

Buy-out

The purchase of a controlling interest in a company, often by its management team or an external investor.

Buy-to-let Mortgage

A mortgage loan specifically for purchasing property to be rented out to tenants rather than for personal occupancy.

Blue Ocean Strategy

A business theory that suggests companies achieve success by creating new demand in uncontested market spaces.

Bond

A debt security that governments or businesses issue to raise money. Bondholders usually get interest payments on a regular basis.

Broker

A third party that helps buyers and sellers make deals, usually in the financial markets.

Buildings Insurance

Insurance coverage that protects property owners against building damage, often including dangers such as fire, theft, and natural catastrophe.

Budget

An organized statement that outlines the expected earnings and expenses in a given financial period.

Bridging Loan

This is a limited funding requirement that is used in the short term, where the borrower needs money for a short period. Such loan is often used in the actual estate transactions organization.

C

Cash Flow

The movement of money into and out of a business, showing how much cash is available at any given time.

Capital

Money or assets used to start or grow a business.

Capital Expenditure

Money spent by a company to acquire or improve fixed assets, like buildings or equipment.

CEO (Chief Executive Officer)

The company decision-maker and chief executive responsible for the overall management of the company.

Cost of Goods Sold (COGS)

A corporation's cost directly associated with creating products for sale on its balance sheet, for example, costs of materials and wages for the employees.

Customer Relationship Management (CRM)

Tools and policies to assist a company in ensuring it has proper records of current and potential clients.

Competitive Advantage

Something that makes the goods or services of a business more appealing than those of its rivals.

Credit Score

A number that shows how creditworthy a person or business is based on their credit history.

Collateral

Things that a borrower puts up as a guarantee for a loan, so the lender can take them back if the borrower doesn't pay back the loan.

Cash Flow Statement

A financial report that shows how much money came into and went out of a business over a certain time period.

Corporate Governance

The set of rules, habits, and procedures that a business uses to run and be guided.

Contract

A legally binding deal between two or more people that spells out their duties and rules.

Consumer Price Index (CPI)

A way to look at how much prices have changed over time for things and services that people buy.

Capacity Utilization

A measure of the competency exhibited by a firm in translating input resources such as human capital and production machinery into tangible products or services.

Cash on Delivery (COD)

An approach to purchasing whereby the amounts are paid at the time of receiving the commodities and services respectively.

Cost Benefit Analysis

Evaluating the potential benefits and costs of a decision, project, or policy to determine its feasibility or profitability.

Corporate Social Responsibility (CSR)

A company's commitment to operating in an economically, socially, and environmentally sustainable manner.

Credit Rating

An assessment of a borrower's creditworthiness based on their financial history and ability to repay debts.

Customer Retention

The ability of a company to keep its customers over time, often through good service and loyalty programs.

Convertible Bond

A type of bond that can be converted into shares of the issuer's common stock at a predetermined price or conversion ratio.

D

Debt

Money borrowed by a company or individual that must be repaid, usually with interest.

Debt Service Coverage Ratio (DSCR)

A financial ratio used by lenders to assess a company's ability to generate enough cash flow to cover its debt obligations.

Default

Defaulting, often on something that is a financial commitment, for example, failing to make payments on a loan or to honor the terms of a contract.

Demand

The ability and commitment of people to purchase goods or services at a particular time at a specific price.

Demand Curve

Graphic display of how much a product is being priced and how much people wish to consume the product in question.

Demand Forecasting

Trying to guess how much of a product or service will be needed in the future by looking at past data, market trends, and other factors.

Demand-pull Inflation

A type of inflation that happens when people want more things and services than are available, which causes prices to go up.

Dependent

In tax files, a dependent is someone who depends on another person, usually for financial assistance or benefits.

Depreciation

The slow loss of value that happens to things over time because of normal wear and tear or becoming outdated.

Direct Costs

Expenses directly attributable to producing goods or services, such as raw materials and labor.

Direct Marketing

Using direct mail or email to market and sell goods and services directly to customers without going through middlemen.

Diminishing Returns

In economics, this means that the application of more quantity of inputs say, labor or capital, results in small proportions of output.

Diversification

To reduce risk, putting money in a number of different securities, goods or markets or operating a number of different businesses.

Divestiture

When a company sells or gives away a business unit, division, or asset.

Dividend

A part of a company's profits is given to its owners, usually in the form of cash.

Dividend Yield

A number that tells you how much of a return on investment a company's stock has based on its current share price and the amount of dividends it pays out each year.

Downsizing

Getting rid of some employees to save money or make the company run more efficiently.

Due Diligence

An in-depth look or study is done before a business deal or agreement is made.

Discount Mortgage

A credit with a rate of interest that is lower than the going rate in the market. This is normally carried out with a view to extending its borrowing base which targets new borrowers.

Digital Marketing

The use of web and social networks, online banners, and other internet facilities to advertise products and services.

Discount Mortgage

An obligation on which a lower amount of interest than the market average has to be paid by the borrower. This is often carried out to win new clients in the market for borrowing money.

Diminishing Returns

This concept in economics indicates that the increase in more factors of production, be it man power or other resources, results in lesser incremental growth.

Demand-pull Inflation

Inflation that results from a persons' demand for goods and services being higher than the actual supply available in the market, leading to a rise in prices of such goods and services.

E

Early Adopter

A consumer who is one of the initial individuals to purchase and begin to use a good or innovative service.

E-commerce

The process of acquiring or offering goods and services through electronic systems such as cyberspace.

Economic Forecasting

The indication of future economic trends of occurrence of certain conditions originating from historical data and current parameters.

Economic Growth

This indicates a period of time when various goods and services are produced and consumed in the economy at large.

Economic Indicator

Relative stock prices and other economic fundamentals like GDP or unemployment rate give an understanding of a certain economy and its trend.

Economic Recession

This is a phase where businesses and consumers spend less money on goods, services and investments respectively.

Employee

A person contracted to work by a firm in return for pay or compensation.

Employee Benefits

Employees get non-wage compensation in addition to their normal income or salary, such as health insurance or retirement programs.

Enterprise Resource Planning (ERP)

ERP software enables firms to manage and connect fundamental functions like finance, HR, and supply chain.

Entrepreneur

An individual responsible for the formation of a business entity and the continuation of the business with the use of capital which is at risk with the intention of gaining returns.

Entrepreneurship

The creation and management of an enterprise that involves using ideas and exercise of various risks to gain profit.

Equilibrium

A state in which the demand for goods and services offered is equal to their supply in the economy.

Equity

Equity refers to ownership of a corporation via shares that entitle the holder to a percentage of its earnings.

Equity Financing

Raising funds for a firm by selling ownership shares (equity) to investors.

Ethics

Ethics refers to moral concepts that influence business decisions and conduct.

Exchange Rate

The exchange rate between currencies utilized in international commerce and investment.

Exchange Traded Fund (ETF)

ETFs are investment funds that trade on stock exchanges and own assets like stocks, commodities, or bonds.

Expense

The expenses spent by a firm in order to produce income.

Exit Strategy

A strategy for selling or liquidating an investment or company interest in order to achieve profits or reduce losses.

Expenditure

The total amount spent on products, services, or investments during a certain time period.

Ex-Dividend Date

The date after which shares purchased no longer include the right to receive the most recently announced dividend.

Externalities

Expenses or benefits resulting from a plan affecting third parties who are not involved in it.

Export

The action of marketing goods produced in one country to consumers in another.

Endorsement

A clearly recognizable character or powerful individual supporting a product or service.

Expansion

A stage of the business cycle marked by economic expansion, higher output, and increasing employment.

F

Factoring

To increase cash flow, sell accounts receivable (invoices) to a third party at a discounted price.

Fiduciary

A trustee or financial adviser is an example of someone or an organization that operates in the best interests of another.

Fixed Costs

Rent and salary are examples of fixed expenses that do not change with output or sales levels.

Franchise

A business model in which a franchisee (person) purchases the right to utilize the parent company's logo and business strategy.

Freelancer

A person who works for themselves and who may offer distinct services to customers within a contractual tone where the service provider can be involved with a number of projects for different clients.

Financial Statement

An official document that contains the financial actions of a company is the balance sheet, the income statement, and the statement of cash flows.

Fixed Assets

Buildings, machinery, and equipment are examples of long-term physical assets owned by a firm and used in its activities.

Fundamental Analysis

Evaluating a company's financial health and performance using metrics such as profits, assets, and market position.

Frictional Unemployment

Workers experience temporary unemployment as they shift between jobs or careers.

Foreign Exchange (Forex)

The currency market which facilitates international commerce and investment.

Fair Market Value

The price at which a property or item would sell in a competitive market, calculated using supply and demand.

Fiscal Year

A 12-month term used by a firm or government for accounting and financial reporting, which does not have to begin on January 1.

Fixed Income

Bonds and some forms of preferred stock are examples of fixed-interest or dividend-paying investments.

Free Cash Flow

The amount of cash available for distribution to shareholders after deducting expenditures, taxes, and fixed asset investments.

Float

The number of shares of a company's stock that are publicly owned and traded.

Fair Value

The projected value of a company's assets and liabilities based on current market pricing.

Forward Contract

An agreement to acquire or sell an item at a defined price on a future date.

Financial Risk

The risk of financial loss or a negative influence on a company's cash flow or profitability.

Fixed Exchange Rate

An arrangement that exists where the value of the domestic currency is pegged, directly or otherwise, to another country's currency or a pool of currencies.

Free Trade

The act or system by which an agreement is made that allows the import and export of goods and services without trade tariffs.

Frictional Costs

Costs that are incurred in acquiring or disposing of securities or other assets, like commissions or other costs incurred at a marketplace.

Financial Leverage

The act of raising the potential payoff on an investment by adding money that is borrowed.

Forecasting

Prognosis or prediction of the respective trends, occurrences, or outcomes starting with the historical and current statistical records.

G

Gatekeeper

An individual or organization that has the authority to grant or deny rights to other individuals or companies to acquire certain assets, information or chances in an organization or certain market.

Global Market

The global system of buyers, sellers, and sources of financing working together in the processes of trade and investment.

Globalization

Globalization refers to the harmonization and interaction of the global systems of economics, business, cultures and societies.

Golden Rule

One of the fundamental rules of ethical behavior in business, which can be described as the golden rule, do unto others as you would like done unto you.

Golden Share

A type of share with special voting rights that can block certain changes to a company's structure or operations.

Goodwill

The value of the business not directly linked to the tangible resources that exist in the enterprise, which include such aspects as reputation, customer loyalty, etc.

Governance

The authoritative framework within which an organization is managed.

Grant

Grants are money that states, foundations, or other groups give to support certain projects or efforts.

Greenfield Investment

Direct investment in a new facility or operation in a foreign country, typically involving construction from the ground up.

Ground Rent

Payment made by a leaseholder to the freeholder for the use of land or property.

Gross Domestic Product (GDP)

The total monetary value of all goods and services produced within a country's borders in a specific time period.

Gross Margin

The percentage of revenue that exceeds the cost of goods sold, indicating a company's profitability.

Gross National Product (GNP)

The total value of all goods and services produced by a country's residents, regardless of where they are located, in a specific period.

Gross Profit

The total revenue minus the cost of goods sold, representing the profit before deducting operating expenses.

Growth Rate

The rate at which a company's sales, earnings, or other metrics are increasing over time.

Guaranteed Annuity Rate

A minimum rate of income provided by an annuity, typically higher than prevailing rates at the time of purchase.

Guarantor

A person or entity legally responsible for fulfilling another party's debt obligation if the debtor fails to pay.

H

Half Year

It usually means six months and is used in business reports to show results or success over that time.

Hedge Fund

A type of investment vehicle that pools money from qualified people or big buyers to buy a wide range of assets.

Horizontal Integration

The acquisition or merger of companies that operate at the same stage of the production chain or provide similar goods and services.

Hostile Takeover

The acquisition of a target company against its wishes by a bidder that bypasses management and appeals directly to shareholders.

Human Resources (HR)

The part of an organization that is in charge of hiring new employees, handling employee interactions, teaching them, and making sure the company follows all job laws.

Hyperinflation

Out-of-control and very fast inflation that often causes the value of a currency to drop sharply.

Hypothesis Testing

A way to use statistics to decide what to do or what to think about a whole community based on selected facts.

Horizontal Merger

The combining of companies that operate in the same industry or at the same stage of production.

Holding Company

A corporation which has a controlling stake in another corporation usually for the purpose of informing the management of varied stakes and investments.

Horizontal Market

A market that comprises customers from different industries as compared to the vertical market that targets particular industries.

Home Reversion Plan

A financial arrangement where a homeowner sells a portion or all of their property to a provider in exchange for regular payments or a lump sum while retaining the right to live there for life.

House Price Surveys

Reports or studies that examine trends and changes in residential property values in a certain market or area.

High-Net-Worth Individual (HNWI)

High net worth individual is an individual that has investable assets with an Initial threshold being $1 million.

Horizontal Analysis

A technique of analyzing financial data that involved the comparison of past money information belonging to different periods with a view of identifying some repetitive pattern and passing a verdict on performance.

Horizontal Diversification

A plan in business where a firm sells its products or services in areas different from its core business or in industries different from the ones it operates in.

I

Income Protection Insurance

Insurance coverage that provides financial support to individuals who are unable to work due to illness or injury.

Income Statement

A financial statement that shows a company's revenues, expenses, and profits over a specified period.

Income Tax

A tax levied by governments on individuals' earnings and businesses' profits.

Independent Financial Adviser (IFA)

A person who gives customers a neutral opinion of management concerning their financial situation.

Individual Savings Account (ISA)

An ISA is an investment product offered to individuals in the UK so they can save or invest in money without making contributions to their income tax or capital gains tax on their investments.

Industrial Output

This is the gross sum of products and services formed in an industry or sector in a certain cycle of time.

Inflation

The pace by which the overall price level of products and services increases and hence reduces the purchasing power of the consumers.

Inflation Measures

Different methods that measure the increase in prices of goods and services and the rate of inflation within an economy. These include consumer price index and producer price index.

Inheritance Tax

A tax levied on properties, cash and other assets that the deceased individual owned before being inherited by other individuals.

Insider Trading

The act of purchasing or selling securities such as shares by using privileged and often undisclosed information about the firm.

Institutional Investor

A legal organization through which individuals come together with their funds with the aim of acquiring securities or other forms of investments.

Interest-Only Mortgage

It refers to a mortgage in which the borrower makes interest repayments throughout a certain period with no changes to the principal amount.

Interim

They are accounts or statements made for half a year or less than a financial year but most commonly for a period of three or six months.

Investment Trust

An investment that gathers funds from the investors and invests them in a portfolio of securities.

Invisible Hand

A phrase originated by the renowned economist Adam Smith to depict the economic process by which individuals' actions that are guided by self-gain contribute to enhanced societal welfare without being the intention.

Irrational Exuberance

A term that was given by the economist Robert Shiller to refer to optimism that at time may result in formation of bubbles in the financial markets.

Inventory

The stock of goods or materials held by a business for production, sales, or distribution.

Initial Public Offering (IPO)

The process through which a private company offers shares to the public for the first time.

Insolvency

The financial state of being unable to pay debts as they come due or having liabilities that exceed assets.

Intangible Assets

Non-physical assets such as patents, trademarks, and goodwill that contribute to a company's value but do not have a physical presence.

J

Job Costing

A cost accounting technique applied in establishing the cost incurred in completing a certain job, normally implemented in manufacturing and construction.

Job Description

This is a legal document that describes all the jobs description, duties, required qualification and working relationship of a certain post in an organization.

Job Satisfaction

The overall satisfaction and comparability of the job and organizational climate that an employee has towards his occupation.

Joint Account

It is a current account where two or more people can transact on the account and withdraw money from that same account since it is jointly owned.

Joint Committee

A group formed by representatives from organizations or groups that work together on certain matters or projects.

Joint Stock Company

A legal structure of a business where the ownership is spread in small portions of the company, known as stocks, which can be bought by different investors in the organization's capital.

Joint Venture

An agreement in business by which two or more people share resources in a common venture to share profit and loss.

J-curve Effect

A pattern characterized by going down or negative effects at the beginning, then rapidly increasing or turning positive effects, commonly observed in investment or economic development.

Jurisdiction

The power given to a legal entity or court to exercise the reception of the law in a geographical region or in a specific subject.

Just-in-Time (JIT) Inventory

A production or purchasing plan that involves obtaining goods in small quantities as and when they are required in production or sales, thus cutting the costs of holding stocks.

K

Key Account Management

The deliberate management of the interpersonal relationship between an organization and its clients or customers for the ultimate objective of enhancing the value and level of satisfaction.

Key Performance Indicators (KPIs)

Business KPIs are measurable indicators that assess the performance of an organization, a department or an employee in relation to key business objectives.

Kickback

This is a type of bribe whereby an individual pays another person in the hope that he will use his influence to benefit him in business matters.

Knowledge Management

The means of collecting, structuring, and managing information and knowledge in an enterprise for the purpose of improving the performance, creativity, and management of an enterprise.

L

Laissez-faire

The political idea stating that markets should be left alone for proper functioning by discouraging government interference.

Leasehold

A property tenure whereby the holder has only a limited right to use the property belonging to someone else although for a limited period of time through leasehold.

Leveraged Buyout

This is the purchase of an organization with the use of a lot of borrowed money, which is usually backed by the purchase assets of the company.

Libor Rate

Stands for London Interbank Offered Rate, the interest rate at which banks can borrow funds in the international interbank market for the purpose of short-term borrowing.

Liquid Asset

A form of property, which can be instantly converted into cash with minimal loss in value or the ability to qualify for sale immediately.

Loan-to-Value (LTV)

It is a financial ratio which lenders employ to determine the risk of extending credit for a particular asset and is given by the amount of credit extended divided by the value of the asset.

M

Macroeconomics

The area of economics that focuses on the analysis of economic systems and activities at the national or international level, considering such indicators as inflation rate, unemployment rate, and economic growth rate.

Managed Fund

A collective investment pool where skilled fund managers undertake complete investment decisions on behalf of the investors, usually in exchange for fees.

Manufacturing Output

The total amount of output of manufacturing industries within a certain period, usually employed to measure an economy's performance.

Margin

The amount by which a product or service is sold above its cost or the portion of the equity needed to get a loan.

Median

A number which divides a set of ordered values into two equal parts where the values arranged in ascending order.

Merger

The process of acquisition when two firms merge with each other through a contractual agreement with a view of realizing a number of benefits mostly-formed in terms of market influence.

Microeconomics

The field of economics that deals with the actions and choices of distinct companies and consumers, centering on supply and demand and resource distribution.

Minimum Wage

The minimum amount of money legally allowed to be paid to the workers for the work they perform for their employers' companies.

Monetarism

An economic theory that specifies the manageability of the supply of money to as being used in management of economic activity with the view of controlling prices.

Monetary Policy Committee

A group of officials entrusted with the duty of formulating instruments of monetary regulations for the realization of economic goals like inflation control or growth.

Money Supply

The sum total of cash and cash-like items in circulation in the economy, including demand deposits.

Monopoly

A market form in which there is the presence of a single seller or producer in the market and who has considerable market influence over the availability of the good or service he offers.

Mortgage Broker

A state-licensed individual who acts as a go-between between borrowers and lenders and assists in providing a mortgage loan with possibly several lenders.

Mortgage Indemnity Protection/Guarantee

A type of credit insurance that helps to minimize possible losses caused by a borrower's failure to repay the mortgage loan – it has a limited purpose that covers a part of the possible losses.

Mortgage Term

The length of time that a mortgage loan was planned to be repaid usually the period of time it takes to complete the mortgage is between 15-30 years.

Mutual

A corporate form in which people who are involved in a similar business venture jointly own the business and control it in the interest of the members or policy holders.

Mutual Fund

A financial tool used to gather funds from numerous buyers for the purpose of purchasing securities on the basis of the defined investment plan.

N

NASDAQ

An international market where securities are traded through the use of electronics.

Negotiation

The discussion that is held in a bid to try and find a middle ground.

Net Income

It is a measure of business profits that results from netting the overall profits earned by a company against the cost of goods sold and other expenses.

Net Present Value (NPV)

Cash flows discounted at a certain rate; the valuation of present value for opportunities that can be invested.

Networking

Developing and nurturing interactions for the attainment of professional or organizational objectives.

Nominal Interest Rate

The raw interest rate charged before making adjustments for inflation.

Non-Disclosure Agreement (NDA)

An agreement in writing that sets out certain information that the concerned parties are not allowed to reveal to other persons.

Non-Profit Organization

This is a business organization that is established with objectives which diverse from the motive of making profits.

Non-Recourse Loan

A loan in which the borrower does not guarantee the repayment of the loan and instead pledges an asset which the creditor can sell to recover the balance in case the former fails to pay.

Normal Distribution

A statistical distribution with the data accumulated at the center of the distribution with equal and identical tails on both sides.

Niche Market

A smaller part of the overall market that has unique requirements and characteristics.

O

Open-market Operations

The process of purchasing and selling government securities to regulate money stock and interest rates in the economy.

Operating Income

Net income from a company's primary business activities, nit including interest and taxes.

Operating Margin

A financial ratio used to determine the operating profitability of a business, arrived at by dividing operating income by total revenues.

Operating Profit/Loss

A company's earnings or losses from its main business activities before accounting for interest and tax expenses.

Option

An agreement that allows an individual or company to purchase or sell an asset at a specific price in the future.

Ordinary Residence

A legal term that establishes where a person principally lives for tax means.

Ordinary Share

A form of share ownership in a business where investors are legally recognized as shareholders with options to vote and be paid dividends.

Organizational Structure

The structure and organization that delineate authority and accountability for tasks within an organization.

Operational Efficiency

A measure that demonstrates the extent of output for any given amount of input in a business process.

Operational Risk

The loss exposure as a consequence of internal controls' shortcomings, including a company's policies, procedures, and people.

Operationalize

Refers to the process of applying a strategy, plan or system in an organization with the aim of achieving a certain goal or an objective.

Opportunity Cost

The value that is lost when an inferior decision is made instead of the other available choice.

Option Contract

A financial contract allowing the buyer to call for an asset at a certain price but not necessarily to purchase it.

Outsourcing

Outsourcing is defined as hiring third-party companies or vendors to carry out activities that were previously done in-house.

Overdraft

An amount that is less than zero in a bank account due to a withdrawal of a larger sum of cash from the account.

Overhead

The business costs that are not related to the creation of the good or provision of services which are incurred continuously.

Over-the-Counter (OTC)

Direct physical transfer of financial instruments from one counterparty to another instead of through a centralized exchange.

Owner's Equity

Percentage of ownership that a particular owner has in a business and, which is obtained by subtracting the liabilities of the business from its total assets.

P

Partnership

This is a structure of a business where two or more people own the venture and also are involved in managing the business.

Patent

The right granted to an inventor entitling him to exclusive control of the use of an invention or product design.

Payroll

The overall sum that an organization spends on the remuneration of its staff as well as various other costs of employing labor.

Pipeline

The target audience a salesperson or business organization is in the process of trying to reach out to.

Portfolio

A group of investments, products or projects planned and operated with some overall organization objective.

Price Elasticity

The extent to which consumers' demand for a certain product or service is affected by changes in its price.

Price Point

The particular price that a firm sets for the product or service that it provides to the consumer.

Process Improvement

Actions taken to improve the cost, quality, or effectiveness of organizational processes in the business environment.

Product Development

It refers to the action of developing or enhancing goods, services, ideas, or methodologies to satisfy customers' needs.

Profit Margin

The number of revenue dollars that once had passed through the company's cost of goods sold line on the income statement.

Profitability

The measure of the efficiency of a business in producing profits and the relationship of such profits in accordance with the costs and expenses incurred in the process.

Promotion

Campaigns designed to promote a specific product or service in the market with the aim of making more sales.

Public Relations (PR)

Coordinating the image a certain company or person seeks to portray and the way in which they communicate this.

Pivot

To realign business strategically in order to adapt to changes in the market environment as quickly as possible.

Procurement

The method through which an organization obtains products, services, or works from a different supplier.

Q

Quality Control

Processes and procedures used to ensure that products or services meet specified standards of quality.

Quality Management

Processes and systems used to ensure consistent quality in products or services.

Qualitative Research

Research methods that explore attitudes, behaviors, and opinions to gain insights rather than numerical data.

Quantitative Analysis

Methods of analyzing data that lend themselves more to numerical information and statistical tools.

Quarter

An arithmetical period of three months commonly applied in preparing the balance of sheets and profit preparations.

Quarterly Report

Quarters financial reports and performance reports that a company comes up with every three months.

Questionnaire

A series of questions designed in a specific manner to obtain information from the respondents.

Qualified Lead

A potential customer who has shown interest and meets certain criteria indicating a higher likelihood of making a purchase.

Quick Ratio

A financial ratio that measures a company's ability to meet short-term obligations with its most liquid assets.

Quota

A predetermined sales target or limit assigned to a salesperson or team.

R

Rally

A sharp rise in the price or value of an asset or a market that has fallen for some time.

Random Walk Theory

A theory in which it is believed that cup price flows and patterns are unforeseeable and random.

Rate of Return

The increase or decrease in an investment during a particular period which is compared to the initial value of the investment as measured usually in percentage.

Ratings Agencies

Companies or institutions that evaluate and rank the credit standing of an individual, corporation, or security.

Real Estate Investment Trusts (REITs)

Business entities that use and possibly pay for real estate with the intention of earning income from it.

Real Interest Rate

The nominal interest rate adjusted for inflation, reflecting the real purchasing power of the return on investment.

Real Values

Figures prepared and updated to represent the importance of money in buying power or worth based on different indicators.

Recession

A drastic decrease in the pace of economic activities throughout the economy, over a reasonably long duration.

Regressive Tax

A tax whose proportion of share is high among the poor people than it is among the rich people.

Regulatory News Service (RNS)

An organization that provides the public and investors with information on regulations and finance.

Repayment Mortgage

This is a home loan in which the monthly payments are used to pay an interest component and part of the principal so that by the end of the agreed time, the entire sum is paid.

Restructuring

Modifications that occur in an organization including its structure, business processes and procedures, people, systems and technology.

Retail Prices Index (RPI)

Indicator of the overall price level in the UK; informs about the changes in the price level for goods and services within a given period of time.

Retirement Age

The time in life when an individual leaves the workforce to possibly depend on their retirement benefits or pension.

Revenue Stream

The activities through which a business makes its income like sales, subscription or licensing.

Reverse Takeover

A method of taking a private company public by having it purchase a public firm instead of the years it will take to go through the process of going public.

Rights Issue

A shareholders' special occasion whereby they are allowed to purchase more shares of the company at a lower price.

Risk Assessment

Assessment of risks and their consequences on business or specific ventures.

Royalties

A payment made to the owner of an intellectual property for using or reselling the property.

S

Sales Forecast

Projection of probable sales for a given time in the future normally through extrapolation of past statistics and trends.

Sales Funnel

These are the steps that a customer follows right from the time they get to know about a particular product until when they buy it.

Scalability

The capacity of a business or system to expand its scale or operations in the future and avoid becoming slow.

Shareholder

A person who possesses stock in the company and therefore has a stake, voice, interest and claim on the firm's properties and earnings.

Share Options

A specific type of inducement whereby the employee is rewarded with the company's shares.

Sole Proprietorship

A business form where one person owns the business and is also directly responsible for managing all the business operations and assumes all the risks.

Stagflation

A condition of inflation existing alongside unemployment and weak demand in a country's economy.

Stakeholder Pension

A pension plan that has features of a defined contribution scheme such that the employer is legally responsible for contributing a specified amount towards the provision of the pension benefits.

Stamp Duty (equity)

A type of tax that is charged on the sale of shares or securities.

Stamp Duty (housing)

An excise tax that is charged on the buying of property or real estate.

Startup

A relatively young company with the primary goal of increasing its sales and market share within a short period, using products or services that are unique in the market.

Stock Exchange

A place where buyers and sellers trade shares, debentures and other securities.

Stockholder

An individual or organization holding stock in a company, entitling them to profits and having a voice in how the company is run.

Strategic Alliance

A business partnership between at least two organizations with the aim of attaining similar goals.

Strategic Management

The strategic planning and executive actions and decisions made by a firm's senior executives to advance shareholder interests.

Strategic Planning

A course of action determined through the delineation of goals and a favourable planning line as a strategic guideline.

Sub-prime Loans

The money that is given to various borrowers with a view of being given to those with a low credit rating and usually charged with higher interest rates.

Supply and Demand

The connection between the supply of a certain product and the demand for it, regulating the price of that product.

Supply Chain

A complex web of people, businesses and functions that organize and facilitate the flow of goods and services from producers to consumers.

Supply Chain Management (SCM)

The management and control of the different materials, information and funds as they flow from the suppliers to the consumers.

Sustainability

Activities that do not limit prospects for future generations to fulfill their wants and requirements in the future.

Swaps

The purchase and sale of cash flows or any other financial assets for a specified price at a particular date in the future.

SWOT Analysis

A business management model that captures the current and potential strengths, weaknesses, opportunities and threats that affect an organization.

Synergy

Synergism is a term used to refer to the concept whereby two or more entities combine their efforts to create a larger outcome than what would have been possible when the individual forces were in action.

Sustainability

Sustainable actions which enable the needs of the current generation to be fulfilled without having an adverse impact on the resources for the next generations.

T

Takeover

The act of one company gaining control over or merging with another through the purchase of its stock.

Takeover bid

A proposal in which one firm agrees to purchase shares that are owned by another firm.

Takeover Panel

An administrative body that supervises takeovers and mergers in some legal systems.

Tangible Common Equity Ratio

This is a metric used in the banking sector to signify how strong a bank is through a comparison between tangible common equity and tangible assets.

TARP (Troubled Asset Relief Programme)

A scheme launched by the US government with the intention of pulling the financial industry out of the pit by buying bad debts from companies.

Tax Haven

A country or jurisdiction whose taxes are friendly to international citizens or corporate entities seeking to pay as little as possible in taxes.

Teaser Rate

The first low interest rate provided on loans or credit cards to make customers borrow from the firm, and when they have borrowed the money and have been using it, the interest rate is adjusted to a higher level.

Term Assurance

A form of insurance that pays money to dependents in the event of the insured's death within the period agreed upon through premiums.

Terminal Bonus

A payment normally made by an insurer at the completion of an insurance policy, such as at their expiry or when the policy has reached the end of the term.

Tracker Funds

It is a kind of investment funds in which a portfolio of securities will be trying to emulate some referenced market index, for instance, the S&P 500.

Trade Balance

The value of the goods and services a country sells to another country minus the value of the goods and services that it buys from the other country.

Treasury

The branch within a firm or government that deals with money, funds, budgets, finances, and risks frequently related to funds.

Turnover

The total revenue realized by a business from the sale of goods, services or both throughout a given period, normally a one year period.

U

Underwriting

The proposal of the assessment of the likelihood of a person or an asset being insured, as well as the pricing of the premium.

Unemployment Rate

The proportion of the active population that is without a job and is looking for work.

Unincorporated Business

An enterprise that has not incorporated itself through the laws of corporations and company Acts, usually carried on by an individual trader or by a partnership firm.

Unique Selling Proposition (USP)

A factor that differentiates a product or service from its competitors.

Upward Communication

The flow of information from lower levels of an organization to higher levels, such as feedback or reports.

User Experience (UX)

The overall experience of a person using a product such as a website or computer application, especially in terms of how easy or pleasing it is to use.

User Interface (UI)

The point of human-computer interaction and communication in a device, application, or website.

Utility

The satisfaction or benefit derived from consuming a good or service.

Utilization Rate

In manufacturing, the percentage of time that equipment is used productively.

Unsecured Loan

A loan that is not backed by collateral, relying instead on the borrower's creditworthiness.

V

Value added tax (VAT)

A tax levied on a product at various production stages and at the final point of delivery to the consumer.

Value Chain

The series of operations which a firm undergoes in order to create value to the final output is known as value chain.

Value Proposition

The value that is created by a product or a service and adds on distinctive value to the customers it targets.

Variable rate mortgage

This is a home loan where the rate of interest is adjusted according to the changes that occur in a particular index.

Vertical Integration

A situation used to mean that a firm has significant influence over more than one stage of a product or industry.

Vertical merger

It is a business consolidation strategy whereby two firms in related industries but in different positions of the value chain combine.

Volume

The volume of goods or services that has been either marketed and sold or manufactured and used within a given timeframe.

Vesting

A method which an employee earns non-forfeitable rights to receive employer contributions or other benefits, often over time.

Virtual Team

A set of people who coordinate their work over time, space, and organizations by means of technology.

Vision Statement

A statement that identifies and describes the aims of an organization with the view of influencing the internal operations and planning processes of the organization.

Viral Marketing

The method which involves leveraging already existing social relationships to pass information about a product or service.

Vulture funds

Funds with the ability to acquire bad debts for better purposes of earning large profits through the rearrangement as well as selling of the debts.

W

Wage

Money or other remuneration given to workers as an exchange for work done or services offered.

Warranty

Seller's assurance to the buyer that a product will be of specified quality, which, if not met, will be fixed/ replaced/repaired.

Wealth Management

It is the process through which individuals, organizations, and other companies delegate the responsibility of managing their finances to other individuals, firms, or even other companies for the sake of achieving their desired profits or targets.

Wholesale

The process of marketing and supplying products mostly in large quantities to users such as retailers at cheaper prices per unit.

White Paper

An extensive document that gives the reader information about a specific phenomenon, often utilized in business and government sectors.

Wildcard

A character employed in search engines and databases to denote any number of characters in a word or a phrase.

Working Capital

The difference between current assets and current liabilities, representing the funds available for day-to-day operations.

Workflow

Steps necessary for the accomplishment of a particular goal or required to undertake a specific process.

Workforce Diversity

Refers to the many aspects through which individuals within an organization can be diverse, such as racial origin, gender, ethnic origin, age, and cultural differences.

X

X-axis

In charts and graphs, it refers to the horizontal axis that usually holds the independent variable or time.

X-branded product

A product that is sold under a different brand than the company that makes the product with special distribution or a selected market targeted.

X-efficiency

It refers to a firm's productivity level that generates optimal outcomes from the available inputs with minimal loss and expense.

X-inefficiency

It is a condition whereby organizational production becomes less effective or economically suboptimal, often due to factors such as bad management, lack of rivalry, or overconfidence.

X-factor

A factor that may be hard to evaluate in numerical terms but is capable of exerting a powerful influence on a business or decision.

Xenocurrency

A domestic currency of one country adopted as a means of payment for goods and services in another nation.

XIRR (Extended Internal Rate of Return)

A kind of Internal Rate of Return that takes into account non-regular patterns of cash inflows and outflows and different periods between them.

XM (Cross Marketing)

This is a branding technique in which two or more businesses agree to endorse each other and exchange customer databases.

Y

Yellow Knight

A merger and acquisition terminology referring to an acquirer that previously used to be a hostile party before switching to a friendly acquirer.

Yield

The money obtained from an investment which is usually calculated as the ratio of income that comes from the investment in relation to the cost basis or from the present value.

Yield Curve

An interest rate that compares the credit quality of bonds of the same type but with varying maturities. It displays the yield to maturity against the bonds' maturities.

Yield Management

A pricing method adopted by companies to increase its revenues; the method involves charging different prices for similar products depending on the level of demand, production costs, time, and other factors.

Yield Spread

The amount earned in excess of the risk-free rate on two different investments used to assess the level of risk for two types of bonds or other instruments.

Yield to Maturity (YTM)

The total return expected on a bond if held till the time of its redemption, taking into account the price at which the bond is bought, the coupon rate that the bond pays, besides the time left before the bond actually matures.

Z

Z-Score

It is a measure that compares the probability of bankruptcy of a company on the basis of its financial status. It is basically an overall measure of the financial soundness of a business that incorporates a number of financial ratios that deal with solvency.

Zero-Based Budgeting (ZBB)

A budgeting approach where every cost in the new period has to be justified from the ground up, arriving from zero as opposed to using the previous period's figure as a starting point.

Zero-Coupon Bond

A type of bond that does not pay periodic interest payments. Instead, it is issued at a discount to its face value and pays the face value at maturity.

Zero Interest Rates

An economic policy in which the central bank of a country fixes the rate for interest, often close to zero level, to prompt borrowing and probable spending.

Zero-Sum Game

An event in game theory and economics in which one player profits while another loses an equivalent amount. In business contexts, it can mean rivalry where one company benefits at the other company's expense.

ZOPA or Zone of Possible Agreement

The zone or area of overlap that exists in any negotiation between two different parties with the potential to reach an agreed solution.

Zombie Funds

Known as zombie companies or zombie banks, these are enterprises that are still active legally in the market despite the fact that they cannot service their debts or their payment for the debt. They sometimes depend on outside resources like bailouts from the government or special discounted loan rates.

www.ingramcontent.com/pod-product-compliance
Lightning Source LLC
Chambersburg PA
CBHW050853150626
46549CB00013B/1433